ARHAT PĀRŚVA AND DHARAṆENDRA NEXUS

B. L. Series No. 11

Arhat Pārśva and Dharaṇendra Nexus

Editor

M.A. Dhaky

LALBHAI DALPATBHAI INSTITUTE OF INDOLOGY
AHMEDABAD
BHOGILAL LEHARCHAND INSTITUTE OF INDOLOGY
DELHI

First Edition: Delhi, 1997

LALBHAI DALPATBHAI INSTITUTE OF INDOLOGY
Near Gujarat University, Ahmedabad 380 009
Phone : 079-6442463

ISBN: 81-208-1485-1

Distributed by

MOTILAL BANARSIDASS

41 U.A. Bungalow Road, Jawahar Nagar, Delhi 110 007
8 Mahalaxmi Chamber, Warden Road, Mumbai 400 026
120 Royapettah High Road, Mylapore, Chennai 600 004
Sanas Plaza, Subhash Nagar, Pune 411 002
16 St. Mark's Road, Bangalore 560 001
8 Camac Street, Calcutta 700 017
Ashok Rajpath, Patna 800 004
Chowk, Varanasi 221 001

B.L. INSTITUTE OF INDOLOGY

C/o Shree Atma Vallabh Jain Smarak Shikshana Nidhi
22nd Km., G.T. Karnal Road, P.O. Alipur, Delhi 110 036

L.D. INSTITUTE OF INDOLOGY

Near Gujarat University, Ahmedabad 380 009

PRINTED IN INDIA

BY JAINENDRA PRAKASH JAIN AT SHRI JAINENDRA PRESS,
A-45 NARAINA, PHASE I, NEW DELHI 110 028

जैनभारती कांगड़ातीर्थोद्धारक श्री वल्लभस्मारकप्रणेता महत्तरा साध्वी
श्री मृगावती श्री जी महाराज

जन्म: ४-४-१९२६ सरधार (गुजरात)
स्वर्गारोहण: १८-७-१९८६ श्री वल्लभ स्मारक दिल्ली

DEDICATION

To

The Sacred Memory

of

Mahattarā Mṛgāvatīśrījī

CONTENTS

FOREWORD

The present volume contains most of the papers read at the Seminar in 1987 organized by B.L. Institute of Indology in Delhi. It was convened by Prof. M.A. Dhaky. The press-ready manuscript had been given over to us by Prof. Dhaky about two-and-a-half years ago. Its printing, regrettably, could not be taken in hand immediately owing to certain difficulties at our end. We crave the indulgence of the contributing scholars for the tardiness in giving them the volume in print.

The Seminar had been attended by such stalwarts like the *āgama*-specialist Pt. Dalsukh Malvaniya, the doyen of Jaina iconography (late) Dr. U.P. Shah, the noted epigraphers like Dr. K.V. Ramesh and Shri Madhav N. Katti, and of course several archaeologists and students of Jaina art and history. The papers in this volume, we feel (and the scholars possibly will endorse), cast fresh light on the problem of the connection between Arhat Pārśva and Nāgarāja Dharaṇendra and thus push forward the frontiers of research on that score by some measure, besides adding information on several facets of research and issues related with the doctrine, sect, followers and representations of Arhat Pārśva. Hopefully, the purpose of organizing the seminar is to a large extent served.

My friend and colleague Shri N.P. Jain, in fact all of us associated with the B.L. Institute of Indology, wish to thank the scholars who participated in the Seminar, as also for their learned contributions by way of papers and by the discussions during deliberations. And we are specially beholden to Prof. Dhaky for competently convening the Seminar and for meticulously editing the volume.

Delhi, December 1996.

Jitendra B. Shah
Vice-Chairman

PREFATORY

When I was asked by the Bhogilal Leherchand Institute of Indology, Delhi, to convene a seminar on any Nirgranthist subject involving art, my initial reaction was politely to decline accepting this responsibility. My major pre-occupation for over two decades with the ongoing project of the American Institute of Indian Studies on the *Encyclopaedia of Indian Temple Architecture* at its Varanasi Center, left very little free time as well as surplus energies for getting involved into any other serious undertaking. However, the persuasive pressure by Pt. Dalsukh Malvaniya, Dr. U.P. Shah, and equally by my friend Shri Narendra Prakash Jain — one of the primal pillars of the BLI — could not be set aside. In the field of Nirgranthist researches, for some years ago now, indeed since 1974, I was deeply engrossed with the problems concerning Arhat Pārśva, his teachings, and the Nirgrantha Church that eventually grew from his foundational creed; the relationships of his Church, its doctrines as well as the monastic discipline with those of the Church of Arhat Vardhamāna *alias* Jina Mahāvīra and, together with it, its basic philosophy, tenets, and ascetic practices were some of the problems that had not been seriously investigated. It had always been taken for granted that Jina Vardhamāna Mahāvīra reformed the old church of Jina Pārśva. However, this view, as is now increasingly becoming clear, represents an oversimplification of a highly complex phenomenon and has had neglected several vital aspects and significant details, and, as its consequence, the issues that arose therefrom. One other problem requiring attention was to find an explanation for the well-known association of Nāgarāja Dharaṇendra with Jina Pārśvanātha. For this Jina remains distinguished from the other Jinas by the presence of this very special feature in his concrete representation, and hence this very specific connection needed explanation. Keeping this exigency in view, I suggested that, the main focus may be on "Arhat Pārśva and Dharaṇendra nexus" for the Seminar under contemplation. Around this thematic pivot may revolve the relevant investigatory papers. Accordingly, four papers providing an intimate background, discussing as they would do Pārśva's teachings and the sect which evolved after him, the āgamic and narrative literary references that may clarify (or at least hint at) the origins of the legend behind the connection of the Jina with the Nāgendra, the anthropological as well as ontological interpretation of this special nexus, and notices taken as well as the portrayal of this feature rendered in the elative hymnic compositions in praise of Pārśvanātha. The mythological, theological, liturgical, and socio-anthropological aspects involved in the investigations would thus largely be taken care of.

This background, as was then rightly envisaged (and now substantiated), could in part also provide the historical and religious backdrop against which the image of Pārśva configures. However, as complimentary to this sketch, the archaeological facts and finds were needed to be brought in, particularly for filling in the colour and adding some realistic and corporeal dimensions to the overall perspective that would emerge. Keeping in view these twin axes of the approach, eminent Nirgranthologists on one side and the epigraphers and historians, and no less important the iconographers (specializing in Nirgrantha iconography) on the other side were invited to present their research papers at the Seminar. As a result, some papers covering the regionwise surveys of the epigraphical data and sculptural material relating to Pārśvanātha by specialists in the field were read at the Seminar and now form part of this small volume. Regrettably, the scholars devoted to Nirgranthist studies are far too less in number than those working in the spheres of Brahmanical and Buddhist studies. Luckily, for our purpose, we could count on the cooperation of a small but competent band of some 16 scholars on the issues and subjects contemplated to be discussed in depth. However, seldom has a blueprint been executed without modifications, compromises, and, inevitably, the gaps due to the failings and shortcomings that the prevailing circumstances customarily generate. The publication, for instance, has to go without three important papers, the one on the "Epigraphical data on Pārśva images and temples in Western India"; the second on the "Pārśva images in Rājasthān", and the third concerning the "Pārśva images in Tamilnadu". Seemingly, the busy schedules (and, as in one case, indifferent health of the scholar concerned) worked against the materialization of these papers. When long waitings (coupled with reminders at intervals by the successive Directors of the BLI) for these vital papers produced no response, it was decided to send the papers on hand to the press even when we were painfully aware of the lacunae that will appear in the published version of the proceedings. One other factor which contributed to tardiness was the ignoring, by some contributors, of the style-sheet for the research papers that was earlier communicated to all scholars invited for the Seminar. Indeed, this eventuality made the task of editing still harder and I had, for want of time, to allow such unconformities and lay the responsibility at the doors of the contributors concerned. (In some papers, even the footnotes and bibliographical references were missing!) Despite these shortcomings, the overall outcome of the Seminar is fairly satisfactory. True, all problems (indicated in the preamble of the Seminar) could not be fully explored, and on some of the very dimly illuminated corners no fresh or further light could be cast. But a breakthrough has been made and the frontiers of the existing knowledge on this subject have been to an extent pushed forward. (After all, perfection in human endeavours and achievements is an impossible, and hence an unattainable, reality.)

If I feel grateful — and I most certainly do— to the scholars for their efforts and the thought-provoking contributions as also for their lively and evocative deliberations when the Seminar was on, the Management of the B.L. Institute of Indology, too, deserves full compliments not only for contemplating and supporting the Seminar but also for ideally carrying it out through all its stages and finally for making available the proceedings volume in print. (I must also admire their patience in seemingly interminable waiting for the edited version of the proceedings manuscript which was, for some of the reasons explained, delayed for so long at my end.) The zeal and active participation at the organizational level by Shri Narendra Prakash Jain, Shri Rajkumar Jain, Dr. Prem Singh, and Dr. Dhanesh Jain proved memorably effective. The staff of the B.L. Institute of Indology including its former member Ms. Aruna Anand wholeheartedly provided assistance at various levels for which the participants had nothing but admiration. And without the active and enthusiastic support of Shri Pratapbhai Bhogilal, the founder and Chairman of the B.L. Institute of Indology (who was present at the occasion of the inauguration of the Seminar), and its Advisory Committee, the Seminar could not have taken shape. Late Professor S.B. Deo, the former Director of BLI had lent substantial help in maintaining the liaison with the contributors.

The Seminar was held at the B.L. Institute from the 21st to 24th March 1987. The deliberations of the Seminar had begun with the blessings of Her Holiness, Āryā Śrī Suvratāśrījī, the chief disciple of the most revered late Mahattarā Mṛgāvatīśrījī. Dr. Kapila Vatsyayan had inaugurated this Seminar and her observations were indeed pertinent in the direction of the emphasis she laid on the "concept" side of the subject, and to the innate imperfection of our methodologies which often fail to lend insights in the underlying "Truth". I, for one, fully concede with this observation. In India, for long decades, the archaeological tradition of "material" investigations has dominated. The "idea" investigations done in the field of disciplines such as philosophy and linguistics and their highly perceptive and systematic procedures have been largely neglected in the field of Nirgranthist studies. However, "Truth" is a singularity which cannot be grasped in its totality by a mind which is not "omniscient". The only path that can be pursued is to lessen the degree of imperfection in knowledge fraction by fraction. And to that extent the Seminar can perhaps be said to have succeeded.

Lastly I must thank M/s Motilal Banarsidass for the care they bestowed in printing and production. Their chief proof-reader Shri S.K. Tyagi must be complimented for the very careful reading of the final proofs.

A profound shadow of gloom over the elation we may feel today is cast by the sudden passing away in late 1988 of our very dear and revered friend, an eminent senior Indologist and the front ranking specialist on Nirgrantha art and iconography, Dr. Umakant Premanand Shah, who had actively participated in the Seminar. He would have been most delighted to see this volume in print. His valuable paper, one of the last from his pen and indeed full of insights, is in the volume.

M.A. Dhaky

ARHAT PĀRŚVA AND DHARAṆENDRA NEXUS: AN INTRODUCTORY ESTIMATION

M. A. Dhaky

I

As is well known, it was thanks mainly to the pioneering efforts and consequent findings of Hermann Jacobi that the originality, antiquity, and distinctness of the Nirgrantha religion *vis-à-vis* the Buddhist, and, together with it, the historicity of Arhat Pārśva—regarded in the tradition as the 23rd Jina in succession—was unequivocally established in Western scholarship.[1] On the 22 Jinas who are believed to have preceded Pārśva, it was largely left to the Indian Nirgranthologists to search out data (which may have bearing upon their identification) in the early Brahmanical and Buddhist literature and speculate about their historicity and, as its consequence, make a few tentative suggestions.[2] The concept of the 24 Jinas, however, does not appear in the earliest Nirgrantha *āgmas*[3] which, alone of the two surviving major Nirgrantha sects, were inherited by and preserved in the Śvetāmbara sect of the Northern tradition. With the sole exception of the *Isibhāsiāiṅ* (compiled *c.* 2nd-1st cent. B.C.),[4] even Pārśva finds no mention in the earliest *āgmas*, such as the *Ācārāṅga* and the *Sūtrakṛtāṅga*, which doubtless had originated in, and embody the doctrines and monastic discipline adopted and advocated by the sect of the last Tīrthaṅkara, Arhat Vardhamāna. Ārya Śyāma I (*c.* 1st cent. B.C.-A.D.) of the Northern Nirgrantha (probably *alpacela*) tradition, who is reported to have composed, along with three other works, a work on the biographics of the 24 Jinas (and other legendary and quasi-historical great personages), called the *Prathamānuyoga*, in which very probably for the first time the concept of the 24 Jinas apparently had figured.[5] His second work, the *Gaṇḍikānuyoga*, is also said to have contained some account concerning the same subject.[6] All subsequent accounts on the lives of the 24 Tīrthaṅkaras plausibly were based on these two primordial works that were, to all seeming, lost several centuries ago. The *Sthānāṅga* and the *Samavāyāṅga*, which in their present enlarged version presumably were finalized at the Mathurā Synod (A.D. 363), possibly, indeed largely, had used Ārya Śyāma's works as sources for the biographical details, of course mostly mythical, of the Jinas including Pārśva.[7] The "Jinacaritra" section of the *Paryuṣaṇākalpa* (A.D. 503/516), in turn, may have depended on the above-cited two *āgmas* for some traditional notings on Pārśva, which in any case, historically speaking, is far from considerable as far as the record goes. The other *āgmas* such as the *Vyākhyāprajñapti* (*c.* 1st-3rd cent. A.D.), the *Jñātādharmakathā* (*c.* 3rd-4th cent. A.D.), and the *Vṛṣṇidaśā* (*c.* 3rd-4th cent. A.D.) give a few more details; also, the *Āvaśyaka-niryukti* (*c.* A.D. 525), the *Āvaśyaka-cūrṇi* (*c.* A.D. 600-650), and the *Tīrthāvakālika-prakīrṇaka* (*c.* A.D. 550) have recorded some interesting additional particulars about him and at least in one case about a few of his followers. There are likewise a few details recorded in the southern Nirgrantha surrogate *āgama*, the *Trilokaprajñapti* (*c.* A.D. 550 with many tenth century additions). The pre-medieval and medieval *caritas* of, and poems and hymns addressed to Pārśva (and the pre-medieval comprehensive purāṇic Digambara work such as the *Uttarapurāṇa* of Guṇabhadra, *c.* A.D. 850), had largely depended on earlier sources. They add nothing more of significance except, of course, in some cases, a poetic description of the famous *upasarga*-episode of Pārśvanatha.

II

The original *āgama* and āgamic works belonging to the sect of Arhat Pārśva, among them were what were called the 14 *Pūrva* texts, a few of which could have thrown clearer (and perhaps considerable) light on the Jina's biography, are largely lost, assumably for many, many centuries. We are today dependent on what scanty references to him are scattered through the *āgmas* of the *alpacela*-Nirgrantha sect,[8] in essence and in a small measure preserving also the books of the more ancient *acela*-Nirgrantha of Arhat Vardhamāna,[9] and now surviving within the fold of the sacred scripture of the *sacela* or the Śvetāmbara sect;[10] these have been mentioned in the foregoing passages along with some relevant āgamic commentarial works, the latter doubtless were the products legitimately of the Śvetāmbara sect.[11] According to all these sources, Pārśva was born in Ikṣvāku/Ugra[12] dynasty in Vārāṇasī; his parents were king Aśvasena and queen Vāmā.[13] His height was 10 *ratnīs* or *hastas* (*c.* 15 ft.?), a dimension for human stature which of course lay in the realm of improbability. He was of blue/black complexion.[14] At the age 30[15], he had renounced the world; had preached till he passed away at the ripe age of 100 on Sammeta (or preferably Sammeda)-śaila.[16]

The *Caturvidha-Saṁgha* or the four-fold congregation of the sect of Pārśva, as was to be with Arhat Vardhamāna, consisted of *munis* and *āryās* (friars and nuns) together with their *gaṇadhara*-apostles and the *upāsakas* or *śrāvakas* and *upāsikās* or *śrāvikās*, lay men and women followers. The *Saṁvāyāṅga* reports that Pārśva had eight *gaṇas* or cohorts of friars and nuns with corresponding eight *gaṇadharas*:[17] the *gaṇadharas* by name were Śubha, Śubhaghoṣa, Vaśiṣṭha, Brahmacārī, Soma, Śrīdhara, Vīrabhadra, and Yaśa. (The names given in the *Sthānāṅga* are the same except for the last two which are Vīrya, and Bhadrayaśa).[18] The chief leader of the friars was Dinna, while the chief of the nuns or mother superior was Puṣpacūlā.[19] The principal man lay-votary was Suvrata[20] while the corresponding position for the lady lay-follower was held by Sunandā. (The highly inflated figures given in the texts for the numbers of friars, omniscients, nuns, and the lay-votaries need not detain us).[21]

During his itineraries, Arhat Pārśva is said to have visited Ahicchatrā, Āmalakappā, Arakkhuri, Campā, Hastināpura, Kāmpilyapura, Kauśāmbī, Mathurā, and Nāgapura; also Rājagṛha, Sāketa and Śrāvastī. Beyond these facts, what little is said, is all mythical. Even the date as to when he flourished is, to my sensing, doubtful. Indeed the separation of as many as 250 years envisaged between him and Arhat Vardhamāna[22] which would place his date somewhere in the bracket B.C. 877-777 or 817-717[23] does not seem to accord with some more tangible facts. For example:

(1) The way Keśī, a patriarch of the sect of Pārśva, is introduced in the opening statement of his dialogue with Gautama, the chief disciple and *gaṇadhara*-apostle of Nātaputta Vardhamāna,[24] seems to indicate that not many years had elapsed between the two Jinas. Also, the manner in, and phraseology by which Vardhamāna refers to Pārśva, which includes "Arahā purisādānīya Pāsa" indicates that he acknowledged Pārśva as senior to him but seemingly not too distant in time from him.

(2) The antiquity of Vārāṇasi where the Jina Pārśva was born does not go beyond eighth-seventh century B.C. Pārśva, therefore, could not have flourished in the ninth-eighth century B.C. Likewise, the antiquity of some of the cities he is said to have visited, like Campā, Mathurā, Rājagṛha, etc. (if the information is correct), does not go beyond seventh-sixth century B.C. on archaeological evidence. Pārśva, therefore, could not have started his ascetic career before the beginning of the sixth century B.C.

(3) The late medieval work, the *Nābhinandana jinoddhāra-prabandha* (A.D. 1337) of Kakka sūri of Ukeśa-gaccha, traces the *gaccha's* origin in the aforenoted Keśī of the Pārśva's sect, his hagiography given there is as follows:[26]

Arhat Pārśva
|
gaṇadhara Śubhadatta
|
Keśī

Although the notice is very late, it, too, curiously seems to fit in the present context. Since Pārśva is believed, as per āgamic records, to have lived for a century, it seems plausible that his disciple (or grand disciple ?) Keśī must have been his contemporary, at least in the his middle and late years of career. On this showing, too, Pārśva may have passed away only a few decades before Vardhamāna had started his preaching career. (Keśī was contemporary of *gaṇadhara* Gautama and hence also of his preceptor Arhat Vardhamāna.)

III

The next question is regarding the monastic discipline formulated by Pārśva and adhered by the votaries of his sect. A point of discussion in the dialogue between Keśī and Gautama (*Uttarādhyayana-23*) is a clear pointer to the fact that, in Pārśva's church, friars were allowed to wear garments. This is further supported by an end-statement figuring after the dialogue between the Pārśva's follower Kālāsyavaiśyaputra and Arhat Vardhamāna (as reported in the *Vyākhyāprajñapti*), when the former ultimately joins the order of Vardhamāna: From it, it seems clear that in the church of Pārśva friars did put on a robe: Not only that: They did not remove their hair on the skullcap; also, they used to clean teeth, did not sleep on floor (or ground); they, moreover, used foot-ware as well as an umbrella.[27] In Vardhamāna's discipline these somewhat lineant practices were not permitted, and those who embraced his order had to accept a much sterner monastic conduct including the *pañcamahāvrata* vows. Pārśva's discipline being not so strict and rigorous, came closer to the moderate asceticism of the Buddhists, and to some extent also to that of the existing Śvetāmbara sect.[28]

As for the beliefs, doctrines, and dogmas of the Church of Pārśva, some information is available. Pārśva preached *cāturyāma-dharma*[29] (called *cāturyāma saṁvara* in the Buddhist canon), as perhaps was followed also by a few other contemporaneous sects. This fact is referred to in some of the *āgamas* of the sect of Arhat Vardhamāna. The most direct evidence of what his other doctrines and beliefs were is recorded in the *Isibhāsiāiṅ*, an early and a very important work emanating from his sect.[30] Two chapters — the second being an alternative and possibly a little later in date,[31] in which Pārśva himself is involved — cast some light on the subject. Pārśva believed in *gati* or transmigration of soul, in the existence of *loka* or cosmos, also he spoke about the five primary verities (*pañcāstikāyas*[32]), the eight kinds of *karmas* and their connection with the *gati* of soul, and the relationship of gravity on the *gati* or motion of matter.[33] And already in his sect there is mention of *siddha-*

buddha which implies the inherent concept of the ultimate liberated souls.

The other *āgmas* that may still survive from Pārśva's sect are the *Sūryaprajñapti* and the *Candraprajñapti*, the texts embodying archaic (and now un-valid) astronomical concepts of the Nirgranthas (plausibly developed further in the long lost *Lokānuyoga* of *Ārya Śyāma* (*c.* 1st cent. B.C.-A.D.). The extant *Jambūdvīpaprajñapti* (*c.* 3rd cent. A.D.), the *Dvīpasāgaraprajñapti* (incorporated in the *Jīvābhigama-sūtra*, *c.* 2nd-3rd cent. A.D.), and the *Sthānāṅga's* cosmographical information represent their elaborated form. While the 14 *Pūrva* texts (meaning "anterior" in relation to the texts developed in Vardhamāna's sect), plausibly by their archaic style, concise size, and undeveloped disposition became obsolete and hence for long time lost: their basic content, however, seems to have been preserved and apparently pervade through the fabric of the highly developed and detailed *āgmas* of the Vardhamāna's Church. For example, the extremely difficult exposition involving complex classifications, the aspects of nature as well as the intricate mechanism of the operation of *karma* noticeable in the *Karmaprakṛti*, the *Śataka*, and the *Sattari* of *Śivaśarmā* (*c.* 5th cent. A.D.) in the Śvetāmbara tradition and the *Ṣaṭkhaṇḍāgama* of the Yāpanīya tradition (now in Digambara fold, *c.* late 5th or early 6th cent.) probably were based on a primordial shorter *Pūrva* text such as the *Karma-prakṛti-prābhṛta*. The Nirgrantha biological classification of the living beings, notable for its scientific approach, also may have its roots in the Pārśvāpatya sect.

The surviving early works (and the later developed texts based on his original teachings) would lead us to believe that Arhat Pārśva was an ascetic-scientist, a systematic and methodical thinker, though speaking through an archaic mould of style. Arhat Nātaputta, by contrast, was an ascetic-philosopher who, as his original words and phrases (resembling the Upaniṣadic *genre*) preserved in the *Ācārāṅga* I reveal, cared more for contemplating on *ātman* or 'Self' and its absolute purification from *kaṣāya*-passions for making it free from the *karma*-latancies so as to attain total salvation. Indeed, he was not so much concerned about the scholastic complexities. These latter began to be cared for and developed in highly elaborate form in his sect only from the post-Mauryan times onwards when the need was felt to know the content of the *Pūrvas* which may by then have been further developed in the post-Pārśva times in his sect whose adherents were progressively absorbed in the Church of Vardhamāna. In the ultimate analysis, it is very likely that, much that the Nirgrantha religion for the past many centuries stands for and preaches is based on the original teachings of Pārśva. Even the well known Nirgrantha methodology of examining the idea or object from four-fold viewpoints, of *dravya*, *kṣetra*, *kāla*, and *bhāva*, is also the gift of Pārśva. As a final note, by way of inference, it may be stated that the rite of *sallekhanā* also comes from him; for he had passed away on the Sammeda Hills, assumably by that rite which apparently had initiated that practice, known and followed till now.

IV

The *upsarga*-episode of Arhat Pārśva has been nowhere mentioned in the *āgamas*, not even in the āgamic commentarial literature. The episode, of course, is much too well-known, indeed needing no detailed description in the present context.[34] Briefly speaking, when Pārśva, after renunciation of worldly life was meditating (on the outskirts of Ahicchatrā[35]), his past enemy, the *tāpasa*-ascetic Kamaṭha, who after his death was reborn as a *vyantara* demi-god called Meghamālī, conjured up a cloud burst, the fiercely gathering waters were intended to drown the Jina. At this juncture Nāgendra Dharaṇa, to whom Pārśva had shown compassion in the former's previous birth as snake, appeared on the scene, lifted up the Jina from the waters, and protectively spread his five-hooded head as a canopy over him. The myth, which is available in a few versions (differing in detail and intensity of phenomenon) in the pre-medieval and medieval Nirgrantha narrative literature as well as in the sculptural representations, believably had been created for explaining away, in a dramatic manner, the intriguing association of Dharaṇendra with Pārśva, concretely evidenced as it is from at least the 1st century B.C.-A.D. The dynamic characters involved in the myth are Kamaṭha and Nāgendra; Pārśva, lost in deep contemplation, was a neutral figure. The selection of Ahicchatrā as a site of the event in some versions of the myth was of course for reinforcing the idea 'Ahi' or serpent and 'chhatrā' canopied (by the 'Ahi'). The medieval writers obviously were not aware that the real ancient appellation of the town was 'Adhicchatrā'. From its Prākṛta form 'Ahicchattā', by back formation, it was rerendered in Sanskrit as 'Ahicchatrā' which altered the connotation.[36]

As for Kamaṭha, the earliest reference to him (without any allusion to the *upsarga*-episode) is in the *Paryanta-ārādhanā*,[37] probably a pre-medieval Śvetāmbara work incorporating several verses which formally, stylistically, and by content seem to be of the seventh-eighth century. The relevant verse says that, thanks to *anaśana-maraṇa* (suspension of aliment unto death), Tāmali was reborn as Īśānendra, *bāla-tapasvī* Pūraṇa became Camara (Camarendra in the nether world), and Kamaṭha became Kamaṭhāsura, probably a godling in the *asura-kumāra* or demon class of beings who are believed to be residing in the subterranean quarters. Since Kamaṭhāsura has no other relevance except in the *upsarga*-episode, it may be inferred that the myth was already known to the Śvetāmbaras at this date though nowhere expositioned in their known literature. The earliest Śvetāmbara work clearly to refer to the *upasarga*-tormentation of Pārśva, indeed graphically, is the *Caüpannamahāpurisa-cariya* of Śīlācārya of Nivṛti *kula*, the work datable to A.D. 869.[38] Kamaṭha in his incarnation as a demon, is, in this work, called 'Meghamālī' as has been found in some subsequent Śvetāmbara works dwelling on this theme.

Dharaṇendra, of course, is known to the *āgamas* as well as in the oldest āgamic commentaries. His earliest reference figures among the comparisons instituted for Jina Mahāvīra in the "Mahāvīra-stava" (*c.* 2nd cent. B.C.) inside the *Sūtrakṛtāṅga* I.[39] He is next mentioned in several *āgamas* seemingly composed between the 1st-2nd and the 3rd-4th century A.D. in their available versions.[40] In some of these works he is specified as the Lord of the Nāgakumāra class of gods. Dharaṇa, obviously, is the Nirgrantha adoption of the Brahmanical 'Śeṣa' who supports the globe of the earth on his polycephalous head.[41]

As far as Meghamālī is concerned, he seems to be the Nirgrantha adoption of the Vedic Parjanya or rain-god identified with Indra, particularly in the purāṇic period. The Śvetāmbara version of narration apparently had borrowed a single element from the Kṛṣṇa-Govardhanadhara episode in which Indra inflicted the rain-*upasarga* on Kṛṣṇa and the inhabitants of the village Gokula.[42] No Nāgendra is involved there: but, for the Nirgranthas, they had to explain the presence of the *nāgachatra* on Pārśva; hence the hill-motif was replaced by the Nāgendra motif and, as a result, the other concerned details differed. Since the shower of rain cannot comfortably be suggested in sculpture, the Śvetāmbara standing images of Pārśva (which in any case are not many) do not show the *upasarga* event. The presence of *nāgachatra* by itself signified here, as it were, the *upasarga* moments just as it also served to identify Pārśva and distinguish him from other Jinas. (Such images occur in very large number both in north and south India in the *acela*-Kṣapaṇaka and Digambara sects, a monumental example of it from Haḷebīḍ is illustrated here on Plate 2.)

The southern Nirgrantha (Digambara) version is first hinted in the *Trilokaprajñapti* (*c.* A.D. 550 with several tenth century additions) and its fuller poetically treated account is first encountered in the *Pārśvābhyudaya-kāvya* of Jinasena of the *Pañcastūpānvaya* order, the work composed in the time of the Rāṣṭrakūṭa emperor Amoghavarṣa in *c.* A.D. 820-830 or so.[43] Next it figures in Jinasena's disciple Guṇabhadra's *Uttarapurāṇa* (*c.* A.D. 850). What is involved, besides the incessant rains, in this southern version, is the throwing of a rock or boulder at Pārśva by Śambara, the *vyantaradeva* who was Kamaṭha in his previous existence. (While

Kamaṭha as *tāpasa* or Brahmanical ascetic when he was in human incarnation is known to both traditions, the Śvetāmbara is unaware of 'Śambara' and the Digambara does not call him 'Meghamālī'.)

The powerful sculptural representations of the southern narrative is first encountered in the *vīthikā*-forelobby of the rock-cut Nirgrantha temples at Aihoḷe (Mīnā-basadi) and Bādāmī (Cave IV), both stylistically datable to *c.* late sixth century. Afterwards, it was in Tamil Nadu in the ninth and tenth centuries that this representation is again met with as in the Pāṇḍyan cave at Kaḷagumalai (*c.* 9th cent.)—this being the most impressive portrayal of the episode[44]—and as carved figural representation in relief on the large boulder faces at Tirakkol[45] and some other places.[46]

A third version is described in the medieval Digambara author Padmakīrti's *Pāsanāhacariü* (Apabhraṁśa: A.D. 1077) where the full-fledged fury of Kamaṭha/Śambara is graphically projected. The demon here conjured up by his magical power a variety of phenomena, now to frighten, now to lure away Pārśva from his meditation, the narration doubtless is strongly reminiscent of the Māravijaya episode of Buddha.[47] Śambara here virtually assumes the role of Māra unknown in the main Śvetāmbara version and only partially appearing in the Digambara narratives as in the Puṣpadanta's *Uttarapurāṇa* (Apabhraṁśa: *c.* 10th cent.) and Vādirāja's *Pārśvanātha-caritra* (A.D. 1025). Padmakīrti's version, however, finds a close correspondence, indeed strong anticipatory echoes, in several rock-cut sculptural representations in the halls' fore-lobbies in Ellorā Nirgrantha caves (*c.* 9th cent. A.D.),[49] in two similar looking steles in the Pārśvanatha temple in Huṁca of the Śāntara period (*c.* 10th cent.) in Karnataka,[50] on an image from the collections of Indian Museum (Plate 1: *c.* late 9th cent.),[51] and a few examples from Eastern India.[52]

The *upasarga*-narratives and corresponding representations doubtless are interesting even when they are somewhat imitative since they follow the paradigms, in one case of the earlier Brahmanical and in the other the Buddhist mythical narrative. In the Nirgrantha context they reflect later perceptions on, and closely corresponding verbal and graphic interpretations for clarifying the association of Pārśva with Dharaṇendra. Although earlier literary narrative on the *upasarga*-myth is today unavailable, its sculptural representations of late sixth century in Karnataka anticipate an earlier oral (and perhaps written) tradition. However, much before that, Pārśva images are met along with Dharaṇendra, but without the *upasarga*-details. What, in those early days must the motive/notion be of this association, remains unrevealed. Here U.P. Shah's guesses seem to best accord, or more likely, even are pertinent as explanations since more rational. As he has pointed out, the *nāgachatra* may be a totemic symbol, and a signifier possibly of the links of Pārśva (his ancestors?) with the Nāga tribe.[53] In any case, there exists plenty of archaeological evidence for the *nāga* worship in north India from the pre-Mauryan times through the early centuries of Christian Era, and in South, particularly in the Sātavāhana-Ikṣvāku periods when steles depicting polycephalous *nāga* figure were worshipped. The legend of the Mucalinda-Buddha in the Pāli canon and the missing (or unreported) early legend in the Pārśvanātha context in the Ardhamāgadhī canon may have derived from the common cultural millieu of the pre-Christian Era times. This, ultimately, is a problem on which perhaps a cultural anthropologist (equipped also with the knowledge of early Indian socio-religious conditions, history, literature, and archaeology) may be able to shed further light.

ANNOTATIONS

1. For discussion, *see* Walter Schubring, *The Doctrine of the Jainas*, reprint, Delhi 1978, pp. 28-31.
2. *Cf.* Pt. Kailashchandra, *Jaina Sāhitya kā Itihāsa Pūrvapīṭhikā* (Hindi), Vārāṇasī V.N. 2489 (A.D. 1962), pp. 107-83; and Pt. Dalsukh Malvaniya, "Prastāvanā", *Jaina Sāhitya kā Bṛhad Itihāsa* (Hindi), pt. 1, Vārāṇasī 1966, pp. 21-27.
3. For example the *Ācārāṅga* Book I (*c.* early 5th-3rd cent. B.C.), the *Sūtrakṛtāṅga* (*c.* 4th-2nd cent. B.C.), the *Daśavaikālika* (*c.* 4th-2nd cent. B.C.), and the *Uttarādhyayana* (*c.* 3rd cent. B.C. to B.C. 1-2nd cent. A.D.).
4. Here I have used the Mahāvīra Jaina Vidyālaya edition, the text incorporated within the compilation *Paiṇṇayasuttāiṁ*, pt. 1, Jain Agama Series No. 17, Bombay 1984, pp. 181-256. The text uses material, a larger portion of which pre-dates the compilation itself by a few centuries, and at least three chapters therein may even go to the times close to Pārśva, Vardhamāna, and the Ājīvika Maṅkaliputra Gośālaka.
5. For detailed discussion, *see* Muni Puṇyavijaya, "Prathamānuyogasaśātra ane tenā Praṇetā Sthavira Ārya Kālaka" (Gujarātī), *Jñānāñjali*, Bombay 1960, pp. 122-29. The other three works of Ārya Śyāma were the *Gaṇḍikānuyoga*, the *Lokānuyoga*, and a bunch of *Saṅgrahaṇīs*. The well-known *Caturviṁśati-stava*, one of the six *āvaśyakas* incorporated, since *c.* fifth century A.D., into what is called the *Āvaśyaka-sūtra*, may have been the inaugural (*nāndi or maṅgala*) hymn of the *Prathamānuyoga* on the analogy of a convention, though somewhat late, of the *Caturviṁśati-stava* figuring in the *Nandi-sūtra* of Deva Vacaka (*c.* A.D. 450), the *Paümacariya* of Vimala Suri (*c.* A.D. 473) as well as in its augmented Sanskrit version, the *Padmacarita* of (the Yāpanīya author?) Raviṣeṇa (A.D. 677), the *Harivaṁśapurāṇa* of (the Yāpanīya?) Jinasena (A.D. 784) of Punnāṭa Saṅgha, etc.
6. Puṇyavijaya 1960, pp. 124-25.
7. For details, *see* Pt. Dalsukh Malvaniya, *Sthānāṅga-Samavāyāṅga* (Gujarātī), Ahmedabad 1955,

index, p. 945. My examination of the *Sthānāṅga* and the *Samavāyāṅga* texts has revealed that, stylistically speaking, only very small portions now survive therein, particularly in the *Sthānāṅga*, of the period of the Pāṭaliputra Synod (*c.* 300 B.C.). The rest largely embodies the highly developed material extracted from the *āgamas* and iso-āgamic works composed between the 1st cent. B.C. to early 4th cent. A.D.

8. A few centuries after Arhat Vardhamāna, the friars, under some compulsions now not clearly known, had started using (while walking in public?), a piece of cloth (*colapaṭṭaka?*) for concealing their private parts (as truthfully demonstrated by the figures of male ascetics carved on the pedestals of the Jina images from Mathurā of the Kuṣāṇa period); they also kept a small *gocchaka*-broom and a single bowl to which sanction apparently had been accorded in the late Mauryan and post-Mauryan monastic rules of the Northern tradition. Thus had derived, from the original *acela*-Nirgrantha sect of Nātaputta Vardhamāna Jina, the *alpacela*-Nirgrantha sect. Most of the existing post-Mauryan to Śaka-Kuṣāṇa period *āgamas* apparently had originated within the fold of this sect.
9. An earlier portion of the *Ācārāṅga* Book I, the larger portion of the *Sūtrakṛtāṅga* Book I, and a little less than half the number of chapters in the *Uttarādhyayana-sūtra* plausibly had belonged to the sect of Arhat Vardhamāna. Other chapters in the above-noted *āgamas* together with the larger portion (Chapters 3-10) of the *Daśavaikālika-sūtra* are somewhat later, the composer of the *sūtra*'s surviving original portions was Ārya Svayambhūva (For details see my paper, "The Earliest Portions of Daśavaikālika-Sūtra," *Researches in Indian and Buddhist Philosophy* (Essays in Honour of Professor Alex Wayman), Delhi 1993, pp. 179-93.)
10. There are the *Sūryaprajñapti*, the *Candraprajñapti;* the larger part of the *Bṛhadkalpasūtra* reflects the rules consistent with the monastic discipline of Pārśva's sect.
11. The Śvetāmbara as Śvetapaṭṭa sect is first referred to in the *Paümacariya* of Vimala Sūri and in one of the copper-plate charters of the Kadamba king Mṛgeśavarmā (*c.* last quarter of the fifth century A.D.) in Karnataka. From the *alpacela*-Nirgrantha, it was gradually taking shape since at least *c.* fourth century A.D. through the friars who had eventually turned abbatial monks (*caityavāsī-sādhus*) in Lāṭa (southern Gujarat) and Valabhī area in western Surāṣṭra. Whether this was due to the impact, in theory, of the monastic discipline of the surviving Pārśvāpatyīya or the monks of the sect of Pārśva, or was it thanks to the optional monastic rules which permitted wearing clothes and small essential possessions given priority, needs further investigation.
12. "Ugra" in the southern tradition: (*Cf. Trilokaprajñapti* 4.)
13. For the details on the sources, see the entry "Pāsa" in the *Āgamic Index Vol.I Prakrit Proper Names,* pt. 1 (Comp. M. Mehta and K.R. Chandra), L.D. Series No. 28, Ahmedabad 1970, pp. 452-53. (According to the southern sources, the name of Pāṛśva's mother was Brāhmī: *Cf. Padmapurāṇa* 27 (A.D. 677); and *Harivaṁśa-purāṇa* 60 (A.D. 784); for further details, *see* Jinendra Varṇī, *Jainedra Siddhānta kośa,* pt. 2, Bhāratīya Jñānapīṭh, New Delhi 1992, p. 380) The explanation offered by the *Āvaśyaka-niryukti* for the appellation "Pārśva" is doubtless unlikely. It states that the Jina's mother in a dream saw a crawling cobra close to (*pārśva*) her bed and hence the boy-prince, after his birth, was named "Pārśva." (In such an event the appellation "Pārśvanāga" would have sounded more in accord!)
14. "Dark" in the southern tradition. "Blue" colouration for human skin is only imaginary; "dark",

as stated in the southern sources, seems a more accurate description since realistic.

15. Vardhamāna, too, in his dependable biographical records, is reported to have renounced the world at the age of 30. Curious coincidence!
16. The genuine or original Sammeda-śikhara (called in the Śvetāmbara Sanskrit works 'Sammeta-śaila') is not the one identified with the famous Pārśvanātha Hill near Hazārībāg in Bihar but the hill known as Kuluvā-pahāḍ near Gayā as attested by the remains of the medieval Jaina antiquities there including a fragmentary inscription mentioning "Sammeda .....". (The source from which I got this information is at the moment not handy for citation.)
17. *See* Malvaniya, *Sthānāṅga-samavāyāṅga,* p. 719. Some of these names could be genuine.
18. *Ibid.*
19. Puṣpacūlā has been referred to in a few other *āgamas* as well. *See* Mehta, *Āgamic Index,* Vol. I, pt. 1, p. 468 for references.
20. *Ibid.*
21. The Nirgrantha numerical conceptions as reflected in the writings, at least from the beginning of the Christian Era, in fact from the days of Ārya Śyāma onwards, reflect megalomania and pampalomania (unbridled flair for antiquity). The limitlessly inflated computed figures shown in these writings often fall in the realm of superhuman and super-astronomical.
22. The *Āvaśyaka-bhāṣya,* 17 (*c.* mid 6th cent. A.D.) so records: (Mehta 1970, p. 453).
23. These alternative dates are due to two different ways of computing Vardhamāna's date of *nirvāṇa,* which, as firmly believed in the tradition, is 527 B.C.; but 477 B.C. as computed by Jacobi after removing the needlessly interpolated 60 years of Pālaka's régime in the former figure and adding a decade more as a correction, seems more realistic.
24. *See* the chapter "Keśī Gautamīya," in the *Uttarādhyayana-sūtra* (chapter 23): Eds. (Late) Muni Puṇyavijaya and Pt. A.M. Bhojak, *Jaina-Āgama Series* No. 15, Bombay 1977, pp. 207-27.

    जिने पासे त्ति नामेनं अरहा लोगपूजिते
    संबुध्घप्पा य सव्वन्नू धम्मत्थिकरे जिने ॥ १ ॥
    तस्स लोगप्पदीवस्स आसि सीसे महायसे ।
    केसी कुमारसमने विज्जा-चरणपारगे ॥ २ ॥

    Stylistically, the date of this versified narrative would lay in the first century A.D., however, it seems to preserve the old authentic memory of an event of Vardhamāna's time. (It does not strike as a "mock fight"!)
25. *Cf.* The *Vyākhyāprajñapti-sūtra,* ed. Pt. Bechardas J. Doshi, *Jaina-Āgama-Series* No. 4 (Pt. 1), Bombay 1974, pp. 227, 228; *Ibid.,* p. 447.
26. The *Nābhinandanajinoddhāra-prabandha* (2. 135, 136), ed. Pt. Bhagvandas Harakhchand, Ahmedabad V.S. 1985 (A.D. 1929), p. 38.
27. For the episode of the Pārśvāpatya Kālāsyavaiśyaputra's joining the church of Vardhamāna and what procedure he then had followed, *Cf.* the *Vyākhyāprajñapti,* pt. 1, Bombay 1974, p. 67.24.
28. The Śvetāmbara friars, however, do not use shoes or umbrella; they, however, permit a few other things including a variety of wooden containers based perhaps on the *Vyavahāra-sūtra.*
29. The reference to *cātujjāme-nigganthe* in the Pārśva's chapter and elsewhere in the context of the statements by a few other Arhats in the *Isibhāṣiyāiṁ* is a clear proof of it. (For the *Isibhāṣiyāiṁ* text, I have used the text figuring in *Paiṇṇayasuttāyiṁ,* Bombay 1984, pp. 181-255. For the *cātujjāme-*

nigganthe, see there the reference on p. 232. It is likely that both these chapters formed the *Pūrva*-related works.)

30. *See Isibhāsiyāiñ,* Bombay 1984, pp. 230-33.
31. As stated there, it is an extract from the *Gati-vyākaraṇa-grantha*, a chapter concerning the exposition of transmigrational motion. (For detailed discussion on Pārśva's monastic discipline and some of his doctrines, *see* here the following Sagarmal Jain's paper.)
32. These are *ākāśa* (space), *dharma* (ether), *adharma* (gravity), *pudgala* (matter), and *jīva* (soul).
33. उध्धगामी जीवा
    अधेगामी पोग्गला।
    कम्मप्पभवा जीवा,
    परिणाम पभवा पोग्गला।

    (*Isibhāsiyāiñ*, Bombay 1984, pp. 231, 232.)

    That *Isibhāsiyāiñ* is not the text of the sect of Vardhamāna is clear from its relatively different and obviously earlier āgamic style of exposition. Also, in the earliest *āgamas* of the Church of Vardhamāna, Vardhamāna Jina is given a prominent position: He has been addressed there as Nātaputta, Kāśyapa, *maharṣi, muni, mahāmuni, vīra,* etc. and finally a whole hymn is addressed to him in the *Sūtrakṛtāṅga* calling him for the first time 'Mahāvīra' and proclaiming him as omniscient (*sarvjña-sarvadarśī*). Nothing of this sort is noticeable in the *Isibhāsiyāiñ*. It is respectable to, and considerate of the views of many sages of other sects as in a few examples inside the *Sūtrakṛtāṅga*. Also, the material of the Pārśva chapters is quite archaic and impresses as authentic. Such intense awareness on Pārśva's teachings is nowhere noticeable in the *āgamas* of the sect of Vardhamāna. (On the subject of Pārśva, there is some useful additional material in Pt. Dalsukh Malvaniya's paper, "Mahāvīra Samayanā Pārśvāpatyo" (Gujarātī), *Jaina Prakāśa*, Utthāna Mahāvīrāṅka, V.S. 1990 (A.D. 1934).
34. For details extracted from the biography of Pārśva by different authors collected by M. Mody and discussed on comparative basis, *see* U.P. Shah's paper in this volume.
35. Only a few texts mention this as a place of the incident.
36. Identified with Ramnagar in Bareily District, U.P.
37. तामील ईसाणिंदो बालतपस्सी विपूरणो चमरो।
    अणसणमरणपभावा कमढो कमढासुरो जाओ ॥ ८३१ ॥

    (In the *Paiṇṇayasuttāiṁ*, pt. 2, Eds. Puṇyavijaya Muni and Pt. A.M. Bhojak, *Jaina-Āgama-Series* No. 17 (Pt. II), Bombay 1984, p. 75.)
38. Ed. A.M. Bhojak, *Prakrit Text Society Series* No. 3, Ahmedabad-Vārāṇasī, 1961, pp. 266-68.
39. जथा सयंभू उदधीन सेट्ठे
    नागेसु या धरणिंद माहु सेट्ठे
    खोतोदगे वा रसवेजयंते
    तवोवधाने मुनिवेजयंते ॥ २० ॥

    (Ed. Muni Jambūvijaya, *Jaina-Āgama-Series* No. 2, Bombay 1978, chap. 6, p. 66.)
40. For example in the *Vyākhyāprajñapti*, the *Jīvābhigama-sūtra*, the *Prajñāpana-sūtra*, the *Sthānāṅga-sūtra*, and the *Jñātādharmakathā*. Details about these references are not so relevant in the present context.

41. Since the earth is not spherical but discoidal in Nirgrantha concept, the central Jambūdvīpa and the surrounding ring-formed oceans alternating with ring-formed mega-continents in transfinite number take its place, a function such as of Śeṣa for Dharaṇendra has no place in Nirgrantha cosmography.
42. U.P. Shah as well as M.N. Tiwari have so suggested. *See* their respective papers in this volume.
43. It was believed that this poem by Jinasena, since admired in one of the *Harivaṁśapurāṇa's* verses figuring there after the inaugural hymn, was composed before A.D. 784, the date of the selfsame *purāṇa*. Those verses, in reality, had been later interpolated. (For details *see* my paper in Hindi, "Dakṣiṇātya Paramparā ke kucha Grantho kī Aitihāsika Samaśyāyeṅ", *Sandhāna,* Vol. V, Varanasi 1992, pp. 15-29.)
44. It has appeared in several publications, the most complete and the best reproduced is in C. Sivaramamurti, *Panorama of Jain Art,* Bombay 1983, frontispiece.
45. *Cf.* K.R. Srinivasan, "South India", *Jaina Art and Architecture,* ed. A. Ghosh, Bharatiya Jnanpith, New Delhi 1975, plate 133. It is of the Pallava period, plausibly ninth century.
46. *Cf.* Sivaramamurti, *Panorama,* Kiḷakuyilkuḍi (Pāṇḍya, 9th cent.), Fig. 85; Citrāl (*c.* 9th cent.), Fig. 94, etc.
47. For details, *see* here U.P. Shah.
48. Vādirāja involves Padmāvatī also in his narration. *See* again U.P. Shah.
49. *See* here M.N. Tiwari's paper.
50. *See* my paper, "Śāntara Sculpture", *Journal of the Indian Society of Oriental Art,* New Series, Vol. IV, (1971-72), plates XVII-XX.
51. This image has been variously dated by different scholars between the Gupta period and the tenth century. I have tentatively suggested late 9th century but it could be somewhat early. Again, about its provenance, there is no unanimity. While it is believed to be originating from Bihar, Amar Singh places it in Madhya Pradesh. It could as well be from Uttar Pradesh. The image has been published in several different publications by different authors.
52. *See* here D.R. Das's paper.
53. *Vide* here U.P. Shah's remarks in his paper here.

LIST OF ILLUSTRATIONS

THE TEACHINGS OF ARHAT PĀRŚVA AND THE DISTINCTNESS OF HIS SECT

Sagarmal Jain

Among the Nirgrantha Tīrthaṅkaras, the historicity of Arhat Pārśva as well as of Jina Vardhamāna Mahāvīra has been fully established. Inscriptional and literary evidence play an important role in establishing the historicity of a person. The earliest inscription relating to Pārśva, of the 2nd or 3rd century A.D.,[1] has been found from the Kaṅkālī Ṭīlā, Mathurā. It is inscribed on an image of Pārśva which was installed by Ghoṣaka, a disciple of Gaṇi Aggahinīya of the Sthānīya-kula of the Koṭṭīya-gaṇa, a sub-order of friars and nuns also noticed in the hagiological list (earlier part, *c.* A.D. 100) of the *Paryuṣaṇā-kalpa* (compiled *c.* A.D. 503/516).[2] Though uninscribed, a more than life size sculpture of Pārśva (upper part mutilated)[3] and a tiny figure of Pārśva as the central focus of an *āyāgapaṭṭa,* both stylistically datable to the period of the Śaka king Ṣoḍās (*c.* early 2nd cent. A.D.),[4] prove that Arhat Pārśva was venerated in, and arguably before, that period. A metal image of Pārśva in the Prince of Wales Museum, variously dated between the 2nd-1st cent. B.C. to *c.* 2nd cent. A.D., is one more early piece in evidence.[5]

The inscriptional as well as the literary references to the Nirgranthas, however, are met with from *c.* third century B.C. The term "Niggantha" is mentioned in the inscription of Maurya Aśoka[6] and is fairly frequently met with in the Pāli *Tripiṭaka*[7] (usually, of course, in hateful and denegatory terms) though this cannot be taken as a conclusive evidence for the earlier church of Pārśva because the term Niggantha by then also had included the sect of Mahāvīra. In point of fact, the Pāli canon confounded a few views and teachings of these two historical Tīrthaṅkaras. As demonstrated in the early days of the Nirgranthic researches by Jacobi,[8] in the *Tripiṭaka* it is said that Nigganṭha Nātaputta (Mahāvīra) preached *cāturyāma-saṁvara,* while in point of fact the preacher of the *cāturyāma-dharma* was Arhat Pārśva and not Mahāvīra according to the Ardhamāgadhī canon of the Nirgranthas themselves.[9] Mahāvīra preached five-fold great vows (*pañca-mahāvratas*) and not the *cāturyāma-saṁvara.*

What we today can know about the teachings of Arhat Pārśva and the distinctness of his sect from that of Jina Vardhamāna is only through the available Ardhamāgadhī canon preserved in the Northern Church of Mahāvīra, because the ancient church of Pārśva was later progressively absorbed in the former and the records and texts relating to its hagiology and history are long lost.

Nirgranthologists like Pt. Sukhlal Sanghvi and others were of the opinion that the *Pūrva* literature (so often mentioned in the canonical literature from the late Kuṣāṇa period onward) had belonged to Pārśva's tradition.[10] At present, however, no texts of that category or specification exists. Today, insofar as our knowledge of Pārśva's teachings and traditions goes, we are dependent on the canonical literature of Mahāvīra's tradition, and, to a very small extent, on the Pāli canon of the Buddhists as well.

In the Ardhamāgadhī canon, the *Isibhāsiyāiṅ* (*Ṛṣibhāṣitani*) [11] the *Ācārāṅga,*[12] the second book the *Sūtrakṛtāṅga,*[13] the *Vyākhyā-prajñapti,*[14] the *Jñātādharma-kathā,*[15] the *Uttarādhyayana*[16] and the *Rāja-Pradesīya,*[17] the *Narakāvalikā,*[18] and the *Sthānāṅga*[19] reveal some significant references to Pārśva, his teachings as well as traditions. In the *Uttarādhyayana,*[20] the *Samavāyāṅga,*[21] the *Āvaśyaka-niryukti,*[22] the *Viśeṣāvaśyaka-bhāṣya* of Jinabhadra gaṇi kṣamāśramaṇa,[23] the *Āvaśyaka-cūrṇī*[24] and in the *Paryuṣaṇā-kalpa*[25] as well as in the *Mūlācāra*[26] of the Yāpanīya Church there are references to some distinctive (and hence distinguishing) features of the sects of Pārśva and Mahāvīra.

On Pārśva's life and the history of his times and of his sect, scanty material is traceable in these works; yet it is significant that they contain sufficient material pertaining to the ethical teachings and philosophical doctrines of Pārśva. They also firmly point toward the distinctness of Pārśva's sectarial tradition from that of Vardhamāna.[27]

The Teachings of Pārśva in Isibhāsiyāiṅ

The earliest and authentic version of Pārśva's philosophy and teachings is encountered in the *Isibhāsiyāiṅ* (*Ṛṣibhāṣitāni*)[28], a text compiled *c.* 1st cent. B.C. but often containing material that goes back to *c.* 4th century B.C., some even perhaps earlier. In a separate article,[29] I had suggested that the *Isibhāsiyāiṅ*, in terms of some of its content, is earlier than the whole of Pāli as well as the Ardhamāgadhī canonical literature excepting of course the first book of the *Ācārāṅga.* M.A. Dhaky opines that this text belongs to Pārśva's tradition. I, however, hold a different view. In my opinion the text, in earlier times, might have been composed in Pārśva's tradition as an independent text, but later on it was assimilated in the *Praśnavyākaraṇasūtra* which is considered to be one of the ten *Daśā* texts as well as the tenth work among the 11 *Aṅga*-books of Mahāvīra's tradition.

The *Isibhāsiyāiṅ* has an independent chapter on Pārśva's doctrines and teachings.[30] The authenticity of the Pārśva's view presented in this chapter cannot be doubted for various reasons. First, the *Isibhāsiyāiṅ* contains the teachings not only of Pārśva but also of Arhat Vardhamāna of the Nirgrantha Church, Maṅkhali Gośāla of the Ājīvaka sect; Vajjiyaputta, Mahākassapa, Indranāga and Sāriputta of the Buddhist Church, and Yājñavalkya, Asita-Devala, and Uddālaka-Āruṇi of the Vedic tradition. When we compare the views of the aforesaid saints mentioned in the *Isibhāsiyāiṅ* with the texts of their own traditions, we notice general similarity between them, which by and large proves the authenticity of the content of the *Isibhāsiyāiṅ*. If the author of the work in presenting had remained faithful to the original teachings of the *ṛṣis* or teachers of the other sects, we must conclude that he also was faithfully presenting the views of Pārśva. Second, we find that the teachings of Pārśva presented in the *Isibhāsiyāiṅ* corresponds to that which is stated of Pārśva's church in other canonical works like the *Sūtrakṛtāṅga*, the *Uttarādhyayana*, and the *Vyākhyā-prajñapti*. Third, the authenticity as well as high antiquity of the Pārśva-chapter in the *Isibhāsiyāiṅ* can also be supported on the ground that this chapter is represented by its two separate versions. It is said that the second version of this book originally was found in the text named *Gati-vyākaraṇa* i.e. the *Praśnavyākaraṇa*. The reference thus runs:

गतिवागरणगंथाओ पमिति जाव सामित्तं इमं अज्झयणं ताव इमो बीओ पाढो दिस्सति

The views of these two versions of the same chapter fully correspond to each other with slight difference in content and to an extent in language, a few details figuring more in one than in the other. Thus, at a very early date, two versions (*vācanās*) of the same subject had existed. This chapter contains philosophical as well as ethical views of Arhat Pārśva. First of all, in this text, the views of Pārśva about the nature of the world are stated. To explain the nature of the world the following five questions were raised:

(1) What is the nature of the world (*loka*)?
(2) What are the different planes of the world?
(3) To whom the world belongs?
(4) What does one mean by (the term) "world"?
(5) What is the meaning of the term *loka*?

Answering these five questions Arhat Pārśva said:

(1) The world consists of the animate beings and the inanimate objects.
(2) There are four different planes of the world:
 (i) Material (*dravya*)
 (ii) Spatial (*kṣetra*)
 (iii) Temporal (*kāla*)
 (iv) Existential (*bhāva*)
(3) World inheres in selfhood. It exists by itself. In the perspective of commandeering position the world belongs to animate beings but in the perspective of its constitution, it belongs to both animate and the inanimate.
(4) As for the existence of the world, it is eternal, with neither the beginning nor the end but is ever changing and (thus) dynamic in nature.
(5) While explaining the meaning of the term *loka*, it is said that this world is called *loka*, because, it is known or experienced or recognized. (The Sanskrit term *lokāyata* means to be known or to be recognized.) To explain the nature of motion the following four questions have been raised:
 (a) What is motion or *gati?*
 (b) Who meets this motion?
 (c) What are the different forms of motion?
 (d) Why is it called *gati,* motion?

Answering these questions about the motion Arhat Pārśva said:

 (a) Any motion or change in existence in animate and in the inanimate beings is called *gati.*
 (b) Animate and inanimate (substances) encounter motion or change. This change is of four types: substantial, spatial, temporal and existential.
 (c) The existence of movement or change is also perennial with no beginning or end.
 (d) It is called *gati* because it has motion.

About the *karma* philosophy and the moral teachings of Arhat Pārśva, it is thus recorded:

1. The animate beings possess an upward motion by their inherent (abstract) nature, while the matter has a downward motion by its intrinsic nature (inertia).
2. The animate beings reap the fruits of their deeds according to their (good or bad) *karmas* or activities, while the changes in inanimate substances take place due to their dynamic nature.

The animate beings are activity-oriented, the inanimate substances are change-oriented or dynamic in nature.

The animate beings have two types of experience, of pain and pleasure. Only those who can get rid of violence and other evils including wrong viewpoint will have the feeling of bliss. A Nirgrantha, who eats only inanimate things, will meet emancipation and thus will end the transmigratory cycle.

In the second version of this chapter the following additional concepts are also mentioned:

(1) The motion is of two types: (i) self-motivated and (ii) generated by external factors.

(2) Whatsoever a person experiences, it is due to his own, and not due to other's deeds.

(3) Those who observe the *cāturyāma* (the fourfold ethical code beginning with non-violence and ending with non-possession) will be free from the eight-fold *karmas* and will not be reborn in the four *yonīs* or generic categories.

The essence of the doctrines and ethical teachings of Pārśva as embodied and expositioned in the *Isibhāsiyāiñ* may be thus summarized:

(i) The world is eternal with no creator behind it.

(ii) Permanence in change is the essential nature of the world. World is dynamic in disposition. It consists of the five *astikāyas*, existentialities.

(iii) Substances are of two kinds, animate and inanimate.

(iv) The animate possesses an upward motion; the inanimate (by law of gravity), downward motion.

(v) The motion is of two kinds: (a) self-motivated and (b) directed by external factors.

(vi) The *gati* or transmigratory motion of animate beings is due to their own *karmas*, while the motion of matter is due to its own dynamic nature and inertia.

(vii) The *karmas* are of eight types.

(viii) Evil and non-restraint activities consequence in pain and in the cycle of births and deaths.

(ix) Those who indulge in passions and violence cannot achieve the eternal peace and bliss.

(x) Liberation can be achieved through the observance of four *yāmas*, self-restraints.

Teachings of Pārśva in other Canonical Works

In the *Sūtrakṛtāṅga*, the *Uttarādhyayana,* and the *Vyākhyā-prajñapti*, we find some explanation of, or minute observations on, what is broadly stated in the *Isibhāsiyāiṁ*. In these texts the views of Pārśva are presented by the followers of Pārśva and not by Pārśva himself. It is in the *Isibhāsiyāiṁ* alone that the original version of Pārśva's teachings is directly and implicitly present. Elsewhere we meet with Pārśva's views by proxy, through the discussions between the followers of Pārśva and that of Mahāvīra or in a few instances by Mahāvīra himself.

In the *Sūtrakṛtāṅga,*[31] for instance, is incorporated a conversation between Gautama and Udaka-Peḍhālaputra, the follower of Pārśva, on the nature and language of the *pratyākhyāna*-vow of non-violence. In this long discussion Udaka-Peḍhālaputra stressed on a technical point that, while taking the vow of non-violence, one must frame it in the language that "I shall not kill the being, who is presently in mobile-form (*trasa-bhūta*) instead of saying 'I shall not kill any mobile being". Similarly, in the *Vyākhyāprajñapti*[32] some observations relating to the difference in minutiae about the nature and meaning of the terms *sāmayika*, the *pratyākhyāna*, the *saṁvara*, the *viveka* and the *vyutsarga* have been made during the discussion of Kālāsyavaiśya-putra, the follower of Pārśva and some *sthaviras* of the Mahāvīra's following.

In the *Vyākhyāprajñapti*[33] we come across a very interesting and pinpointed discussion between the lay-followers of Mahāvīra and the *śramaṇas* of Pārśva's tradition on the outcome of restraint and penance. It had been questioned: If the outcome of restraint is to stop the influx of fresh *karmas* and of penance to liberate the soul from the kārmic bondage, then why the souls are born as *devas* in the celestial regions? To this question different answers were given by the *śramaṇas* of the Pārśva's church. At last Kaśyapa said it is due to the adherence to pious deeds such as penance and restraint that the souls are born as *devas* in celestial quarters. In the *Uttarādhyayana*[34] we also come across an interesting dialogue between Gautama and Keśī on aspects relating to the monastic disciplines and spiritual practices; as a result, some distinctive features of Pārśva's teachings surface.

Distinctness of Pārśva's Sect

Pārśva as well as Mahāvīra belonged to the Nirgrantha section of the Śramaṇic traditions which had several similarities in doctrines, philosophy, and religious practices. So far as the philosophical aspect of their teachings is concerned, the traditions of Pārśva and Mahāvīra have much in common. Scholars of Nirgranthology like Pt. Sukhlal Sanghvi and others are of the opinion that the Mahāvīra's sect has considerably borrowed from that of Pārśva in the field of metaphysics and *karma* philosophy.[35] The concepts such as the world is eternal as well as dynamic, that it exists by itself and has no creator are common to both traditions. The concept of permanence in change as the nature of Reality, which is the foundational tenet of the later Nirgrantha doctrine of *anekāntavāda* or non-absolutism is also met with in its embryonic form in, and in point of fact is central to, the teachings of Pārśva as well as Mahāvīra. Similarly, the concept of the five *astikāyas* and the eight-fold *karmas* are found in the philosophy of Pārśva as well as Mahāvīra. We encounter brief references to these concepts in the Pārśva-chapter of the *Īsibhāiyāiṁ* and more detailed ones in the standard canonical works of Mahāvīra's tradition.

Similarly, the concepts of *āsrava, saṁvara, nirjarā, sāmayika, pratyākhyāna* and *pauṣadha* are also common to both traditions, though there were some differences in the minutiae of these concepts and observances. The difference in opinion about the nature of *pratyākhyāna* between Gautama and Udaka Peḍhālaputra in the *Sūtrakṛtāṅga* has been earlier noticed. Similarly, the differences in te¬ms of detail on the practices are noticed in the relevant dialogues in the *Vyākhyāprajñapti* and in the *Uttarādhyāyana* also. However, these differences were related mostly to the code of conduct and not to the doctrines, philosophy, and principles of ethics as such. The distinctness of Pārśva's sect lies in its code of conduct, and not in dogma or philosophy, since it somewhat differed from that of Mahāvīra. We shall notice and discuss at this point the distinctive features of the Pārśva's tradition.

(1) Pārśva propounded *cāturyāma-dharma*, while Mahāvīra preached the *pañcayāma-dharma* or the five *mahāvratas.*[36] According to the Ardhamāgadhī canon, Mahāvīra added celibacy as an independent vow to the *cāturyāma-dharma* of Pārśva. The *Sūtrakṛtāṅga* mentions that Mahāvīra prohibited having woman, and eating during night hours.[37]

The question arises: Why did Mahāvīra add celibacy as an independent vow? The answer to this question can be read in the *Sūtrakṛtāṅga*. In the times of Pārśva, woman was considered a property or possession and it was taken for granted that prohibition of possession implied the prohibition of sexual relationship, for no one can enjoy the woman without having her. But, as the *Sūtrakṛtāṅga* informs, in the time of Mahāvīra, there were some *pāsatthā* (wayward) *śramaṇas,* who believed that the prohibition of possession did not imply (or include) the prohibition of sexual enjoyment. "If any woman invited or offered herself for enjoyment to a *śramaṇa*, than the fulfillment of her sexual desire was no sin, just as the squeezing of a blister or boil (causes relief) for some time (and has no dangerous consequences); so it is with (the enjoyment of) attractive (woman). How could, then, there be sin due to that ?"[38]

From this stanza it follows that some *śramaṇas* were interpreting the concept of non-possession in their own way. It only meant that, for the one who takes the vow of non-possession, cannot have a wife or woman. So it became necessary for Mahāvīra explicitly to add celibacy as an independent vow and to lay considerable stress on the observance of this vow.

If we contemplate this question historically, we notice that the ancient Vedic *ṛṣis* used to marry and had had progenies. After that state in life, on the one hand is followed the concept of *vānaprastha*, in which a *ṛṣi* did have a wife but observed celibacy; on the other hand, as informed by the Nirgrantha canonical literature, there were *śramaṇas* who were of the view that to enjoy a woman without possessing or getting her married was no sin: which is why Mahāvīra included in the fold a separate, clear, definite and uncompromising vow of celibacy.

In Pārśva's tradition, repentance was not accepted as an essential daily duty. Only when a monk committed sin or transgression of his vows may he repent. But Mahāvīra made repentance an obligatory daily-duty. A monk must repent every morning and evening whether he committed a sin and violated his vows or not. In the *Sūtrakṛtāṅga*[39] and in the *Vyākhyāprajñapti*[40] as well as in other canonical works of Mahāvīra's discipline it is known as *pratikramaṇa-dharma*.

One more difference in monastic practice was that Pārśva did not lay stress on nudity; he rather allowed one or two apparels for his monks (who thus were *sacelaka*), while Mahāvīra stressed on nudity and so Mahāvīra's tradition was known as *acela-dharma*. Though the medieval commentator of the *Uttarādhyayana* holds that Pārśva allowed his *śramaṇas* to wear expensive or coloured robe,[41] we possess no early textual support for such an assumption.

These three were the main features distinguishing the monastic code of conduct of Pārśva and that of Mahāvīra. Along with these three major differences, there also were some minor differences which are found in the concepts of the ten *kalpas* or planes of asceticism.[42] For instance, in Pārśva's tradition a monk could accept the invitation for food and also could take food prepared for him; but Mahāvīra forbade this practice. Pārśva allowed his monks to accept the meals prepared for the king; Mahāvīra prohibited it. In Mahāvīra's tradition it was vital for a friar (or nun) to move from one place to another, except during the rainy season: Also, an ascetic, he had said, must not stay at one place for more than a month. But, according to Pārśva's tradition, a friar could stay at one place as long as he wished. In short, to keep on wandering was essential in Mahāvīra's but was optional in Pārśva's disciplinary code. Again, Mahāvīra had stressed that an ascetic must stay on at one place during the four months of the rainy season; in Pārśva's tradition this practice was also optional.

According to Mahāvīra an aspirant to friarhood must be initiated probationally. After this testing period, if he is proven eligible, then he may be allowed to be ordinated second time and his seniority was fixed accordingly in the Order or Saṁgha.

These are some of the distinctive features of Pārśva's philosophy, teachings, and monastic discipline as can be traced out from the early literature. The belief that all Jinas teach the same code of conduct, and that the ascetics of the Pārśva's Order had become wayward by Mahāvīra's time receives no support from the evidence locked in the earlier canonical books.

NOTES AND REFERENCES

1. *See Epigraphia Indica,* Vol. X. Appendix. A list of Brāhmī Inscriptions S.N. 110, p. 20.
2. *Kalpasūtra* 216. In the various inscriptions of Kaṅkāli Ṭīlā, Mathurā, we have two readings about this kula of the Koṭṭiya-gaṇa: (1) Ṭhāniya-kula (2) Sthānīya-kula. While in the *Kalpasūtra* we have a third reading, Vāṇijja-kula.
3. Preserved in the Government Museum, Lucknow.
4. This date is after the recent researches by Gritli v. Mitterwallner.
5. *Cf.* U.P. Shah, *Studies in Jaina Art,* Varanasi 1955, plate 1, fig. 3.
6. *Me Kaṭe ime viyāpata hohonti ti niganṭhesu Pi* — Inscription No. 7, line 16, Delhi-Topara Inscription.
7. *See* G.P. Malalasekere, *Dictionary of Pāli-Proper names,* Vol. II, London 1974, pp. 61-65.
8. Hermann Jacobi, *Jaina Sutras,* Part II, (S.B.E. Vol. XLV), Introduction, p. xxi.
9. (A) *Cāujjñame niyanṭhe — Isibhāsiyāiṁ,* 31.
   (B) *Cāujjāmo ya jo dhammo jo imo paṁcasikkio — Uttarādhyayana* 23/12.
10. *See* Pt. Sukhalal, *Cāra Tīrthaṅkara* (Hindi), (sec. edn.), Varanasi 1989, pp. 141-43. *See also* "Introduction", the *Sacred Books of the East,* Vol. XXII, p. xliv.
11. *Isibhāsiyāiṁ,* 31.
12. *Ācārāṅga* II, 15/25.
13. *Sūtrakṛtāṅga* II. 7/8.
14. *Vyākhyāprajñapti* 1/9/21-24; 2/5/95; 5/9/254-255.
15. *Jñātādharma-kathā* 2/3/1-6.
16. *Uttarādhyayana* 23.
17. *Rājapradeśīya* 2/3.

18. *Narakāvalikā (Niryāvaliya-sūtra)* 3/1.
19. *Sthānāṅga* 9/61.
20. *Uttarādhyayana* 23/12-13; *see also* commentary of Śāntyācārya for these verses.
21. *Samavāyāṅga* 8/8, 9/4, 16/4, 38/1, 100/4.
22. *Āvaśyaka-niryukti* 238 and 1241-1243.
23. *Viśeṣāvaśyaka-bhāṣya.*
24. *Āvaśyaka-cūrṇi.*
25. *Paryūṣanā-kalpa (Kalpa-sūtra)* 148-156.
26. *Mūlācāra.*
27. *See Arhat Pārśva.*
28. *Isibhāsiyāiṅ,* 31.
29. *See* Sagarmal Jain, *Rishibhasit: A Study,* Jaipur 1988.
30. *Isibhāsiyāiṅ,* 31.
31. *Sūtrakṛtāṅga* II, chapter 7th.
32. *Vyākhyāprajñapti* 10.9. 33. *Ibid.*, 2.5.
34. *Uttarādhyayana* 23.
35. *See Cāra Tīrthaṅkara* for detailed discussion.
36. *Uttarādhyayana* 23/12.
37. *Se vāriyā ithi saraibhattam—Sūtrakṛtāṅga* 1/6/28.
38. *Ibid.*, 1/3/4/9-10.
39. *Ibid.*, 2/7/81.
40. *Vyākhyāprajñapti* 1/9/123. *See also Āvaśyaka-niryukti* 1241.
41. *Uttarādhyayana* 23/12. *See also* Śāntācārya's *ṭīkā* on the above verses.
42. *See* (a) *Āvasyaka-niryukti,* 1241-1243.
    (b) *Bṛhat-Kalpa sūtra-bhāṣya,* 6359-6366.

JINA PĀRŚVA IN JAINA CANONICAL LITERATURE

Dalsukh D. Malvaniya

After surveying the available Nirgrantha canonical literature, I am convinced that the biography of Jina Pārśva was in a continuous process of growth and consequently reflects stages of development. In the earliest canonical work like the *Ācāra* Book I (*c.* 5th-3rd century B.C.) and the *Sūtrakṛta* Book I (*c.* 3rd-1st century B.C.), no reference to Jina Pārśva is noticeable. Only in the *Vyākhyāprajñapti* (*c.* 2nd-3rd century A.D.) do we find a reference to him as a "respected person (*arahā, arhat*)" designating him also as winsome (*puruṣādānīya*)[1]. Therein his view on the cosmos or universe (*loka*) is reported to be shared by Jina Mahāvīra.[2] Earlier, in the *Ṛṣibhāṣitāni* (compiled *c.* 2nd-1st century B.C. from earlier sources), Pārśva is included among the 45 *ṛṣis*. Correspondingly in the text are 45 brief chapters on these *ṛṣis*'s sayings and aphorisms, hailing as these holymen are from the Vedic, the Buddhist, the Ājīvika and the Nirgrantha traditions. Pārśva here is included,[3] alongside Vardhamāna (Jina Mahāvīra), as an *arhat*. In the later notices concerning the *Ṛṣibhāṣitāni*, these teachers are recognized, several of course wrongly, as *Pratyeka-Buddhas*;[4] for Pārśva, Mahāvīra, and Gośāla were a little later recognized as *tīrthaṅkaras* or Founders of Church, the last two also noted that way in the Buddhist literature. Moreover, most of them are designated as *arahā* or *arhat*, a Vedic term which originally was commonly applied to all great men and was not the sole prerogative of the Nirgranthas (or for that matter Buddhists either) as it lately had become.

In Pārśva's sayings in the *Ṛṣibhāṣitāni* (Ch. 31), the theories about the cosmos (*loka*) and the transmigration (*gati*) are discussed where it is clearly mentioned that the conscious beings (*jīvas*) and non-living verities (*ajīvas*) constitute the *loka*. *Loka* is without the beginning or the end, and is subject to change or modification (*pāriṇāmī*). *Loka* is amenable to viewing from four standpoints or aspects: substance (*dravya*), region (*kṣetra*), phenomenic time (*kāla*) and sentience-reaction (*bhāva*). The conscious beings, *jīvas*, are abstract in form. *Jīvas* are mentioned as sublimatory (*ūrdhvagāmī*), and matter (*pudgala*) as being gravity-bound (*adhaḥ-gāmī*). It is also noted that the present state of the *jīvas* or beings depend on *karma* and that of the *pudgalas* on consequential change, *pariṇāma*.

The Nirgrantha is mentioned as *maḍāī* or eating things that possess no life, and is a person who is without the next birth. Pārśva also refers to the eight types of *karmas* (without naming them) and the five universal verities (*pañcāstikāyas*, also without further elucidation). The well-known principal doctrines of the Nirgrantha-darśana are thus rooted in the teachings of Pārśva as deducible from the notices in the *Ṛṣibhāṣitāni*. However, nothing here is said about his life.

In the *Sūtrakṛta* Book II (*c.* 3rd century B.C.-1st century A.D..), the *Vyākhyāprajñapti*, the *Rājaprasenīya* (*c.* 1st century-3rd century A.D.), the *Jñātādharmakathā* (*c.* 2nd-3rd century A.D.) and the *Ācāra* Book II (*c.* 1st century A.D.) refer to the followers of Pārśva; since I have discussed the concerned particulars elsewhere,[5] I here shall omit enlarging upon this subject.

Mention of some of the particulars of Pārśva's life story is first found in the "Jina-caritra" section of the famous *Paryuṣaṇā-kalpa* (compiled *c.* A.D. 503/516); but, there too, we do not find the biographical narrative as such but only the reckoning of a few basic personal particulars. In point of fact, in the *Paryuṣaṇā-kalpa*, the chapter concerning the lives of the 24 *Tīrthaṅkaras* were added later, the time by which the concept of the 24 *Tīrthaṅkaras* was a settled fact. (The *Paryuṣaṇā-kalpa*, which actually is an elaboration of a small section of the *Daśāśruta-skandha olim Ācāra-prakalpa*, is traditionally held to have been written by Ārya Bhadrabāhu, 170 years after the *Nirvāṇa* of Mahāvīra (about 300 B.C.). In the *Paryuṣaṇā-kalpa* the following facts about Pārśva are noted:[6]

1. For his five *kalyāṇakas*—auspicious occasions such as *cyavana* (transmigration for taking the new birth), *janma* (birth), *niṣkramaṇa* (renunciation), *kevala* (omniscience), and *nirvāṇa* (liberation) — Viśākhā is noted as the constellation for each of the *kalyāṇaka*-occasion.
2. The following dates are given for the above-mentioned five *Kalyāṇakas:* (1) *Cyavana* — *Caitra Kṛṣṇa* 4 in the womb of Vāmā, the consort of Aśvasena, king of Vārāṇasī; (2) *Janma* — *Pauṣa Kṛṣṇa* 10; (3) *Dīkṣā* — after 30 years in *Pauṣa, Kṛṣṇa* 11 with 300 other persons; (4) *Kevala* — *Caitra Kṛṣṇa* , 4; and (5) *Nirvāṇa* — at the age of 100 years on *Śrāvaṇa śukla* 8.
3. According to non-āgamic notices, Pārśva endured the *upasargas* or sufferings but whether through mortal or divine agency is not mentioned though on the basis of the pre-medieval and medieval narrative literature it may be inferred that the tormentations inflicted by Kamaṭha probably were implied.
4. Names of his eight *gaṇadharas* or chief apostles have been mentioned.
5. The number of his disciples — friars and nuns — is mentioned.
6. Some 1230 years had passed since his *nirvāṇa* when the "Jina-caritra" was codified. (This would correspond to 813 B.C. according to the tradition of 527

B.C. for the date of the *nirvāṇa* of Mahāvīra, or 753 B.C. if the *Vīra-nirvāṇa* took place in 477 B.C. as Jacobi had reckoned.)

An attempt at the reconciliation of the Church of Mahāvīra with the Church of Pārśva is recorded in the *Uttarādhyayana-sūtra*. (This chapter [23], in my opinion, is anterior to the formulation of the conception of 24 *Tīrthaṅkaras*).

The belief about the sequence of the 24 *Tīrthaṅkaras* is first met with in the *Caturviṁśati-stava* (*c*. 1st century A.D.) — one of the six *āvaśyakas* — and next in the *Samavāyāṅga* (24) (present version *c*. A.D. 363). There, Pārśva finds mention before Mahāvīra as last but one *Tīrthaṅkara*. Some more information about Pārśva (along with that of the other Jinas) is also found there as well as in the *Sthānāṅga* (likewise enlarged *c*. A.D. 363). (For detailed information inside these two *āgamas*, one may refer to my *Sthānāṅga-Samavāyāṅga*, 696-745).[7] Here I must add that some of this information in the *Sthānāṅga* and the *Samavāyāṅga* possibly may have been extracted from an earlier source like the *Prathamānuyoga* of Ārya Śyāma I (*c*. last quarter of the 1st century B.C.). And the *Paryuṣaṇā-kalpa* may have used the same source or the *Sthānāṅga* and the *Samavāyāṅga*, or perhaps all the three.

The *Jñātādharma-kathā* II (*c*. 3rd-4th century A.D.) deals with the female disciples of Pārśva but, from the description, they happen to be of lax character (*vis-à-vis*, of course, the stern and strict practices enjoined in the Church of *Arhat* Vardhamāna Mahāvīra.)

Though the *Paryuṣaṇā-kalpa* does not mention, the earlier source *Ācārāṅga* II.15.25 (*Bhāvanā*) mentions that the parents of Mahāvīra were the follower of Pārśva (*Pāsāvaccijjā, Pārśvapatya*). It must, however, be noted that the *Āvaśyaka-cūrṇi* (*c*. A.D. 600-650), which treats the life of Jina Vardhamāna Mahāvīra at some length, does not so report.

In the *Paiṇṇaga* or the *Prakīrṇaka* list of the *Samavāyāṅga* (p. 943) are quoted some *saṅgrahaṇī-gāthās* in which the personal appellations in the previous births of the 24 *Tīrthaṅkaras* are mentioned and in that Sudaṁsaṇa (Sudarśana) is the name of Pārśva's in his penultimate birth. Seemingly, this *paiṇṇaga* part had been somewhat lately added to the *Samavāyāṅga*.

The first attempt to give some general information on the 24 *Tīrthaṅkaras* is found in the *Āvaśyaka-niryukti* (198, *c*. A.D. 525; *see also* the *Viśeṣāvaśyaka-bhāṣya*, 1636).[8] About five decades earlier, it had been noted in the *Paümacariya* (*c*. A.D. 473) as well.

Here we are concerned with the narrative on Pārśva's life, and as far as my knowledge goes, Jinasena's *Pārśvābhyudaya-kāvya* (*c*. A.D. 825 or after A.D. 815)[9] is the earliest to have been written on this subject, the next being the *Uttarapurāṇa* of Guṇabhadra (c. A.D. 850). These two Southern Nirgrantha works apparently are the source for most of the later narrative works in South on the legendary life of Pārśva.

From all these references it is clear that a direct mention of Dharaṇendra's nexus with Pārśva is first met with only in the Nirgrantha-Digambara *purāṇas* and not in the Northern Nirgrantha canonical works nor in their exegetical literature.[10] The only Northern work which says that Pārśva and Mahāvīra alone of the *Tīrthaṅkaras* had to encounter the *upasarga*-tormentations. This is the *Śattarī-saya-ṭhāṇa* (*Saptati-śata-sthāna*); and it is a medieval work, indeed fairly posterior to Southern Nirgrantha notices.

NOTES AND REFERENCES

1. *Bhagavatī-sūtra* (*Aṅgasuttāṇi*, Vol. II), 5.255; 9.122, Ladnun V.S. 2031 (1975).
2. *Ibid.*, 5. 255.
3. *Isibhāsiyāiṅ*, ch. 31, L.D.S. No. 45, Ahmedabad 1974.
4. *See* Intro. to *Isibhāsiyāiṅ*, 1.
5. "Mahāvīra Samayanā Pārśvāpatyo", (Gujarātī), *Jaina Prakāśa*, Utthāna Mahāvīraṅka, V.S. 1990 (1934 A.D.), 46.
6. *Kalpasūtra*, 148-160, 4th edn., ed. Devendra Shastri, Udaipur 1985.
7. Published in the *Aṅga Suttāni*, Vol.I, Delhi V.S. 2031/A.D. 1975. *See* note 1.
8. Included in the *Viśeṣāvaśyaka-bhāṣya*, Vol.II, L.D. Series Vol.14, Ahmedabad 1968.
9. *Cf.* Madhusudan Dhanky (M.A. Dhaky), "Dakṣiṇātya Nirgrantha Paramparā ke Kucha Granthoṅ kī Aitihāsika Samasyāyeṅ", *Sandhāna*, V (1992), 15-19.
10. *See* the word "Dharaṇa" in Mohanlal Mehta, Prakrit proper names (L.D. Series No. 28), Ahmedabad 1970; and "Dharaṇendra" in the *Jainendra Siddhānta Kośa* (Bharatiya Jñāna Pīṭha), New Delhi 1992.

THE HISTORICAL ORIGIN AND ONTOLOGICAL INTERPRETATION OF ARHAT PĀRŚVA'S ASSOCIATION WITH DHARAṆENDRA

U.P. Shah

Arhat Pārśva—Jina Pārśvanātha—is reported in the "Jina-caritra" of the *Paryuṣaṇā-kalpa* (*PK*) (*c.* A.D. 503/516) to have flourished 250 years before the *nirvāṇa* of Mahāvīra. He is reported there to have spent his first 30 years as a layman and after that led the life of an ascetic for 70 years and attained *nirvāṇa* on Mt. Sammeta. According to the *PK* (149 ff), Pārśva was born as a prince, as son of king Aśvasena and queen Vāmādevī in the city of Vārāṇasī. No explanation is given there for the appellation Pārśva, nor there is any mention of a snake by the side of the queen mother in her dream or in waking state as recorded in the medieval works of the Northern Nirgrantha tradition which purport to deal with his (mostly legendary) biography. Nor Pārśva's association with Dharaṇendra is referred to in the *PK*. According to the *PK* (159), "The bhagavān (Arhat Pārśva) passed 83 day-nights in meditation on Self on the way to liberation ...... on the 84th day-night, ... under the *dhātakī*-tree, ... while in meditation, he attained the total cognition and conation, *kevala*." The austerities practiced and the hardships suffered by Mahāvīra and Pārśva are described in almost identical terms and there is nothing in the *PK* account indicative of the episode of Kamaṭha who had attempted to obstruct Pārśva in meditation. (Pārśva's austerities before his attaining Kevalajñāna are of course mentioned therein, *vide* 157-159.)

Pārśva was an historical personage; but, as Schubring puts it, "what else we are told of him in *Jinac.* 149 f. is merely a copy of Mahāvīra's biography with the exception that Pāsa is said to have been born in Benares and to have died on Sammeya mountain in Bihar. Nor do we learn anything of importance of Pāsa's role from *Nāyādh.* II.1, and *Puppha.* 1.3. (What in *Isibhās.* 31 is given as his utterance has no individual character). But he is attested as a historic personality by other passages in rendering his teaching and reporting on his followers. Mahāvīra's parents are said to have belonged to Pāsa's lay-followers (*Pāsāvaccijjā samaṇovāsagā*, Āyara., II.15.16.) and in his life-time — as is confirmed by the *Sammaññaphala-Sutta* of the Dīgha-Nikāya — there have been teachers (*P. jjā therā bhagavanto*, *Viy.* 134b., 247b.) and monks (*aṇagāra*, *Viy.* 99a, 439a) in accordance with Pāsa's intentions ..... Pāsa was obviously of a winsome nature, for he bears the constant title of *puriṣādānīya* which seems to be the oldest precursor of the modern occasional title of Lokamānya, Deśabandhu, Mahātman etc...."[1] (The term *puriṣādānīya* is often translated as the "beloved one", or as the "celebrated one".)

Pārśva and his disciples are noticed in some *āgamas* and āgamic commentaries. For instance the *Āvaśyaka-cūrṇi* incidentally mentions several ascetics of the Pārśva sect, who were there during the course of Mahāvīra's wanderings as an ascetic. Uppala was a *Pāsāvaccijjā* (disciple of Pārśva), who, after giving up the monastic order, had entered the house-holder's life and lived in Aṭṭhiyagāma. His two sisters, Somā and Jayantī, had joined the Order of Pārśva, but, being unable to live the stern ascetic life of his Order, became Parivrājikās of the Brahmanical Order.[2] Municandra, a follower of Pārśva, dwelt in a potter's shop in Kumārāya-sanniveśa in company of his disciples. Asked by Gosāla (as to who they were), Municandra had replied that they were *Samaṇa Nigganthas*. Mahāvīra told Gośāla that they were the followers of Pārśva.[3] Vijayā and Pagabbhā (Pragalbhā ?), two female disciples of Pārśva (*pāssāntevāsino*) rescued Mahāvīra and Gośāla during their predicament in Kuvīya-sanniveśa.[4]

Pārśvanātha is said to have visited a number of cities, prominent among which were Adhicchatrā,[5] Āmalakappā[6] , Śrāvastī, Hastināpura, Kāmpilyapura, Sāketa,[7] Rājagṛha and Kauśāmbī.[8] Buddhist texts refer to the existence of a large number of Nigaṇṭhas who followed *cāturyāma saṁvara*.[9] The *Vyākhyāprajñapti*[10] records a discussion that took place between Mahāvīra and Śramaṇa Gāṅgeya, a follower of Pārśva in Vāṇijyagrāma. Gāṅgeya gave up the *catujjāma-dhamma* and embraced the *Pañcamahāvrata* disciplinary vow of Mahāvīra. Kālāsyavaiśyaputra, also a follower of Pārśva, became a follower of Mahāvīra. The *Jñātādharmakathā*[11] refers to Puṇḍarīka who plucked out his hair and accepted the four vows. The city of Tuṅgiya is stated to have been the centre of *theras* (*sthaviras*) who were followers of Pārśva and who moved in a congregation of 500 monks. Names of some of these *theras* mentioned are Kāliyaputta, Mehila, Ānandarakṣita, and Kāśyapa.[12] The *Sūtrakṛtāṅga*[13] mentions Udaya Peḍhālaputta, a Nirgrantha follower of Pārśva, of the Meyañña (Maitreya) *gotra*. Gautama Indrabhūti had discussions with him after which Gautama took him to Mahāvīra where he gave up the doctrine of four restraints (of Pārśva) and took to five great vows as ordained by Mahāvīra. The *Rāja-Prasenīya*[14] refers to a *kumāra-śramaṇa* Keśī who was a pontiff or patriarch of the Pārśva's Church and knew 14 *Pūrvas*. Keśī visited the town of Śrāvastī in a congregation of 500 monks. Later Keśī visited Śvetāmbī where a discussion took place between him and king Pradeśī who afterwards became a follower of the (Nirgrantha) *śramaṇa*. Possibly he is the same Keśī who had had the historical meeting with Gautama, the *gaṇadhara* of Mahāvīra, in Śrāvastī, as reported in the *Uttarādhyayanasūtra* (23).[15]

In none of these references to Pārśva, to his teachings, and to his followers do we find any reference to the *upasarga* of Kamaṭha to Pārśva, nor do we meet with any specific reference to, and explanation of Pārśva's association with Dharaṇa, the lord of the Nāgas. This association is first met with in the images of Pārśva from Mathurā (*c.* 1st or 2nd and 3rd centuries A.D.); also in an early much corroded bronze from Causā hoard (*c.* 2nd-3rd cent. A.D.), and in an early metal image of Pārśva in the Prince of Wales Museum which I have assigned to *c.* 2nd-1st century B.C. But there is no evidence that the images of Pārśva or any other *Tīrthaṅkaras* existed in the age of Mahāvīra and his *gaṇadharas*. No mention of a worship of, or to the temples of Jinas is found in the older strata of the available Nirgrantha canon.

In the Nirgrantha canonical literature, we for the first time come across references to the previous births of each of the 24 *Tīrthaṅkaras* in the *Samavāyāṅga-sūtra* (157/11-14). Accordingly, in the previous birth, the soul of Pārśva was called Sudarśana. *PK* does not refer to any previous birth of Pārśva and only says that Pārśva descended into his mother's womb from the Prāṇata Kalpa (heaven). The Digambara cosmographical work, the *Trilokaprajñapti* (*c.* mid-6th cent. A.D.), too, follows this tradition. According to Raviṣeṇa, the author of the *Padmacarita* (A.D. 676) (20.35), Pārśva descended from Vaijayanta heaven. In his previous birth he was called Ānanda, son of Vītaśoka Ḍāmara of Sāketa. Modi in his Introduction to his edition of the Digambara Padmakīrti's *Pāsanāhacariū* (S.S. 999/A.D. 1077) has given an interesting Table (on pp. 33-36) giving comparisons of the main details of the nine previous existences of Pārśva from the *Uttarapurāṇa* of Guṇabhadra (*c.* mid-9th cent. A.D.), the Apabhraṁśa *Mahāpurāṇa* of Puṣpadanta (*c.* 865-874.), *Śrī-Pārśvanātha-carita* of Vādirājā (A.D. 1025), and *Siri-Pāsanāhacariū* of Padmakīrti (A.D. 1077) — Digambara authors all — next *Siri-Pāsanāhacariya* of Devabhadra Sūri (Śve. A.D. 1111), Hemacandra's *Triṣaṣṭiśalākāpuruṣacarita* (Śve., 3rd quarter of the 12th century), *Pāsacariya* of Kavi Raidhū (Dig., 15th cent. A.D.) and *Pārśvanāthacaritra* of Hemavijaya Gaṇī (Śve., 17th cent. A.D.). The differences among them are only on a few points and are mainly about the names of the parents of Pārśva's previous births or about the heavens from which Pārśva descended in different births and the names of Pārśva in some of his earlier births. Modi has given an analysis of the various details in the life of Pārśvanātha as reported in the above texts. The study shows that there are two different traditions concerning the life of

Pārśvanātha and of his previous births, the Southern or Digambara (also perhaps Yāpanīya) and the Northern or Śvetāmbara. Whereas the Śvetāmbara accounts mainly follow the tradition of Devabhadra, the Digambara accounts often follow Guṇabhadra. But there are some differences in the tradition of the *Uttarapurāṇa* and of the *Padmacarita* of Raviṣeṇa as well. (I omit giving details; those have been already given by Modi.) Modi's study brings out one salient fact: Detailed accounts of the life of Pārśvanātha and his previous existences have originated possibly after *c.* 4th century A.D. These perhaps were based on some earlier traditions not yet traceable. But there is at present no explanation for the absence of the account of Kamaṭha even in the relatively later strata of the Northern canonical texts.

Both Digambara *purāṇas* and the Śvetāmbara *caritas* give elaborate descriptions of the *upasargas* caused to Pārśva in meditation by a demi-god who in his previous existence was the soul of Kamaṭha, the younger brother of Marubhūti, who was the soul of Pārśva in the earlier existence of Pārśvanātha. According to the *Uttarapurāṇa*, the *Mahāpurāṇa* of Puṣpadanta, and the *Pāsacariya* of Raidhū, this demi-god was called Śaṁbara. Vādirāja has called him Bhūtānanda. In the Śvetāmbara tradition, in the *Pāsanāhacariya* of Devabhadra, the demi-god is Meghamālin. The Digambara Padmakīrti, too, in his *Pāsanāhacariü* calls him Meghamālī, an "Asurendra".

It is indeed difficult to say when this tradition of the *upasarga* caused by the demi-god had started. The total absence of the depiction of this episode in the sculptures from the Kaṅkāli Ṭīlā, Mathurā, probably suggests that the belief came into currency some time after the Kuṣāṇa period, perhaps not long after the fourth century A.D. An elaborate sculpture depicting this episode preserved in the Indian Museum, Calcutta, supposed to have originated in U.P. or Bihar, is often assigned to the Gupta age on account of the carving reminiscent of Gupta art. But the figure of the snake-queen holding the umbrella is clearly post-Gupta in character, reminding as it also does one of the Buddhist representations of the attack of Māra. As the material evidence goes to indicate, it cannot be earlier than the later part of the sixth century A.D. (For illustration see *Panorama of Jain Art,* figs. 38-39[16] and the frontispiece of my recent book, the *Jaina Rūpa-Maṇḍana,* Vol. I).[17] Elsewhere I have published various sculptures depicting this episode of Kamaṭha's attack, from both northern and southern India in a paper entitled "A Pārśvanātha Sculpture in Celeveland Museum".[18] Dhaky has published two beautiful and elaborate sculptures from Karnataka in his article on the Śāntara sculptures.[19] I need not go in the details of these sculptures since some of the participants in this Seminar have discussed them region-wise. A study of almost all sculptures depicting this incident shows that the earliest datable are: (1) the Indian Museum sculpture referred to above and assigned to *c.* late sixth century; (2) the relief panel in the Aihoḷe cave assignable to *c.* A.D. 600[20] and (3) the large panel in the Jaina cave (No. IV) at Bādāmī assignable to the end of the late sixth century A.D.[21]

Kamaṭha (also called Kaṭha)-tāpasa who was reborn as Śaṁvara or Śaṁbara (Dig.), or Meghamālī (Śve.), tried hard to shake Pārśva from his trance. For seven days he poured heavy rains, made terrifying sounds and hurled rocks at him. To frighten Pārśva he conjured up lions, scorpions, terrific Vetāla-genii and ghouls who spit fire from their mouths. But the great sage, unaffected by these harassments (*upasargas*), remained steadfast in meditation. Dharaṇa, the Indra of the Nāgakumāra gods, remembering the good turn done by Pārśva in his previous *āśrama*, came to his rescue. Standing behind the Jina, the Nāgendra held a canopy of his seven hoods over the Jina's head in order to protect the Lord from rains, bombardment of rocks, etc. Dharaṇa's chief queens (four) staged dance with music before the meditating sage but the great sage was equally unmindful of the pleasure of music and dance and of the pain inflicted by Śambara or Meghamālī. His villany going fruitless, the lord of the demons relented, and bowing down before the Lord, seeking as he did the Jina's forgiveness, returned with remorse to his celestial abode. It is said that Meghamālī had so much flooded the area that the water level rose up to the tip of the nose of Pārśva and that Dharaṇendra, wrapping his coils all around the body of Pārśva and holding the hoods as a canopy over the sage's head, had lifted up the body of Pārśva above water.

According to both sects, the Jina Pārśvanātha was dark-blue in complexion and had the snake as his cognizance, *lāñchana*. Hemacandrācārya as well as Āśādhara (*c.* 2nd quarter of the 13th cent. A.D.) have made it clear that the *lāñchanas* are (the symbols on) the *dhvajas* of the Jinas. Thus the snake was originally the heraldic sign of Pārśvanātha. Does it suggest Pārśvanātha's intimate association with the race or tribe that had the Nāga as its totem or symbol? Or, did Pārśva himself belong to the Nāga race or tribe? According to the Śvetāmbara tradition, the Jina was called Pārśva because his mother had seen, in dream, a cobra by her side (Pārśva) during the period of confinement.[22]

When Pārśva grew up, he once saw an ascetic (*tāpasa*), variously called Kaṭha, Kaḍha, or Kamaṭha, practicing penance called *pañcāgni-tapa*, by burning logs of wood in four groups in four directions around him and the fifth fire being the scorching sun above. In one of the logs was a pair of snakes which was being burnt alive. Pārśva rescued the snakes and remonstrated the ascetic who was no other than Kamaṭha, the soul of the younger brother of Pārśva in his previous existence as Marubhūti. The snake couple, half burnt, died immediately after prince Pārśva chanted before them the *Namaskāra-maṅgala* and were reborn as Dharaṇendra (Indra of the Nāgakumāra class of Bhavanavāsī gods) and his queen (called Padmāvatī in medieval texts). In the *Pāsanāhacariya* (3, p. 167), Devabhadrācārya speaks of only one snake, and he was reborn as Dharaṇendra after death. The Digambara texts speak of a pair of snakes. However, in the *Pāsanāhacariü*, 13.11. pp. 111-12, Padmakīrti speaks of only a single snake saved by Pārśva.

Both sects agree in stipulating cobra as the *dhvaja* or *lāñchana* of Pārśvanātha and generally represent five or seven snake-hoods as a canopy over the Jina's head. In the images of Pārśvanātha the snake cognizance is shown on the pedestal and often the coils of the snake's body are shown behind the body of Pārśva either standing or sitting in meditation. The snake-hoods as well as the coils suggest Nāgendra Dharaṇa protecting the body of Pārśvanātha.

It may be recalled that Supārśvanātha, the seventh *Tīrthaṅkara,* is also said to have a canopy of snake, but having either one, three, or nine hoods over his head. But no known account explains the presence of cobra-hoods over Supārśvanātha's head. The difference in the number of hoods help differentiating the images of Pārśva from those of Supārśva. But no canonical allusion in this matter is known. Amongst the earliest known images, all known heads of sculptures with snake-hoods are identified as Pārśva because of seven snake-hoods shown. This would show that the late medieval written tradition and modern belief that the *stūpa* of Kaṅkāli Ṭīlā was of Supārśva seems unreliable. In all likelihood that was the *stūpa* of Pārśvanātha.

However, as I have shown in the Jaina *Rūpa-Maṇḍana,* the reliefs of Pārśva at Aihoḷe and Bādāmī show five snake hoods and not seven. Technically speaking, all Jina figures with snake-hoods overhead, with coils of a snake behind the body and below the seat of the Jina (as in a sculpture at Rājgīr), should certainly be identified as representing Pārśvanātha on account of the legend of Dharaṇendra protecting Pārśvanātha from rains etc. during Kamaṭha's attacks.

Another way of differentiating images of Pārśva from those of Supārśva is to take help of the cognizance wherever it is shown, because the cognizance of Supārśva is the symbol *Svastika* and not the snake. This further lends doubt about the original association of snake with Supārśva.

The much corroded early bronze of Pārśva from Causā hoard (now in Patna Museum)[23] seems hardly later than the first century A.D. This figure has seven snake-hoods. The standing Pārśvanātha bronze in the Prince of Wales Museum (which I still maintain that it is not later than *c.* first century B.C. against the views of Moti Chandra and Sadashiv Gorakshakar),[24] has the snake-hoods partly mutilated but they suggest that the figure had a canopy of five snake-hoods. Since the body of the Dharaṇa Nāga is shown at the back of this figure there is no doubt that the image represents Pārśvanātha.

From all that has hitherto been said, it is obvious that there is no early literary or archaeological evidence before *c.* A.D. 400 to support the prevalence of the belief in the *upasarga* by Kamaṭha. However, as is clear from the earliest available examples, the association of the Nāga with Pārśva is definitely older and possibly has some historical or an early mythological basis of which we as yet know nothing.

But even here we have some interesting comparable material from the Brahmanical and Buddhist sources. I have earlier shown close correspondence between the representations of Kamaṭha's *upasargas* and those of the assault of Māra on the Buddha.[25] At the end of the attacks both Buddha as well as Pārśva got enlightenment, the supreme wisdom. Both themes have been popular in Indian Art,[26] but as yet we have not been able to discover any representation of Kamaṭha's attack which is earlier than, or even contemporary with, the known earliest Buddhist representations concerning the assault of Māra. Both Śvetāmbara as well as the Digambara pre-medieval and medieval literary sources give graphic accounts of the *upasarga* by Kamaṭha. For a comparison with Buddhist accounts the following few passages may be noted:

(1) रोषात्कृतमहाघोषो महावृष्टिमपातयत् ।
व्यधात् तथैव सप्ताहान्यन्याँश्च विविधान्विधी: ।
महोपसर्गात्शैलोपनिपातानिवान्तका: ॥
तद्ज्ञात्वावधिबोधेन धरणीशो विनिर्गत्त: ।
धरण्या: प्रस्फुरद्रत्नफणामंडपमंडित: ।।
भर्तारमस्थादावृत्य तत्पत्नी च फणातते: ।
उपर्युच्चैस्समुद्रधृत्य स्थिता वज्रातपच्छदम् ।
—**उत्तरपुराण**, 73.137.41.

(2) Also *see*, *Pārśvanāthacarita* of Vādirāja, XI.57-87.

(3) The *upasarga*, by Dharaṇendra (soul of Kamaṭha) is very elaborately described in Padmakīrti's *Pāsaṇāhacariū*, *sandhi* 14, pp. 117-32.

बहु-विह-वण्ण पओहर पवर-मणोहर गयण-मम्मि थिर णिम्मिय ?
जक्ख-रक्ख सुर णरवर गह-गण विसहर जोयवि णह-यले विभिय ॥11॥
पच्चंड-गरुअ-दूसह-रवेण णवि झाणहां चांलिड मारुवेण ।
तें तकखणि पहरण कोडि-लक्ख किय कर-चलि भासुर दुण्णिरिक्ख ।
सर झसर सत्ति सव्वल विसाल मुग्गर भुसुंढि पट्टिस कराल ।
रेवंमि फरिस घण कणय चक्क पजलंत जिणिंदहो सयल मुक्क ।
जिणवरहो चित्तु अविचलु णिएवि सुर-विलय-रुड असुरे मुएवि ।
दक्खवि हुआसणी धम-धमंतु चउ-दिसिहिँ असेसु वित्तरु उहंतु ।
हुववहु णहे पसरंतउ दाहु करंतउ रत्त-वण्णु-दुप्पेच्छउ ।
जिणवर-सलिल-पवाहें अविचल-भावें भाविउ तुहिण सरिच्छउ ॥
उवसमिउ हुवासणु ज रउद्दु असुरेण पयासिउ चं समुद्दु ।
छुडु छुडु जिण-चलणाहिँ उवहि पत्तु आवंतु महंतु जवेण मुत्तु ।
तव-किरणहिँ डवहि खणंतरेण सोसिड असेसु जिण-दिणरयेण ।
मच्झत्यु णिराउहु गय-कसाउ जं चलिउ ण जाणहो वीय-राउ ।
तं असुरु विरुध्दड किलि-किलंतु कोहाणल जालहिं पज्जलंतु ।
उध्दाविउ सावय दक्खवंतु बहु-विविह-सद्दु भीसणु लवंतु ।
सद्दूल-सीह-णंगूल पवर खग साण रिंछ उम्मिण्ण-णहर ।
अहि अजयर सूअर महिस चंडे दीहर-कर मयगल महिस संड ।
पेक्खनि परमेसंरु भद-विमुक्कु सावय-रउद्द-उवसग्गु चुक्कु ।
असुरिंदे दारुणु दुह-विसावु आढत्तु पुणु वि उवसग्ग-जालु ।
वेयाल-भूय-जंभय पिसाय पेयाहिव विंतर गरुव-काय ।
डाइणि गह पण्णय गरुड जकख कुंभंड वाण दक्खिय असंख

(4) And Vādirāja:

पापाचारस्य दुश्चेष्टामुद्वीउच चरिचक्षुषा ।
पद्मावत्या समं देवमुपंतस्थौ फणीश्र्वरः ॥
तस्य विस्तारयामास स धैर्यस्तवपूर्वकम् ।
स्फुरन्मिणिरुचिस्फास्फुटामंडलमंडपम् ॥
आविर्बभूव देवस्य तत्अणादेव केवलम् ।
अनन्यशरणास्तदा प्रभुमुपेत्य बध्दाञ्जलि-
र्जिनेन्द्र जगतांपते जय जयाभिरक्षति माम् ।
ननाम मुकुटोल्लसन्मणिभिरुल्लिख-

न्नुर्वरां जगन्त्रदगुरूं रिपुर्विबोधलक्ष्मीनिधिम् ॥

At Aihoḷe, Bādāmī, Kaḷugumalai, Tirakkol, and Ellorā, we find Kamaṭha repenting and kneeling before Pārśvanātha, the sculptures range in date from the late sixth to the late 9th century A.D.

(४) श्रीपार्श्वनाथमुद्रोतुं भेत्तुमद्रिमिव द्विषः ।
समाययौ अमर्षान्धो मेघमाली सुराधमः ॥
दंष्ट्राऋकचभीमास्यान श्रृण्याकारनखांकुरान् ।
शार्दूलांन्पिंगलदृशो विचक्रे तत्र सोऽमरः ॥
पुच्छैराच्छोटयामासुर्भूपीठं ते मुहुर्मुहुः ।
चक्रुर्बूत्कारमुच्चैश्च मृत्योर्मन्त्राक्षरोपम् ॥
विकृतास्येन चापेतुर्गर्जन्तो मदवर्षिणः ।
उत्कराः करिंणस्तुंभाः पर्वता इव जंगमाः ॥
हिक्कानादापूर्णदिक्का भल्लूकाः शूकवर्जिताः ।
अनेकराश्चित्रकाश्च क्रूरा चमवसूजिभाः ॥
शिला अपि स्फोटयन्तः कंटकाग्रेण वृश्चिकाः ।
तरूनपि निर्दहन्तो दृष्टया दृष्टिविषा अपि॥
वेतालान्कर्त्रिकाहस्तान्स विधुतईवाम्बुदात् ।
उच्चैःकिलाकिलारावानुदंष्ट्रान् व्यकरोत्वत्तः ॥
प्रलम्बजिह्वशिशनास्ते सविसर्पा इव द्रुमाः ।
दीर्घजंघाङ्घ्यस्तालद्रुमारूढा इवोच्चकैः ।
प्रभुस्तैरपि नाक्ष्युभल्लीनो ध्यानसुधाह्रदे ॥
विशेषेण ततः क्रुद्धो मेघमाल्यसुरःस्वयम् ।
मेघान्विचक्रे नभसि कालरात्रिसहोदरान् ॥
स्वानी रत्नशिलास्तम्भ इवांभस्यपि निश्चलः ।
नासाग्रन्यस्तदृग्ध्यानान्मनागपि चचाल न ॥
आनासाग्र भावदंभः श्रीपार्श्वस्वाभिनोऽभवत् ।
धरणस्योरगेन्द्रस्यासनं तावदकम्पयत् ॥
धरणः स्वामिनं नत्वाऽधस्तात्तत्पादयोर्न्यधात्?
उन्नालमंबुजं तुंगं केवल्यासनंसन्निभम् ॥
पृष्ठपार्श्वौरः पिदधे स स्वभोगेन योगिराट् ।
फणैश्चसप्तभिच्छत्रं चकार शिरसि प्रभोः ॥
धरणेन्द्रमहिष्योऽपि श्रीपार्श्वस्वामिनः पुरः ।

विदधुर्मीतनृत्यादि भक्तिभावितचेतस: ॥
ध्यानलीन: प्रभुश्चास्थान्निर्विरोषो द्वयोरपि ।
नागाधिराजे धरणे मेघमालिनि चासुरे ॥
तत्र प्रभो: गर्भस्थे सति शयनीयस्था माता पार्श्वे सर्पन्तं कृष्णसर्पं ददर्श तत: पार्श्वेति् नामकृति: । स्पृशति ज्ञानेन सर्वभावानिति पार्श्व: । तथा गर्भस्थे जनन्दा निशि सर्पो दृष्ट: इति गर्भानुभावोयमिति मत्वा पश्यतीति निरुक्तत्वात्पाश्र्व: । पार्श्वोऽस्य वैयावृत्यकर: यक्ष: तस्य नाथ: पार्श्वनाथ: ।

—**त्रिषष्टिशिलाकापुरुषचरित्र**, IX. 3. 249-81.

The above references demonstrate the role of Dharaṇendra Nāga in the life of Pārśvanātha. The association of Nāga with him probably dates from very early times. It is, then, reasonable to concede to Pārśva's early connection with the Nāga cult (serpent-worship) and/or with the Nāga tribe. Mathurā, where we find so many figures of Pārśva (either singly or in the Caumukha representations) is known from the Brahmanical sources as a haunt of the Nāgas (compare the account of Kālīya-damana and Kṛṣṇa); the recovery of the icons of Dadhikarṇa Nāga, also of Balarāma who, too, is associated with Nāga and who is regarded as an incarnation of Śeṣa—his earliest known image (*c.* 2nd cent. B.C.) has been found in the Mathurā area—is one more significant point. Also, recent excavations at Soṅkh near Mathurā have revealed the existence of a Nāga-shrine and of a beautiful long stone panel with a Nāga king enthroned in the centre.[27]

The association of Pārśva with the Nāga cult and the fact that he lived in the seventh or sixth century B.C. should suggest a further line of investigation into the origin of his sect. It is said that the ancient city of Ahicchatrā was so-called because, at this place, as mentioned by Devabhadra,[28] Dharaṇendra came to worship Pārśva standing in meditation and in order to protect the Jina from the heat of the tropical sun the snake-king (*ahi*) held his expanded hoods as an umbrella (*chatra*) over the head of the Jina engaged in meditation. Since then, the place, formerly known as Śivapurī, came to be called Ahicchatrā.[29] (The true appellation is of course Adhicchatrā. The conversion of the Sanskrit "dha" into "ha" in Mahārāṣṭrī Prākṛta and its subsequent retention in Sanskrit gave scope for the formulation of this explanatory myth.)

Pārṣva, as all writers agree, hailed from Vārāṇasī and is reported to have widely travelled in the eastern parts of India as far as Kaliṅga. Both Uttar Pradesh and Bihar were known to have been inhabited by Nāga tribe and by followers of the Nāga cult from ancient times. In the *Vasudevahiṇḍi* of Saṅghadāsa Gaṇī (*c.* mid-6th century A.D.), it is said that, when Bhagīratha brought the Gaṅgā to the plains, abodes of the Nāgas were swept away in the swift and forceful current of the divine river.

Buddha is also associated with snake; Mucalinda Nāga protected him during a storm. Images of Buddha with cobra-hoods over the head are known from sites like Nāgārjunikoṇḍa, Amarāvatī, etc. At Bhārhut, the scene of Elāpatra Nāgarāja's visit to the Buddha is represented; at first Elāpatra is here shown in his serpent form and next in the anthropomorphic form with of course the snake-hoods attached behind his head.

The story about Mucalinda Nāga[30] has some interesting parallels with the account concerning Dharaṇa protecting Pārśvanātha. It is related at the starting portion of the *Vinaya-piṭaka* that the Lord Buddha, after achieving enlightenment, once betook himself to the Mucalinda-tree, and sat cross-legged at the foot of that tree for seven days enjoying the bliss of enlightenment. At that time a huge cloud appeared out of season, and for seven days the cloudy weather prevailed as it also was with rain and a cold wind. The Mucilinda (Mucalinda), the serpent king, issued from his abode, and enveloping the body of the Blessed One seven times with his coils, kept his large hood spread over the Master's head, thinking to himself, "May no cold touch the Blessed One .... no wind or heat come near the Blessed one." Now, at the end of seven days, the serpent king Mucilinda, seeing the sky clear and free from clouds, loosened his coils from the body of the Lord, and changing his own appearance into that of a brāhmaṇa youth, stood before the Blessed One, raising his joined hands and did reverence to him. The story of Mucilinda is also given later in the *Nidānakathā*.[31] The Sanskrit text *Lalitavistara* (*c.* 4th-5th cent. A.D.)[32] gives a slightly differing and indeed later version of the myth. Here the Buddha is protected not only by Mucilinda but also by a number of other Nāgarājas who have come from the four directions. They all enveloped the Buddha with their coils and formed a canopy over his head with their crests. Also in the *Mahāvastu* the story is briefly related.[33]

The story of the Buddha subduing the fiery dragon of Uruvilva is found in the *Mahāvagga*, i. 15; *Vinaya Piṭaka*, Vol. I, pp. 24ff. S.B.E. Vol. XIII, pp. 118ff. (This miracle is also narrated in the *Mahāvastu*, Vol. III. pp. 428 ff.) The victory of the Buddha over the wicked Nāga in the fire-hut is represented in a well-known bas-relief on the eastern gateway at Sāñcī. The Mucalinda story is also represented in a piece of sculpture from Sāñcī, now in the local museum, and perhaps came from the southern gateway according to Vogel.

While the subduing of the fiery snake manifests the malefic, the Mucilinda incident demonstrates the benefic aspect of the Nāga. We find both these aspects of the Nāga cult also in the Nirgrantha legends. The story of Mahāvīra subduing Caṇḍa-Kauśika[34] refers to the malefic aspect of the Nāga; while the Dharaṇendra demonstrates the benefic aspect. When the Vedic Āryans came in contact with the native tribes and/or autochthonous races and their beliefs and cults as also what we may call folk deities and their cults, the first reaction obviously was to treat the deities of these tribes as malefic. Gradually, with the closer associations with these tribes, such cults and deities came to be regarded as benefic. The Yakṣas, the Nāgas, etc. were worshipped by the masses. Bhandarkar had cited an interesting reference from the *Niddesa*-commentary which referred to several peoples worshipping different deities and following different cults. "The deity of the lay followers of the Ājivakas is the Ājivakas, of those of Nigganṭhas is the Nigganṭhas, of those of the Jaṭilas is the Jaṭilas, of those of the Paribbājakas is the Paribbājakas, of those of the Avaruddhakas is the Avaruddhakas, and the deity of those who are devoted to an elephant, a horse, a cow, a dog, a crow, Vāsudeva, Baladeva, Puṇṇabhadda, Māṇibhadda, Aggi, Nāgas, Supaṇṇas, Yakkhas, Asuras, Gandhabbas, Mahārājas,. Canda, Suriya, Indra, Brahmā, Deva, Diśā, is the elephant, the horse, the crow, Vāsudeva, Baladeva, Puṇṇabhadda, Māṇibhadda etc. in order."[35]

The trampling of the serpent Kālīya by Kṛṣṇa reflects belief in the malefic nature of the Nāgas, but in the life of Vāsudeva-Kṛṣṇa we also find that a large snake sheltered the newly-born babe Kṛṣṇa when he was carried in a basket through the Yamunā in flood with torrential rains. Thus in Brahmanism, Buddhism as well as in Nirgranthism we find the Kṛṣṇa, the Buddha and the Jina given protection from rains by a Nāga.

The iconic representations of cult objects such as those referred to in the *Niddesa*-commentary (and probably referring to the existence of such worship in the time of Buddha), "were probably the direct outcome of the gradual incorporation of most or all of the lower divinities in the ever expanding Brahmanic pantheon and their association with, and absorption into, different cults. The Kālīya-damana episode in the mythology of the Vāsudeva cult can also be compared in this connection."[36]

Marshall refers to two seals found at Mohenjo-Daro, which bear figures of a god seated in yoga posture, on whose either side kneels a half-human, half-animal form of a Nāga with hands uplifted in prayer (M.I.C., Vol. III. CXVI, 29 and CXVIII, 11).[37] Do these seals suggest the origin of later adoption of the idea of Nāgas adoring and protecting the Buddha, the Jina, or Vāsudeva (regarded as incarnation of Viṣṇu)? Śiva is also associated with snakes. Viṣṇu rests on the coils of the Śeṣa-Nāga whose thousand heads are shown as a canopy over Viṣṇu. In the *vīthikā* (forelobby) of the Bādāmī Cave III (A.D. 578) is the famous figure of Viṣṇu sitting on the coils of the Nāga Ananta spreading his heads as a canopy over the Lord.

During the Vedic period we have the famous battle between Indra and Vṛtra. Here Vṛtra figures as a malevolent being, like Kālīya of Yamunā river or the Caṇḍa-Nāga subdued by the Buddha or the Caṇḍa-Kauśika brought to saneness by Mahāvīra. There is an ever-existing contest between the forces of light and of darkness, good and evil, gods and demons, life and death. Kṛṣṇa-Viṣṇu, Śiva, Buddha, Pārśva, and Mahāvīra represent powers of good, light, and life; Vṛtra, Kālīya, Māra, Kamaṭha, Caṇḍa and Caṇḍa-Kauśika represent the opposite, the powers of darkness and death.

Nāga with his thousand snake-heads possibly represents "human mind" with its innumerable evil instincts, attitudes, feelings, tempers and thoughts. When subdued, reformed and sublimated, the same mind is transformed from a malevolent to a benevolent force. Mythology of the Buddha, Pārśvanātha, or Kṛṣṇa-Viṣṇu plausibly represents an advancement upon the earlier Vedic conception of Indra-Vṛtra fight.[38] In later conceptions, it is recognised that the mind which is a bondage and an obstacle can be transformed into a protector, friend or benefactor. So says the *Gītā*: ***mana eva manuṣyāṇāṁ bandha-mokṣayoḥ.***

NOTES AND REFERENCES

1. Walther Schubring, *The Doctrine of the Jainas*, Delhi 1962, p. 28.
2. The *Āvaśyaka-cūrṇi*, pp. 273, 286.
3. The *Āvaśyaka-cūrṇi*, pp. 285, 291; *Bṛhat-Kalpa-Bhāṣya*, I. 1328-57.
4. The *Āvaśyaka-cūrṇi*, p. 291.
5. The *Āvaśyaka-niryukti*, 335.
6. The *Nāyādhammakahāo*, II, p. 222.
7. *Ibid.*, p. 229.
8. *Ibid.*, p. 230.
9. *Idha Mahārāja Nigaṇṭho Nāthaputto cāturyāmaśaṁvara saṁvuto hoti /—Dīgha-nikāya*, I. 57 (*Śamaññaphala-sutta*)
10. The *Vyākhyā-prajñapti*, 9.32.
11. The *Nāyādhammakhāo*, 19.
12. The *Vyākhyā-prajñapti*, 2.5.
13. The *Sūtrakṛtāṅga*, 2.7.
14. The *Rāyapasenīya-sūtta*, 147 f.

15. *Also see*, Jagdishchandra Jain, *Life in Ancient India as depicted in Jaina Canon and commentaries*, sec. edn., New Delhi 1984, pp. 20-21; also Padmanabha Jaini, The *Jaina Path of Purification,* Delhi 1979, pp. 14-20 for some remarks on this meeting and the meaning of *cāturyāma saṁvara.* For a new interpretation by P.K. Modi, see his "Introduction", *Pāsanāhacariü* of Padmakīrti, Prākṛta Texts Series, Vol. VIII, Vārāṇasī 1965. Also *see* W. Schubring, *The Doctrine.*, pp. 28-31; and Muni Nāgaraja, *Āgama aur Tripiṭaka eka Anuśīlana*, (Hindi),Vol. I, 213, 411, 428, 454-55.
16. The fuller reference is C. Sivaramamurti, *Panorama of Jain Art*, New Delhi 1983.
17. Published in Delhi 1987.
18. *The Bulletin of the Cleveland Museum of Art,* December 1970, pp. 303-11.
19. M.A. Dhaky, "Śāntara Sculpture", *Journal of the Indian Society of Oriental Art*, New Series, Vol. IX, 1971-1972, plates XVIII (9) and XIX.
20. Sivaramamurti, *Panorama.*, p. 91, plate 121.
21. For illustration, *see* here Dhaky's Introductory essay and the relevent plate thereof.
22. तत्र प्रभोः गर्भस्थे सति शयनीस्था मात पार्श्वे सर्पन्तं कृष्णसर्पं ददर्श ततः पार्श्वेति नामकृतिः।

    —— *Kalpa-sūtra-Subodhikā*, p. 128.

    स्पृशति ज्ञानेन सर्वभावानिति पार्श्वः। तथा गर्भस्थे जनन्या निशि सर्पो दृष्टः इति गर्भानुभावोऽयगिति मत्वा पश्यतीति निरुक्तत्वत्वार्श्वः पार्श्वोऽस्य वैयावृत्याकरः यक्षः तस्य नाथः पार्श्वनाथः

    Commentary on Abhidhāna Cintāmaṇi, I, 26 ff. *Also see,* the *Āvaśyaka-niryukti gāthā* 1091; *Siri-Pāsanāhacariya*, "prastāva" 3, p. 152. The *Uttarapurāṇa*, 73, 92, says that the name Pārśva was given to this Jina by Indra.
23. Umakant P. Shah, *Akota Bronzes*, Bombay 1959, plate 1b; also the author's *Jaina-Rūpa-Maṇḍana*, plate V (Fig. 8).
24. Shah, *ibid.,* plate III (Fig. 3).
25. *Cf.* "A Pārśvanātha Sculpture.", *BCMA*, Dec. 1970, p. 305.
26. For some Buddhist representations, *cf.* Benjamin Rowland, Jr., *Gandhara Sculptures from Pakistan Museums*, New York 1960, p. 32, showing a sculpture from Peshawar Museum and pl. on p.55 showing hosts of Māra, from Central Museum, Lahore. Also Harold Ingholt, *Gandharan Art in Pakistan,* New York 1957, figs. 61-66; and N.P. Joshi, *Mathura Sculptures*, Mathura1966, pl. 86.
27. Herbert Hartel, "Some Results of the Excavations at Sonkh: A Preliminary Report", *The Excavations at Sonkh: An Exhibition at the National Museum*, New Delhi 1976, fig. 44.
28. *Siri-Pāsanāha-cariyam,* "prastāva" 3, 1-7, pp. 187 f.
29. Ahicchatrā is modern Ramnagar in Bareilly district, U.P. For Ahicchatrā, with Ādi Nāga as its presiding deity and for Nāga-worship in India from Vedic times, see, *The Age of Imperial Unity* (Bharatiya Vidya Bhavan's History and Culture of the Indian People Volume II), Bombay 1960, pp. 471 ff.; also James Fergusson. *Tree and Serpent Worship in India*, Vārāṇasī 1971; and Vogel, J. Ph., *Indian Serpent-Lore or the Nāgas in Hindu legend and Art*, Vārāṇasī 1972.
30. *Mahāvagga,* i.3. *Vinaya-piṭakam* (ed. Oldenberg), Vol. I, p. 3; *S.B.E.*, Vol. XIII, p. 80; Vogel, *Indian Serpent Lore*, pp. 102 ff.
31. *Jātaka* (ed. Fausboll), Vol. I, p. 80. Rhys Davids, *Buddhist Birth Stories,* p. 109.
32. *Lalitavistāra,* Vol. I, pp. 379 f.

33. *Mahāvastu* (ed. Senart), Vol. III, pp. 300 f. *cf. Buddhacarita*, xv. 49-53. The Buddha is also said to have subdued Caṇḍa-Nāga, see Muni Nāgarāja, *Āgama aur Tripiṭaka.*, Vol. I, pp. 179-81.
34. Mahāvīra, while he was proceeding to Śvetāmbikā, met the deadly cobra Caṇḍa-Kauśika who is described as *āśiviṣa*. Poisonous breath of the serpent, however, had no effect on Mahāvīra. Caṇḍa-Kauśika even encircled the body of Mahāvīra who still remained unperturbed in meditation. See *Āvaśyaka-niryukti* with Malayagiri's *Vṛtti, gāthās* 466-67, pp. 273-74 and the *Triṣaṣṭiśalākāpuruṣa-caritra.*, X. 3.
35. R.G. Bhandarkar, *Vaiṣṇavism, Śaivism, and Minor Religious Systems.*, Delhi 1965, p.3; and J.N. Banerjea, *The Development of Hindu Iconography,* (sec. edn. 1956), Calcutta 1956, pp. 76-77.
36. Banerjea., *ibid.*, p. 102.
37. About these seals, Banerjea (*ibid.*, p. 161) adds: "It is not quite clear, however, from these two seal devices whether the snake-body is attached to the back of the kneeling human votaries of the god; in the early Kushana and subsequent representations of the Nāgas at Mathurā and other sites, the whole serpent-body and sometimes only its one or many hoods (five or seven) are invariably attached behind the human body (the latter mode is also adopted in the Śuṅga art of Central India). But on these seals, the technique of showing the Nāgas might have been somewhat similar to the one followed by the Bharhut artist in his presentation of the scene of Elāpatra Nāgarāja's visit to the Buddha; at first Elāpatra is shown in his serpent form, then he is given the human shape with the snake-hoods attached behind his head. On these Indus-valley seals, the snakes appear on the far sides while the kneeling human figurines, without any snake-hood, on the near sides of the god."
38. "The Vedas not only knew of the serpent (*ahi*) but also of its harmful nature (Vṛtra being conceived as such) as well as its beneficent character (Ahirbudhnya being a beneficent agent)." *The Age of Imperial Unity,* pp. 471 f.

    The emergence of the Nāga as a cult object has been traced back to the Mohenjo-Daro age in the two seals referred to above, where the Nāga appears in an attitude of devotion to a figure in yogic posture. "That Śiva and serpents should simultaneously get recognition as important cult-objects in the *Yajurveda* when both are absent as objects of veneration in the *Ṛgveda,* may not be a mere accident. The region in which the *Yajurveda* was followed included the land of the Pāñcālas, whose later capital Ahicchatrā...with Ādi-Nāga as the presiding deity, may not unreasonably be associated with the cult of serpents...... In the *Atharvaveda* and the later Saṁhitās serpents (*sarpāḥ*) appear as semi-divine beings, and in the Gṛhya-sūtras, Nāgas, called for the first time by this term, and supposed to belong to earth, sky and heaven, as also to the quarter receive adoration and worship." — *Age of Imperial Unity,* p. 472.

    The Nirgrantha canonical works refer to Indramaha, Skandamaha, Yakṣamaha, Nāgamaha, Bhūtamaha, etc. The worship of Nāga (Nāgajanna) is specially mentioned. "In the north-east of Sāgeya there lay a Nāga shrine (Nāgaghara) with an image of a serpent. The festival of Nāga (nāgajatta) was celebrated with great pomp and ceremony by the queen Paümavai .... a flower-house was made near the shrine where a beautiful garland was suspended .... the queen .... bathed in the lake and with still moist robe plucked the lotuses and with various flowers, fruits and the incense pot in her hand, entered the temple, where she cleaned the image with a brush, burnt incense and worshipped the deity." (Naya, 8). (J.C. Jain, *Life in Ancient India.*, pp. 219-20).

ARHAT PĀRŚVA WITH DHARAṆENDRA IN HYMNIC LITERATURE

M. A. Dhaky

I

The earliest known Nirgrantha psalms and hymns figure in the books of the first two phases of the sacred *śruta* literature in Ardhamāgadhī and of the northern tradition. Among these the theme of the *Mahāvīra-stava* (*c.* 2nd cent. B.C.) inside the *Sūtrakṛtāṅga* Book I is exclusively "Nātaputta" (Jñātṛputra, Jina Mahāvīra).[1] Of slightly lesser antiquity is the *Namostu-stava* (the so-called *Śakra-stava*)[2] in the Daṇḍaka form, incorporated in at least five *āgamas*—four of the middle phase[3] and the fifth belonging to the latest:[4] it possesses phrases which may possibly hark back to the early literature of the sect of Jina Pārśva.[5] However, there is in this hymn no reference to Pārśva since it is addressed aggregationally to all "venerable Arhats as well as Tīrthaṅkaras". The composition thus belongs to a psalmic category known as the "*sarva-sādhāraṇa-Jina-stava*". The third ancient hymn is the famous *Caturviṁśati-stava* which figures among the six brief texts known as the *Ṣaḍ-Āvaśyakas*. From the later decades of the fifth century A.D., the *Ṣaḍ-Āvaśyakas* formed the main mass of the *Āvaśyaka-sūtra*. The *stava,* as its theme indicates, must have been composed only after the conception of the 24 *Tīrthaṅkaras* was crystallized and this must have been before the formation of the Acela-kṣapaṇaka sect which separated from the main, Alpacela, northern Nirgrantha stream around A.D. 200.[7] This *stava,* of course, includes Pāsa—Pārśva as the 23rd Jina in the series of 24—but has no reference to Nāgendra's association with him.

The next phase of the hymnic (and a little later also litanic) formulations begins from the fifth century A.D., and thus after a hiatus of almost four centuries. The earliest known is an invocatory composition in Prākṛta for the 24 Jinas which occurs amid the inaugural verses of the *Nandisūtra* of Deva Vācaka (*c.* mid 5th century); it, however, makes no allusion to Dharaṇendra in association with Pārśva. From the Gupta period onward, Sanskrit began to be employed alongside Prākṛta and eventually dominated the field. The first writer in Sanskrit, Vācaka Umāsvāti (*c.* mid 4th century A.D.), did resort to metrical compositions, very largely in Āryā meter, which, however, are doctrinal, didactic, and essentially non-hymnic; and his inaugural *kārikās* of the *Tattvārthādhigama-sūtra* invokes Siddhārtha-nandana (Arhat Vardhamāna Mahāvīra) but makes no allusion to Pārśva.[8] And from among the extant 21 (out of the original 32) *dvātriṁśikā*-compositions of the great dialectician and epistemologist, Siddhasena Divākara of the northern Nirgrantha stream (active *c.* A.D. 400-444),[9] six alone are genuinely hymnic; among these the first five (numbered 1 to 5) are addressed to Jina Vīra, and the sixth (numbered the 21st), the *Parātmā-dvātriṁśikā*, is a "*sādhāraṇa-Jina-stotra*" even when in its verse 31 it mentions Mahāvīra as *netā* or leading figure (of the Nirgrantha religion). (The rest of his *dvātriṁśikā's* are topical compositions, *prakaraṇas*.) It is then clear that none of the available hymnal compositions of Siddhasena refers to Pārśva.

The first reference to the association of Arhat Pārśva with the Nāgarāja shining with gems atop his hoods is in a Prākṛta work, the *Paümacariya* of Vimala Sūri of Nāgendra-kula (*c.* A.D. 473), figuring as it does in the inaugural hymn to the *Caturviṁśati-Jinas* in the initial chapter of this work: *Nami Nemi taha ya Pāsaṁ uraga-mahaphaṇi-maṇisu pajjaliyam* (I.6).[10] Next, Svāmī Sāmantabhadra (active *c.* A.D. 550-600)[11] of the southern Nirgrantha tradition, of a stature and fame equal to Siddhasena (but employing more sophisticated and much more ornate form of poetry), in his well-known hymn in Sanskrit, the *Svayambhū-stotra*, addressed his prayer to the 24 Jinas where the *upasarga* of Pārśva together with the manifestation of Dharaṇendra finds a clear mention in association with Jina Pārśva.[12] The concerned two verses are replete with power and are symptomatic of the true poetic calibre of this brilliant "chief among the debaters (*vādi-mukhya*)" and an ace epistemologist:

तमाल-नीलैः सधनुस्तडिद्गुणैः
प्रकीर्ण-भीमाऽशनि-वायु-वृष्टिभिः ।
बलाहकैर्वैरि-वशैरुपद्रुतो
महामना यो न चचाल योगतः ॥ १ ॥
बृहत्फणा-मण्डल-मण्डपेन
यं स्फुरत्तडित्पिङ्ग-रुचोपसर्गिणम् ।
जुगूह नागो धरणो धराधरं
विराग-संध्या-तडिदम्बुदो यथा ॥ २ ॥

— **श्रीबृद्दहृस्वयंभूस्तोत्र**

Returning to northern Nirgrantha tradition, one notices that the second phase of Prākṛta compositions continues further in time. To begin with, the famous church-litany, the *Ajita-Śānti-stava* of Nandiṣeṇa (*c.* late 5th or early 6th cent. A.D.), as the title of the hymn implies, is devoted exclusively to two Jinas, the second *Tīrthaṅkara* Ajitanātha and to the 16th Jina Śāntinātha.[13] The next hymnist, Mānatuṅga Sūri (*c.* late 6th-early 7th cent. A.D.), the author of the very famous Sanskrit hymn, the *Bhaktāmara-stotra*, a prayer addressed to Jina Ṛṣabha, had also composed a Prākṛta litany in praise of Jina Pārśva whose very name he extols as "dispeller of calamities". It, regrettably, fails to take cognizance of Dharaṇendra. The very popular *Uvasaggahara-thotta* regarded as the composition of Ārya Bhadrabāhu (active *c.* B.C. 310-290 B.C.) or his namesake, the so-called Bhadrabāhu II (the supposed brother of Varāhamihira: *c.* early 6th century A.D.) in the northern, but of Mānatuṅga Sūri in the southern tradition,[14] is in reality a quasi-magical hymn in Prākṛta, of the ninth or better still of tenth century, composed by some unknown northern *caityavāsī* or abbatial monk, revolving around Jina Pārśva; it, to all seeming and according to its commentator Pārśvadeva of the 12th century, notices Jina's attendant Pārśva Yakṣa (but does not allude to Nāgendra Dharaṇa[15]). Similarly, the *Vairoṭyā-stava* (*c.* 9th or 10th cent. A.D.) (wrongly ascribed to Ārya Nandila of the Kuṣāṇa period[16]), praises Vidyādevī Vairoṭyā (who had been come to be looked upon, again of course wrongly, as the consort of Dharaṇendra from pre-medieval times on), likewise fails to invoke the Lord of the Nāgas or Jina Pārśva either.

Turning once again to the hymnal compositions in Sanskrit, in the *Stuti-Caturviṁśatikā* (*c.* A.D. 775-800) of Bhadrakīrtti *alias* Bappahaṭṭi Sūri, an extensive hymn which uses the ornament *pādānta-yamaka* in each stanza and is addressed to the 24 Jinas, a reference to Nāgarāja Dharaṇendra in context of Arhat Pārśva is likewise missing. Bhagavaj-Jinasena of Pañcastūpānvaya, a luminary of the southern Church, on the other hand, does portray and indeed graphically, the famous Pārśva-Śaṁbara-Dharaṇendra episode in his elegant as well as powerfully rendered composition, the *Pārśvābhyudaya-kāvya* (probably some time before A.D. 839).[17] Śaṁbara's (Kamaṭha's) tyranny unleashed on the meditating Pārśva and the consequent epiphenic manifestation of Nāgarāja Dharaṇendra for the Arhat's protection have been graphically described there in 11 verses (4.48-58). But the *Pārśvābhyudaya-kāvya* is a legendary-biographical, and not a hymnical work. This is also true of the *Pārśvanātha-caritra* (A.D. 1025) of Vādirāja of Drāviḍa Saṅgha, one other great figure of the southern church which does describe in brief the *upasarga*-episode but contains no hymn which describes the figure of Pārśva canopied by Dharaṇendra even when he alludes to his appearing on the scene at the right moment along with Padmāvatī.[18]

Among the composers of hymns after Sāmantabhadra, neither the dialectician Pātrakesari (early 7th cent. A.D.) nor for that matter Pūjyapāda Devanandi (active *c.* A.D. 635-680), nor does the poet Dhanañjaya — three other great figures of the southern Nirgrantha Church — refer to Pārśva or Dharaṇendra since the first and the third composer's hymns fall in the category of the "*sādhāraṇa-Jina-stava*"; and those severally known as the Ten *Bhakti*-compositions that have been attributed by the commentator Prabhācandra (active *c.* A.D. 1025-1060) to Pūjyapāda Devanandi, have among them only one which stylistically can be ascribed to that great grammarian and commentator and none of them refers to Pārśva.[19] Next in time, Guṇabhadra, the disciple of Bhagavaj-Jinasena in his *Uttarapurāṇa* (*c.* mid-9th cent. A.D.), and Śīlācārya of Nivṛtti-kula of the abbatial Śvetāmbara branch of the northern Church in his "Pāsasāmi cariya" inside the *Caüpanna-mahāpurisa-cariya* (A.D. 869), graphically portray the *upasarga*-tormentations inflicted by Śaṁbara (called Meghamālī by Śīlācārya and in all subsequent Śvetāmbara writings) and the consequent appearance on the scene of Dharaṇa for the protection of Pārśva lost in meditation. However, these works do not fall in the hymnal category of compositions and hence out of consideration. After Guṇabhadra, the epistemologist Vidyānanda (*c.* first half of the tenth century A.D.)[20] in his *Śrīpura-Pārśvanātha-stotra*, a hymn structured largely in epistemological terms, for certain includes a couple of feelingfully composed verses; but Dharaṇendra finds no allusion there. And even when a devotional hymn on Pārśvanātha was composed in the medieval southern India, such as the famous *Kalyāṇamandira-stotra* of Kumudacandra (*c.* first quarter of the 12th century A.D.), it does not hint at Dharaṇendra's connection with the Jina.

II

The medieval and late medieval Nirgrantha devotional compositions, which overwhelmingly are of the western Indian and of Śvetāmbara persuasion, on the other hand, abound in hymns devoted to Pārśva which contain very telling verses pertaining to the images of the Jina canopied by the jewel-crested hoods of the polycephalous Lord of the Nāgas, Dharaṇa. Also, during this period, two peculiar trends lending powerful impetus to the promotion of the worship of Pārśva comes to the fore. The first is the favoured position accorded to Pārśva in the tāntric worship, due mainly to his special attendants—Nāgendra Dharaṇa and Yakṣī Padmāvatī — who appeared in southern India in association with the Pārśva imagery from at least the late sixth century onward (Bādāmī Cave IV, Aihoḷe Jaina Cave).[21] Of the two, Padmāvatī was adopted in the religious art of the northern tradition (eventually replacing Vairoṭyā) from the time perhaps not before the later part of the tenth century.[22] As a result, several tāntric hymns invoking Padmāvatī (and also in a few cases Dharaṇendra sometimes with, but generally without Pārśva) were composed in this period. The second trend may be sought in the prevalence of the belief in the miraculous power of the images of Pārśvanātha enshrined in the temples of certain specific sites. For some of these at least we know through the medieval anecdotes and legends that the original images were interred in relatively remoter past, under the compulsion presumably of some political exigency or adverse socio-religious circumstances, that accidentally came to light in the medieval times. Most of these relate to the western Nirgrantha or Śvetāmbara Church. Foremost among them were the Stambhana-Pārśvanātha, the Śaṅkhapura-Pārśvanātha, and the Pārśvanātha images of Cārūpa, Jīrāpalli, Goḍi, Phalavarddhi, Karaheṭaka, Ajāharā and Ghoghā; one at least at Kalikuṇḍa on the Kaligiri in Magadha and likewise a single isolated example of the pre-medieval Karnataka empire, the Antarikṣa Pārśvanātha of Śrīpura. Special hymns, in honour of some of these *tīrthas*, in some cases also in Prākṛta (and at least one in Apabhraṁśa) were composed, some tāntric, some normal and innocuous, that range in date from about the beginning of the 11th to about the middle of the 18th century.

We shall begin with the citations from the *Dharṇoraga-stotra*, a tāntric hymn addressed to the Pārśvanātha of Kalikuṇḍa by the lay-follower Śivanāga (*c.* A.D. 1000-1010), a contemporary of Vīrācārya of the northern (western) Nirgrantha (Śvetāmbara) Church:[23] It invokes Pārśvanātha as worshipped by Lord of Nāgas; it also alludes to the *upasarga* caused by the Daitya (Kamaṭha):

सकलभुनाभिवन्दित ! गरुडस्त्वं पन्नगेन्द्रकृतपूज ! ।
विषमविषानलशमनो जलद इव जलप्लुतालोकः ॥ १२ ॥
दैत्योपसर्गभीषणजलधरधरा विधौतकर्मकल ! ।
सर्वज्ञ ! नागवन्दित ! सर्वविपाक्षेफण ! नमस्ते ॥ १३ ॥

— **श्री धरणोरगस्तोत्र**

The illustrious āgamic commentator Abhayadeva Sūri of Candra-kula, in his hymn in Apabhraṁśa addressed to the Pārśvanātha of Stambhana (said to be consecrated by him in *c.* A.D. 1054 but may be later by some years), a highly emotive portrayal of Pārśva with the figure of Dharaṇendra with his full splendour occurs:[24]

फणिफणफारफुरंतरयणकररंजियनहयल,
फलिणीकंदलदलतमालीलुप्पलसामल ।

कमठासुरउवसग्गवग्गसंसग्गअगंजिय,
जय पच्चक्खजिणेस पास थंभणयपुरट्ठिय ॥ १७॥

— **श्री जयतिहुअण थोत्त**

(संस्कृत छाया)
फणिफणस्फारस्फुरद्रत्नकररञ्जितनभस्तले,
फलिनीकन्दलदलतमालनीलोत्पलश्यामल ।
कमठासुरोपसर्गवर्गसंसर्गाऽगञ्जित,
जय प्रत्यक्षजिनेश पार्श्व स्तम्भनकपुरस्थित ॥ १७॥

— **श्री जयत्रिभुवनस्तोत्र**

Next in time is the *Pārśvanāthāṣṭaka* by Mahākavi Bilhaṇa, the famous Kāśmīrī *brāhmaṇa* poet who was in Aṇahillapāṭaka, capital of Gujarat, with the Nirgrantha-Śvetāmbara Daṇḍanāyaka Śāntu or Śāntuka as his patron, some time between c. A.D. 1065-75. His praise and portrayal of the splendour of the visionary image of Pārśvanātha protectively canopied by Dharaṇa (whom he variously addresses as *bhujagarāja*, *pannagasvāmi*, and *phaṇipati*) is, for its vibrancy, cadence, and sonorousness perhaps unexcelled in the entire lore of the medieval Nirgrantha Sanskrit hymnic compositions addressed to that Jina:[25]

जयति भुजगराजप्राज्यफुल्लत्फणाली-
मणिकिरणकदम्बाडम्बरी पार्श्वनाथः ।
भुवनभवनमर्दिभ्रमोहन्धकार-
च्छिदुरतरुणदीपोद्दीपने कौतुकीव ॥ १ ॥
कमपि कमठदैत्याकालकालम्बुवाह-
व्यतिकरविधुरेऽपि श्रीविशेषं दधानः ।
मदनमदविकारम्भोरुहम्लानिहेतु-
र्जनयति स जिन्नदुर्युष्मदाशा प्रकाशम् ॥ ३ ॥
जयति भवदवाग्निव्याप्तिनिर्दह्यमान-
स्त्रिभुवनवनरक्षादेशकः पार्श्वनाथः ।
घनमयवि देहं पन्नगश्यामचूडा-
मणिविरचितचञ्चन्नाकिचापं दधानः ॥ ४ ॥
फणिपतिफणरत्नोद्योतविद्योनित श्री-
र्दिशतु शिवगतिं वः पार्श्वनाथस्य मूर्तिः ।

रणरणकविशेषक्षोभवन्मोक्षलक्ष्मी-
सरभसपरिरम्भात् कुङ्कुमेनारुणेव ॥ ८ ॥

— श्री पार्श्वनाथाष्टकम्

The stanza 8 of the hymn refers to the image of Pārśvanātha and the luminescence cast by the gems on the hoods of *phaṇipati* or Nāgarāja Dharaṇa. It likewise alludes to the deluge created by Daitya Kamaṭha.

Among the western Indian medieval Nirgrantha hymnists, Jinavallabha Sūri of Kharatara Gaccha (active *c.* A.D. 1060-1110) was perhaps the greatest. He, too, graphically describes Jina Pārśva, protected by the polycephalous Nāgendra in the ***Pārśva-Jina-Stotra*** he composed in Sanskrit:[26]

पायात् पार्श्वः पयोदद्युतिरुपरि फणिस्फारफुल्लत्फणालीं
बिभ्रद विस्फूर्जदूर्जस्वलमणिकिरणआसूत्रितेन्द्रायुधां वः ।
संरूढप्रौढकर्मद्रुमवनगहनप्लोषपुष्यद्विशुद्ध-
ध्यानाग्निज्वालमालानुकृतिसकृतया सप्तधा प्रोल्लसन्ती ॥ १ ॥
श्रीमान् यः पापतापप्रशमहिमरुचिः सप्तभिः पन्नगेन्द्र-
स्फारोत्फुल्लस्फटाभिः स्फुटफलितमणिप्रांशुरश्मिच्छटाभिः ।
भाति भ्रान्तिच्छिदायै जगति सुनयसत्तत्त्वसत्सप्तभङ्गी-
सङ्ख्याव्याख्यानबद्धक्षण इव स जिनः श्रागनिष्टं पिनष्टु ॥ ४ ॥

— श्री पार्श्वजिनस्तोत्रम्

Also, in his Prākṛta hymn to Pārśva he displays equal mastery on the power of description: Indeed he is soulfully expressive on this favourite theme in his *Pāsa-Jiṇa-thavaṇa*[27]:

फारुप्फुल्लं तुह उवरि फणिफणासत्तयं फुरंतं मे ।
कयसत्ततत्तसंखा वक्खाणखणं व पडिहाइ ॥ ६ ॥
उवरि परिफुरियफणिवइचूडामणिकिरणरइयसुरचावं ।
अइभीसणभवदवतवियभवियवणपसमणसमत्थं ॥ ७ ॥
गुरुकोवफारफुक्कारभासुरो फणिवई वि फुल्लफणो ।
चित्तंमि तुमं जेसिं तेसिं कीडु व्व होइ फुडं ॥ ११ ॥

— सिरि पासजिणथवणं

Next notable among the ecclesiastical composers was the great dialectician Dharma

Sūri of Rāja-gaccha (*c.* 2nd-3rd quarter of the 12th century A.D.): Two verses from his *Pārśva-Jina-stavana* pertinent to the present discussion may be cited:[28]

स्वामिन् ! दुर्जयमोहराजविजयप्रापविण्यभाजस्तव
स्तोत्रं किं कमठोरुदर्पदलने श्रीपार्श्व ! विश्वप्रभो ! ।
तिग्मांशोर्यदि वा स्फुरद्ग्रहमहःसन्दोरहोहद्गुहः
खद्योतद्युतिसंहतिश्रुतिपदे वर्त्तेत किं कोविदः ॥ ७॥
सश्रीकान् तव वक्त्रदुग्धजलधेरुद्भूतमत्यद्भुतं
मोहोच्छेदकतत्त्वसप्तकवचः पीयूषमित्यादृतः ।
विश्वेभ्यः फणभृद्विभुः फणिमणिव्याजात् प्रफुल्लत्फणा-
पात्रीभिः पृथुभिर्विभाति परितः स्वामिन् ! प्रयच्छन्निव ॥ ८॥

– **श्री पार्श्वजिनस्तवनम्**

It was perhaps Ācārya Jinavallabha's grand disciple Jinapati Sūri (active *c.* latter half of the 12th century A.D.), if not some other and later composer, who had addressed a hymn to the Antarikṣa-Pārśvanātha of Śrīpura; a pertinent verse therefrom is quoted below:[29]

प्रस्फूर्जत्फणमण्डलीचलमणिश्रेणीसमाविर्भव-
च्चञ्चच्चन्द्रमरीचिसञ्चयपरित्रस्यत्तमोमण्डलः ।
उन्मीलन्नवनीलनीरजदलश्यामाभिरामद्युतिः
श्रेयःश्रेणिमनुत्तरां प्रथय नः श्रीपार्श्व ! विश्वप्रभो ! ॥ ९॥

— **श्री अन्तरिक्षपार्श्वनाथस्तवनम्**

In the opening decades of the 13th century, the most notable hymnist to meet with was the blind poet Muni Rāmacandra of Bṛhad-gaccha. Among the several hymns he composed, at least six are in praise of the Jina Pārśvanātha of Jābālipura or Jālor in the surroundings of which he was perhaps permanently residing. (The temple to this Jina was founded on Jābālipura's Kāñcanagiri Hill by the Solaṅkī emperor Kumārapāla in A.D. 1166 and was given over by him to the monks of the Bṛhad-gaccha). Rāmacandra interweaves the *śabdālaṅkāras* and the *arthālaṅkaras*, the two classes of grace-ornaments with considerable skill, with equal attention to *prasāda* and *oja* qualities. The configurations he creates of Jina Pārśva and Dharṇoraga are almost as evocative as of his predecessors who portrayed Pārśva and Nāgarāja Dharaṇendra in their hymnical compositions, indeed with considerable force. His style is based on the classical Sanskrit poetry and the flow of his portray is quietly elegant:[30]

इदं न फुल्लत्फणभृत्फणामणीमहस्तवोच्चैः शमिनामधीश्वर ! ।
समुल्लसद्ध्यानसुधाभयात् त्वहेर्विषार्चिरेतन्मिषतः पलायतिम् ॥ १६ ॥

— **श्री अपह्नुतिद्वात्रिंशिका**

मौलिमण्डलविलासमण्डनं दर्शयन् शतिफणीशमुत्फणम् ।
सन्तनोत्यहिभयज्वरक्षयं चित्रमेव चरितं महात्मनाम् ॥ १६ ॥

— **श्री अर्थान्तरन्यासद्वात्रिंशिका**

प्रमदयन्नमृतेन कृताञ्जलीन् गततृषः शिखरिश्रियमावहन् ।
अकलुषः कमठाम्बुदवृष्टिभिस्त्वभिनवः किल यः कमलाकरः ॥ १५ ॥
प्रकटयन्नवनस्थितिपाटवं भुवि कलां कलयन्निह हारिणीम् ।
सकलकामसमुद्भवसौहृदः श्रयति यो नवकेसरिणः श्रियम् ॥ १६ ॥
दधदहो विबुधाश्रितपादतां भुजगराजिविराजितमौलिताम् ।
किमपि यः स्वगुणैर्भुवनाद्भुतैर्दिविषदामचलादतिरिच्यते ॥ १७ ॥

— **श्री व्यतिरेकद्वात्रिंशिका**

पुन्नागभङ्गिसुभगालिविनीलमूर्त्तिरुतुङ्गभूरिशिखरश्रियमादधानः ।
भूयादशोकतरुभूषितभूमिभागः श्रीमान् वसन्त इव सम्भृतसिद्धिरागः ॥
व्याक्रोशमेचककुशेशयकाननश्रीर्वामाङ्गभूर्जिनपतिर्जगती पुनातु ।
उन्मीलदुत्पलदलद्युतिमेति यस्मिन्नालायितस्ववपुषः फणिनः फणाली ॥ १८ ॥
वैरायमाणकमठोल्बणदृष्टिसृष्टौ छत्रीभवद्भूजगराजफणासमाजः ।
शालस्तमाल इव बालदलप्ररोहचेतोहरस्थितिररोचत् यः स पोऽव्यात् ॥ २८ ॥
त्रैलोक्यमाङ्गलिकभूप इवेन्द्रनीलप्रोन्मीलदंशुचयमेचकितः स पार्श्वः ।
चूलावलम्बिसहकारलतानुकारप्रोत्फुल्लपन्नगफणः फलतु श्रियं वः ॥ २९ ॥

— **श्री पार्श्वजिनस्तुतिद्वात्रिंशिका**

मौलो तवाऽयं शमधातुवादिनः फुल्लत्फणास्फारमणीरुचारुणः ।
विश्वस्य कल्याणकृते प्रकल्पते स्यान्नागरङ्गो हिमार्थसिद्धिकृत ॥ २४ ॥

— **श्रीदृष्टान्तगर्भस्तुतिद्वात्रिंशिका**

सर्पद्दर्पोत्फणमभिसरन्नागलोकाधिराज–
स्फूर्जच्चूडाभरणधरणस्याज्ञयेव स्थिरात्मा ।
कालव्यालः स्थलकुलयोल्लासलीलामुपैति

श्रीमत्पार्श्व ! त्रिभुवनपते ! त्वत्पदाम्भोजभाजाम् ॥ २० ॥

– **श्री प्रसादद्वात्रिंशिका**

Some time in the middle of the 13th century, Ālhādana, a Nirgrantha-Śvetāmbara minister of the Gallaka community at the court of the Vāghelā monarch Vīsaladeva of Gujarat, had composed a serene and quiet hymn in praise of Pārśvanātha in which he invokes the Jina Pārśva of Śaṅkheśvara and of Serīṣaka (Serisā), both *tīrtha's* situated in north Gujarat:[31]

अम्भोदरूपिणि रुषा कमठे हठेन
वृष्ट्या विकुर्वति भवन्तमवन्तमूर्वीम् ।
लीलातपत्रधरणे धरणेन्द्रनाग-
स्त्वत्पर्युपासिषु विभो ! परमार्गमाप ॥ ९ ॥

– **श्री पार्श्वजिनस्तवनम्**

Next in sequence and significance may come the *Pārśvanātha-stavana* of the eminent scholiast and hymnist, Dharmakīrti *alias* Dharmaghoṣa Sūri of Tapāgaccha (latter half of the 13th cent. A.D.). The particular verse is addressed to the Jina Pārśva of Śirīṣa-nagara (Serisā), the *tīrtha* referred to in the foregoing discussion:[32]

भोगिस्कन्धनिबद्धपादयुगलं स्फूर्जत्फणाडम्बरं
कायोत्सर्गजुषं शिरीषनगरप्रासादलब्धोदयम् ।
ध्यानस्थं कमठोपसर्गविगमे कैवल्यलक्ष्मीयुतं
श्रीपार्श्व जगतां विदारितरुजं पश्यन्ति धन्या जनाः ॥ ६ ॥

– **श्रीपार्श्वनाथस्तवनम्**

In his *Stuti-Caturviṁśatikā*, Dharmaghoṣa Sūri once more attempted the portrayal of Pārśva with Dharaṇarāja:[33]

अहिपतिवृतपार्श्वं, छिन्नसमोहपार्श्व,
दुरितहरणपाषर्श्वं सन्नमद्यक्षपार्श्वम् ।
असुभतम् उ पार्श्वं, न्यकृतामं सुपार्श्व,
वृजिनविपिनपार्श्व, श्रीजिनं नौमि पार्श्वम् ॥ २३ ॥

– **श्री स्तुतिचतुर्विंशतिका**

A composition in the Daṇḍaka form addressed to Pārśvanātha by an unknown author, possibly of the 13th century, refers to the Arhat with Dharaṇendra in the first stanza and describes Dharaṇendra in its last or the fourth stanza:[34]

विपुलविमलकलसकलकमलदलनयनयुगलवरममितकलं,
रुचिर-रुचिर-करकमनतुहिनकर-सुरगज-समगुण-गणममलम् ।
फणिफण-पृथुमणि-गुरुतर-शुचि-रुचि-मतिशय-विलसन-महिमधरं,
विकसित सरसिजवदन-विजितविधुमभिमतमभिनुत जिनपगुरुम् ॥ १ ॥
सुरवरपरदृढसुदृढगगनचरशुभकर-परिकर-परिकलिता,
सुघटित-जटित मुकुट मणिकरभर-निरुपमलवणिम-गरिमयुता ।
अगणितमदशठकमठकमठहठघनघनरिपुजनकदनपरा,
जयति जगति जय-सुविनयनययुतसधरधरणिधर युवतिवरा ॥ ४ ॥

– श्री पार्श्वनाथदण्डकमयस्तुति

In the late medieval period also, the learned pontiffs and friars of the Kharatara-gaccha, the Añcala-gaccha, and of the Tapā-gaccha had produced considerable hymnic literature. The 14th century, with which begins the late medieval epoch, introduces several hymns which contain brief but memorable portrayals of Dharaṇa and Jina Pārśva. The references from this time onward often pertain to the images of Pārśva of the haloed *tīrtha*-sanctuaries, some of these celebrated for their miraculous powers. Among the famous composers of this period, the seniormost was Jinaprabha Sūri of Kharatara-gaccha (active *c.* A.D. 1290-1245), celebrated both as an āgamic scholar but also as an historian of Jaina *tirthas* and a most prolific producer of hymns, some of which are indeed of high quality, such as a verse from his *Pārśvanātha-stava* symptomatically illustrates:[35]

संसाराम्भोधिवेला निविडजडमतिध्वान्तविध्वंसहंसः
श्यामाश्यामाङ्गधाना (?) शठकमठतपोधर्मनिर्माथपाथः ।
स्फारस्फूर्जत्फणीन्द्रः प्रगुणफणमणिज्योतिरुद्द्योतिताशा-
चक्रश्चकिध्वज त्वं जय जिन विजितद्रव्यभावारिवार ॥ २ ॥

– श्री पार्श्वनाथस्तव

Also in his *Yamakamaya Pārśva-Jina-stavana* he refers to that episode:[36]

फुल्लत्फणिफणारत्नरुचिराजितविग्रहे ।
त्वयि प्रीतिः स्फुरतु मे रुचिरा जितविग्रहे ॥ ८ ॥

A *caturviṁśati-Jina-stuti*, ascribed to Jinaprabha Sūri,[37] also contains a telling description of Pārśva with Dharaṇendra and Pārśva Yakṣa:

स्फारस्फुत्फणिफणामणि-दीप्त-दीप्ति-
चित्रीयित-त्रिजगतीजनचित्तवृत्तिः ।
श्री अश्वसेनतनयः श्रितयक्षपार्श्वः,
पार्श्वः श्रिये भवतु वः सुरसेव्यपार्श्वः ॥ २३ ॥

Surprisingly, the compositions in Prākṛta in this age went side by side with those in Sanskrit, though in diminishing number. A verse from one Kamalaprabha Sūri's *Pārśva-prabhu-stavana* (*c.* early 14th century A.D.) may be cited as an example:[38]

जस्स फणिंदफणोहो सोहइ सोसम्भि पणयमणुयाणं ।
मणिदित्तिहिं दलणो दुरियतमं जगपईवु व्व ॥ १ ॥
वज्जसारिक्खनहे सरणागयवज्जपंजरब्भहियं ।
तं झाएमि तिसंझं पासजिणं परमभत्तीए ॥ २ ॥
– **सिरि-पासपहु-थवणं**

Next is the pontiff Bhāvadeva Sūri of Khaṇḍilla-gaccha who, in a hymn to Jina Pārśva in his *Pārśvanātha-caritra* (A.D. 1356), refers to the Jina with Dharaṇendra in eloquent terms:[39]

प्रभोः फणिमणिज्योतिः, प्लुष्टाऽन्तर्वैरिभूरुहाम् ।
तत्पल्लवनिभाः पुंसां, अये सन्त्येव नाऽरयः ॥ ७ ॥
– **श्रीपार्श्वनाथस्तवनम्**

Immediately next in time is Mahendraprabha Sūri of Añcala-gaccha (*c.* last quarter of the 14th cent. A.D.) whose *stava* in honour of the Pārśvanātha of Jīrāpalli has the following verses relevant to the present discussion. The *stotra*, not particularly striking for the quality of style, is notable for its reference to Pārśva's famous *upasarga*-episode at the Kali Hill (in Magadha):[40]

कलौ नाम शैले सरः कुण्डमस्ति स्वयम्भूर्भवांस्तत्तटे स्माविरस्ति ।
तदासन्नभूपालभक्त्येति चित्रं पवित्रं च तद् वेद कस्ते चरित्रम् ? ॥ २५ ॥
तडित्पातघातस्फुटच्चैलश्रृङ्गास्तरत्तूलनीला लुठद्ग्रावश्रृङ्गाः ।
अदभ्राभ्रगर्जहतप्राणिताशाः स्फुरद्दुर्दिनासाररुद्धाखिलाशाः ॥ २६ ॥

तबांहोमठा: कामठा वारिवाहा न निर्वापयामासुरापूर्णबाहा: ।
स्वचेतोऽभ्रकागारगं ध्यानदीपं भजन्तं चिदानन्दसौख्यं समीपम् ॥ २७ ॥
यदूर्ध्वं फणा: सप्त नागाधिराज: स्फुरद्रत्नचूडा बभुर्भक्तिभाज: ।
विजित्येवतान्नारकान् दुर्गमारीन् सदीपा ध्वजा उच्छ्रिता दुर्गमारीन् ॥ २७॥
विद्योर्येन्महो यच्च वा चण्डभानोर्मणीनां तु यच्चाविरासीत् कृशानो: ।
यन्महो ज्योतिषां विश्वभर्त्त: ! स सर्वोऽपि ते ज्ञानतेजोविवर्त: ॥ २९॥
– **श्री जीरापल्ली-पार्श्वनाथ-स्तवनम्**

The contemporary pontiff Devasundara Sūri of Tapā-gaccha (latter half of the 14th century A.D.) had composed a beautiful hymn addressed to the Stambhana-Pārśvanātha. The initial invocative verse from this hymn may be cited in the present context:[41]

स्फुरत्केवलज्ञानचारुप्रकाशं फणामण्डपाडम्बरोद्द्योतिताशम् ।
महाकर्मपङ्कौद्यनाशे दिनेशं स्तुवे स्तम्भनाधीशपार्श्वं जिनेशम् ॥ १॥

A composition in Prākṛta by an unknown author of this period, refers to the same miraculous phenomenon in the description of Pārśva in his *Caturviṁśati-Jina-stuti*:[42]

अससेणनरेसमहागुणवं,
सेवियदेवियवामभिहा ।
तस पुत्तु सुहावउ सफणातुफणा,
फणिधारणु तारणु पासजिणो ॥ २४॥

We are now in the early 15th century. From the compositions of Devasundara Sūri's most famous disciple, one of the greatest *ācārya's* of Tapā-gaccha, namely Somasundara Sūri, the following citation from his Navakhaṇḍā Pārśvanātha of Ghoghā on the east coast of Saurāṣṭra, which vividly portray Dharaṇendra and Pārśva, is relevant in the present context:[43]

स्फूर्जन्नागफणामणीगणसुद्भूतप्रभूतप्रभा–
भारोद्भासितभूमिण्डलमहं मन्दोऽपि मोहोदयात् ।
स्वामिंस्त्वां नवखण्डपिण्डिततनुं श्रीपार्श्व ! विश्वेश्वरं,
घोघासन्नगरप्रधानवसुधालङ्कारभूतं स्तुवे ॥ १॥

Also remarkable is the verse relating to Pārśva (with Supārśva) from his *Pārśva-Supārśva-stuti*:[44]

पार्श्वसुपार्श्वाभिख्यौफणमणिघृणिगणविभासिताकाशो
स्तोष्ये ऋभुक्षिमुख्यस्तुपदपद्मौ जिनौ भक्तया ॥ १ ॥

Among Somasundara Sūri's worthy disciples, the foremost was Munisundara Sūri: from among his many hymnic compositions, a few are addressed to, or include, Jina Pārśva; the notable stanzas from his *Caturviṁśati-stava* and from his hymns addressed to the Pārśvanātha of Nāgahṛda (Nāgadā) and of Phalavarddhi (Phalodi) — the three hymns figuring in his *Jinastotraratnakośa* — are cited below:[45]

वितरतु भवतं श्रीपार्श्वनाथः स मुक्तिं
फणिपतिफणमालश्लिष्टपादारविन्दः ।
कमठहठविमुक्ताऽवारवारिप्रवाहै-
रपि सपदि यदीयो दिद्युते ध्यानवह्निः ॥ २४॥

– श्री चतुर्विंशतिस्तव

जय श्रीमन्नागहदपुरवरालङ्कृतिमणे !
जिनेन्द्र ! श्रीपार्श्व ! त्रिभुवननुतानन्तमहिमन् ! ।
तव स्तोत्रं कुर्वे फणिफणमणीद्योतितपद !
प्रभो ! पद्मावत्यर्चित ! शिवफलं प्राप्तुममलम् ॥ १ ॥

– श्री नागहृदपार्श्वनाथ स्तुति

धत्ते कल्पलताः स्वमूर्त्तिशिरसि प्रोद्यन्मणीपल्लवाः
सप्ताहीन्द्रफणाच्छलात्रिजगतीभीतीः क्षिपन् सप्तधा ।
सप्तद्वीपसमियृदङ्गिनिकराभीष्टार्थदानाय यः
संसाराम्बुधिसेतवेऽस्तु विभवे पार्श्वाय तस्मै नमः ॥ २२॥

– श्री फलवर्ध्धीपार्श्वनाथस्तुति

One other learned disciple of Somasundara Sūri, namely Bhuvanasundara Sūri, had produced notable hymns: his *Jīrāpallī-Pārśvanātha-stavana* (*c.* 2nd quarter of the 15th century) has a fine verse relevant in the present context.[46]

सदा पुन्नगश्रीः प्रभवति विभो ! दुर्भगतमा
लभन्ते सौभाग्यं प्रसरति हिमाली जनततौ ।

जनः प्रौढज्योतिःपटलपरिपेवी स्फुटतमा-
नुभावाद्यस्यासौ त्वमसि गुरुहेमन्तविभवः ॥ १५॥
– श्रीजीरापल्ली पार्श्वनाथस्तवनम्

The glory of the Pārśvanātha of Cārūpa has been sung by Ratnaśekhara Sūri (*c.* 2nd-3rd quarter of the 15th cent. A.D.), one other famous disciple of Somasundara Sūri, in his *Cārupa-maṇḍana-Pārśvanātha-stavana*. Therein, at least six verses are as pertinent as are good instances of the evocative description of Pārśva with Dharaṇendra:[47]

श्रीचारूपपुरप्रधानवसुधालङ्कारचूडामणि-
प्रायं स्फारफणामणिद्युतिभरैराभासिताशामुखम् ।
कल्पक्षोगिरुहातिशैशववयः पत्रालिवित्रासकृत्-
कायच्चायमहं स्तवोमि मुदितः श्रीपार्श्वविश्वेश्वरम् ॥ १ ॥
फणाग्रजाग्रन्मणिराजिराजमानेन्द्रनीलामलनीलकायः ।
सत्पुष्पभृत् पत्रलहेमपुष्पमहीरुहौपम्यमशिश्रियस्त्वम् ॥ ८ ॥
विभिद्य माद्यद्दुरपोहमोहमहान्धकारं प्रकटानि कुर्युः ।
ससापि तत्त्वानि विभो ! फणाग्रजाग्रत्तमास्ते मणिदीप्रदीपाः ॥ ९ ॥
स्फुरन्मणिस्फारफणान् दधान अपि प्रदर्पास्तव देव ! सर्पाः ।
हर्षं प्रवर्षन्ति जनय दृष्टाः स्पृष्टाश्च सङ्गो हि सतां शमाय ॥ १५ ॥
श्रिताः फणास्त्वां मणिराजिभाजौ रेजुः कृतार्थीकृतभव्यसार्थ ! ।
अतुल्यवल्ल्यः कुसुमाभिरामाः कल्पद्रुमं नन्वधिरूढवत्यः ॥ १६ ॥
अतुल्यकल्याणमहानिधानं लभ्यं लसद्भाग्यभरोदयेन।
प्रभो ! भजन्ते भुजगा भवन्तं युक्तं मणीमण्डितमौलिमध्याः ॥ १७ ॥
स्फारस्फूर्जत्फणानामनणुमणिगणोद्योतविद्योतिताशा-
चक्र चारूपनामप्रवरपुरमहीमण्डनं पार्श्वनाथम् ।
यः स्तौत्येवं तमालद्रुमदलपटलस्पर्द्धमानामलाङ्ग-
ज्योतिर्जालं स शर्माण्यनुभवति भवाम्भोधिपारस्थितात्मा ॥ १८ ॥
– श्रीचारूपमंडनपार्श्वनाथस्तवनम्

The same Sūri's *Tribhāṣā-Pārśva-Jina-stava* also has a fine verse:[48]

फणिगुरुफणमालालम्बिचूडामहीयो-
मणिगणकिरणालीसङ्गरङ्गावगाढम् ।

अरिहमुरुमहेलासिद्धिसम्पन्नरागा-
रुणमिव गुणगेयं चित्तधेयं धरेयम् ॥ २३ ॥

– **श्रीत्रिभाषामयपार्श्वनाथस्तुति**

Ratnaśekhara Sūri's unnamed disciple was no less able in delineating the glory of the combined imagery—Pārśva-Dharaṇendra—as amply evidenced by the verses in his hymn on the Pārśvanātha of Mahīśānaka (Mehsāṇā) in north Gujarat:[49]

सप्तस्फूर्जत्फणमणिलसल्लोचनोद्यल्ललाम-
व्याजात् प्रामृत्यकृत किमिह स्वस्वमेकैकरत्नम् ।
दिक्पालौघो दशहरिदधीशस्य यस्य प्रसत्यै
शैवं शर्म प्रदिशतु सतामाश्वसेनिर्जिनोऽसौ ॥ ९ ॥
श्रीवामेयः प्रथयतु ममामेयमाहात्म्यगेयः
प्रेयः श्रेयस्तिलकनयानाद्यत्फणारत्नदम्भात् ।
धत्ते दातुं दश सुरमणीन् भास्वरांस्तुल्यकालं
चेतोऽभीष्टान्यधिदशहरित्तस्थुषां नेमुषां यः ॥ १० ॥
पोपोषीति स्वयमविरतं पोषयेच्चापरैर्नः
स्वामी विश्वेऽप्ययमिति मुदा किन्त्वमान्तो यदङ्गे ।
एतेऽभूवन् बहिरनिभृताः साधुधर्मप्रकाराः
प्रेङ्खत्पुण्ड्रेक्षणफणमणिव्याजतः पातु सोऽर्हन् ॥ ११ ॥
अष्टानां यः शुभमृगदृशांकेलये सिद्धिनाम्नां
धत्ते रात्नान् प्रवरमुकुरान् स्वेन पाणौ कृतानाम् ।
प्रोद्यत्पुण्ड्रस्फुटमणितनून्नुनमन्यूनऋद्धयै
भूयाद् भृतोऽतिशयभवनं वः स वामाङ्गजोऽर्हन् ॥ १२ ॥
एकाग्रोऽष्टौ प्रवचनमताः पालयेद् यः किलाम्बाः ।
स स्यान्मद्वत् परमपदसम्प्राप्तिमात्रं किमेतत् ।
ज्ञीप्सुर्न्यस्ताः स्वशिरसि सतां दर्शयेद् यः सफुटास्ताः
प्रोद्यत्पुण्ड्रस्फुटमणिनिभाद् भूतय स्तात् स पार्श्वः ॥ १३ ॥
नन्द्याद् विद्याधरनरसुरारब्धपादाब्जसेवः
पार्श्वो देवः फणमणिलसत्पुण्ड्रसङ्क्रान्तियोगात् ।
दध्रे मूर्तीर्नव हितमनाः किं नु सत्वादितत्त्वा-
न्याख्यातुं यः कृतिजनततेर्विस्तरेणैककालम् ॥

– **श्रीमहीशानकमंडन-पार्श्वनाथस्तवनम्**

A hymn by Somasundara Sūri, which I lately came across, is addressed to Jina Pārśvanātha; it consists of stanzas composed in six different languages. Two verses—one in Mahārāṣṭrī-Prākṛta, and the second in Śaurasenī-Prākṛta—are useful in the present context:[50]

फणिफणमणिमाला रेहए जस्स सीसे
तमतिमिरपणासे दीवपंतिव्व दिव्वा ।
परममहिमवासो पावराई व राई
घणतमहिमवासो देउ सुक्खं स पासो ॥ २॥
वोलिज्जंत कुलाचलाहि पयलं भोदप्पभाहिं तदा
वुट्ठीहिं कमठासुरस्स भरिदब्वंभंडभांडाहिवि ।
जस्स ज्झाणहुदासणो पजलिदो सित्तोविही माणहे
सामी पासजिणो स भोदु भगवं तेलुक्कमुक्खप्पदो ॥ ३॥

– श्री पार्श्वनाथस्तवनम्

Ācārya Devasundara's great grand disciple Jinasoma (*c.* 3rd quarter of the 15th cent.), too, had composed a hymn to Pārśvanātha, in this instance of Stambhana. The opening verse elegantly refers to Dharaṇendra with Pārśva:[51]

श्रीस्तम्भनं पार्श्वजिनं निरञ्जनं स्तुमः समग्रातिशयाश्रयं वयम् ।
फणीश्वरस्फारफणागणोल्लसन्मणिप्रभाडम्बरमण्डिताम्बरम् ॥ १॥

– श्री स्तम्भन-पार्श्वनाथस्तवनम्

And plausibly some time late in that century, Muni Lakṣmīlābha, perhaps of the Tapā-gaccha, had addressed a hymn adoring the Navapallava Pārśvanātha of Maṅgalapura, Māṅgaroḷ, at the west coast of Saurāṣṭra:[52]

उद्यत्फणामुकुटभूषितमस्तकान्त ! त्रैलोक्यलोकनयनामृतपूर्णचन्द्र ! ।
विख्यातमङ्गलपुरस्थित ! वीतराग ! मां पाहि पाहि नवपल्लवपार्श्वनाथ ! ॥ १॥

– श्री नवपल्लव-पार्श्वनाथस्तुति

Next in sequence comes Hemahaṁsa Gaṇī, disciple of Jayacandra Sūri of Tapā-gaccha (*c.* last quarter of the 15th century A.D.), who was a prolific producer of hymns, some notable for their simple but elegant expressiveness, such as his *Caturviṁśati-Jina-stava* from which a verse that concerns with Pārśva is cited below:[53]

एकस्य दत्तां पदवीमुदीक्ष्य किं,
तदर्थिनोऽष्टौ फणभृत्-कुलाग्रिमाः ।
भजन्त्यमी यं फणलांछनच्छलात्,
पार्श्वप्रभुः रातु स वांछितानि वः ॥ २४॥

– श्री चतुर्विंशतिजिनस्तव

Contemporaneous pontiffs of the Kharatara-gaccha did not lag behind in composing hymns to Pārśva, the one by Jinasamudra Sūri (*c.* mid 15th century) addressed to the Pārśvanātha of Jaisalmer (founded in A.D.1417), has a fine verse pertinent to the present survey of Pārśva hymns.[54]

यत्ते व्याधायि कमठेन कठोरघोरधाराकरालजलवृष्टिरिहोपरिष्यात् ।
तेनैष केवलमवीवृधदात्मनो वै दुःकर्मवल्लिवनमेव चिरप्ररूढम् ॥ ४॥
स्फूर्जत्फणामणिधरं धरणं भजन्तं यच्चापि पातकमठं कमठं द्विषन्तम् ।
त्वं मन्यसे सदृशमीदृशमीश ! लोको नीरागताविलसितं लसितं तवैव ॥ ५॥

– श्री जैसलमेरुमंडन-पार्श्वनाथ स्तुति

The Sūri was equally at home, even in that late age, with Prākṛta as is clear from the *Stuti-caturviṁśitikā* in which he refers to Pārśva with Dharaṇendra:[55]

पायडियसत्ततत्तो, धरणिंदसरीरफणकडप्पेणं ।
तुट्टभववासपासो, पासो मह मगलं देउ ॥ २३॥

– सिरि थुतिचउविसी

That reminds us of the references to Pārśvanātha and Phaṇīndra in two other Prākṛta compositions by unknown authors and possibly of this general age — the second definitely was composed between A.D. 1437 and 1459 — both possessing poetic pretensions:[56]

देही वत्तविवत्रपत्रगफणा-छत्तेण छन्नंबरो,
सामासामसरीरओ रयतमोमुक्को समुक्कोसओ ।
वामाए विसुओऽसुरामरनई-नीहारसेलोवमो,
सो पासो भववासपासयसमं सज्जो पसाहिज्ज मे ॥ २३॥

– श्री स्तुतिचतुर्विंशतिका

कमठ दाणव दलि-अमाहप्प,
फणमंडविमंडिउ भुवणज्झिमहिमाहि गज्झइ,
पउमावइ वयरुट्ट जुअ धरणराय जस पाय पुज्जइ,
थंभण सामीसर हसया जइ इच्छह भवपार,
दुक्खभार चूरइ सयल भविअहं मंगलकार ॥ ८ ॥

– श्री बहुतीर्थस्तुति

Next may be quoted a relevant verse from the *Mantrādhirāja-kalpa* of Sāgaracandra, an author of an unknown *gaccha* and date (but probably of the 15th century if not of earlier times):[57]

अन्तःस्फुरद्रुचिरसञ्चितसप्तत्त्व-
कोटोपतिर्जिनपतिः प्रकटध्वजोऽस्तु ।
वामासुतः फणमिषात् फणिपस्य विश्व-
विश्वार्तिसंहतिहरो व्यवहारिवद् यः ॥ ४ ॥

– श्रीमन्त्राधिराजकल्प

In the 17th century, too, there are a few instances of good hymnical compositions: Upādhyāya Yaśovijaya (A.D. 1622-1689), the last of the Nirgrantha luminary in the field of epistemology, had also composed some hymns; of these the one on the Saṅkheśvara-Pārśvanātha is brilliantly eloquent. From this hymn some six resonant verses may be cited as illustration:[58]

फणामणीनं घृणिभिर्भुवीश ! मूर्तिस्तवाभति विनीलकान्तिः ।
उद्भिन्नरक्ताभिनवप्रवालप्ररोहमिश्रेव कलिन्दकन्या ॥ ३१ ॥
तेवश ! मौलौ रुचिराः स्फुरन्ति फणाः फणीन्द्रप्रवरस्य सप्त ।
तमोभरं सप्तजगज्जनानां धृता निहन्तुं किमु सप्त दीपाः ॥ ३२ ॥
त्वन्मौलिविस्फारफणामणीनां भाभिर्विनिर्यत्तिमिरासु दिक्षु ।
स्वकान्तिकीर्तिप्रशमात् प्रदीपाः शिखामिषात् खेदमिवोद्गिरन्ति ॥ ३३ ॥
ध्यानानले सप्तभयेन्धनानि हुतानि तीव्राभयभावनाभिः ।
इतीव किं शंसितुमीश ! दध्रे मौलौ त्वया सप्तफणी जनेभ्यः ॥ ३४ ॥
अष्टापि सिद्धिर्युगपत् प्रदातुं किमष्ट मूर्तीस्त्वमिहानतानाम् ।
सप्तस्फुरद्दीप्तफणामणीनां क्रोडेषु सङ्क्रान्ततनुर्दधासि ॥ ३५ ॥

स्फुरत्फणाडम्बरभीमकायः फूत्कारभारैरुदयद्विषायः ।
उल्लालयन् क्रूरकृतान्तदंष्ट्राद्वयाभजिह्वायुगलं प्रकोपात् ॥ १०० ॥

And finally a hymn addressed to Arhat Pārśva, although composed in times as late as the 18th century by a disciple of Guṇavijaya of Tapā-gaccha, is replete with poetic grace and apparently recaptures the style of the previous centuries:[59]

कमठविहितज्वालाजिह्वप्रतप्ततनुः फणि-
र्धरणपतितां यस्यालोकद्गतः परसंसृतौ ।
स्फुरति महिमा [तत्रा]ऽद्यापि प्रवृद्धकलौ युगे
भवभयभिदो वामेयोऽसौ स एव भवे भवे ॥ ८ ॥

III

The above-cited portrayals of Arhat Pārśva canopied by the pentacephalous or septacepalous Dharaṇendra—in a few cases also noticing the *upasarga* of the demon Kamaṭha or Śambara or Meghamālī—are symptomatic of the authors' exalted visualization of the unshakable, dignified, and tranquilly awesome image of the Jina standing in deep trance, and its sharp reflection on their minds and consequently in their hymnal invocations, each of which is delineated in the personal style of the author concerned. If these medieval hymns succeed in conjuring up the highly emotive visions of Pārśva, what the Nirgrantha poets of the Gupta-Vākāṭaka Age could have configured, if they had focused on this mythical episode, may be imagined. In default of such early compositions, in all fairness, let us pay tribute to and admire what the medieval and late medieval hymnists, with their profound devotion coupled with the poetic skills they commanded (which included sensitive control on the ornamental niceties in Sanskrit poetics) had created and is before us to see, sense, and feel. The sculptor-artists correspondingly had attempted, to represent concretely the resplendent imagery of Pārśva with Nāgarāja Dharaṇendra and in few cases in association with the *upasarga*-legend. They also occasionally, indeed faithfully as well as convincingly, captured the mythico-mystical vision of the hymnists as a tri-dimensional reality, following as they did the modular rules and employing the skills of their own sphere of craft: some of the extant examples, particularly of the post-Gupta and pre-medieval times, are witnesses that authenticate this conclusion.

NOTES AND REFERENCES

1. I have discussed, with Jitendra Shah, the subject of early Nirgrantha hymnology in the "Introduction" in Gujarati of *Śri Bṛhad-Nirgrantha-stuti-maṇi-mañjuṣā* (BNSMM) currently in press.
2. In the "Jinacaritra" inside the *Paryuṣaṇā-kalpa* (*c.* A.D. 503/516), Indra is shown as praying Jina Vīra with this *stava*; hence it is sometimes called the *Śakra-stava*.
3. The *Rāja-Pasenīya* Book II (*c.* 2nd-3rd cent. A.D.) in the context of Sūryābha-deva and the *Aupapātika* (*c.* 3rd cent. A.D.) in the context of king Kuṇika of Magadha, the two references are more important. The *stava* also figures in the *Jñātādharmakathā* (*c.* 3rd cent. A.D.).
4. The above-mentioned *Paryuṣaṇā-kalpa*.
5. I have traced the end-phrases of the *Caturviṁśati-stava* of the *Āvaśyaka-sūtra* (with slight variations in the text) at several places in the *Isibhāṣiyāiṅ* (compiled *c.* 2nd-1st cent. B.C.), a work for certain belonging to the sect of Pārśva. (The details of these have been noted in BNSMM.)
6. Up to the period of the autocommentary on the *Tattvārthādhigama-sūtra* of Vācaka Umāsvāti (*c.* A.D. 350-400), and the *Ṣaḍāvaśyakas*, though enumerated in serial formation, originally were independent works. From the period of the *Anuyogadvāra-sūtra* (*c.* late 5th cent. A.D.) and more decisively from before the time of the *Āvaśyaka niryukti* (*c.* A.D. 525), the *Āvaśyaka-sūtra* had come into existence. The Yāpanīya sect, however, even in later times (*c.* 8th-9th cent. A.D.), apparently looked upon the *Ṣaḍāvaśayakas* as serially ordered but not forming a single book, the *Āvaśyaka-sūtra*.
7. I had discussed, with Pt. Sagarmal Jain, the origin of the Yāpanīya sect (the better term would have been *acela-kṣapaṇaka* rather than Yāpanīya in the northern Indian context I now realize) in the *Aspects of Jainology*, Vol. III (*Pt. Dalsukhbhai Malvaniya Felicitation Volume I*), Varanasi 1991. A Śaurasenī version of this *stava* is known from the Digambara sect. (Its source understandably may have been Yāpanīya.)
8. For example the 31 *Sambandha kārikās* at the end of Umāsvāti's *Sabhāṣya Tattvārthādhigama-sūtra* and his *Praśamarati-prakaraṇa* which consists of as many as 304 verses. The style of the two is close enough and indeed is archaic compared to that of Pūjyapāda Devanandi (*c.* A.D. 635-680), Svāmī Samantabhadra (*c.* A.D. 550-600), and even when compared to that of Siddhasena Divākara who is supposed to be contemporary of the Gupta emperor Candragupta II (A.D. 378-414).
9. I have examined the problem of the date of Siddhasena Divākara and have reached the conclusion that he flourished after Umāsvāti and before Diññāga. On certain historical hints and the synchronisms involved, his life-span can be confidently placed some time between A.D. 360-450. He nowhere refers to Pārśva as such, though his allusions to Mahāvīra are very clear and done directly in Jina's name.
10. *Paümacariya*, pt.1, sec. edn., Ed. Muni Shri Punyavijayaji, Varanasi 1962, p. 1.
11. I have discussed the date of this great southern luminary in my article in Gujarātī, "Svāmi Samantabhadra-no Samaya," to appear shortly in the second issue of the *Nirgrantha*, Ahmedabad, in 1997.
12. Ed. Jugal Kishor Mukhtar, Vīrasevāmandira-granthamālā, Vol. 7, Sarsava 1951.
13. For detailed discussion on this *stava*, see my article, "The Date of the Ajita-Śānti-stava of Nandiseṇa",

Pathways to Literature, Art, and Archaeology: Pt. Gopal Narayan Bahura Felicitation Volume, Jaipur 1991.

14. Unlike the *Bhaktāmara-stotra* as well as the *Bhayahara-stotra*, there is no inclusion of the nomen Mānatuṅga in the end-verse or anywhere inside this *stotra*. The style of composition is also definitely later than the *Bhayaharastotra* which, like the *Uvassagahara*, is in Prākṛta.
15. The inclusion of the Pārśva Yakṣa along with Jina Pārśva would suggest a date not earlier than the late ninth century for this *stotra*. Several years ago, I had pointed out this fact when the subject of the so-called Bhadrabāhu II was discussed with Pt. Dalsukh Malvania in Varanasi when Pt. Sagarmal Jain was also present.
16. The date and authorship of this *stava* are being discussed in the "Introduction" of the first part of the BNSMM.
17. For discussion on the probable date of this work, *see* my article "Dākṣiṇātya Nirgrantha Paramparā ke kucha Granthon kī Aitihāsika Samasyāen", *Sandhāna*, Vol. V, Varanasi 1992, 15-19.
18. पापाचारस्य दुश्चेष्टामुद्वीक्ष्य चरिचक्षुषा ।
    पद्मावत्या समं देवमुपतस्थौ फणीश्वरः ॥ ७७ ॥
    तस्य विस्तारयामास सधैर्यस्तवपूर्वकम् ।
    स्फुरन्मणिरुचिस्फारस्फुटामंडलमंडपम् ॥ ७८ ॥
    — श्रीपार्श्वनाथचरित्रम्
19. My studies on these important compositions will appear in print elsewhere, in part also in the Introduction to BNSMM earlier alluded.
20. Vidyānanda has been by past scholars assigned to early 9th century, a date not upheld by facts. Some five years ago, I had discussed the date of this great scholiast in my article, "The Date of Vidyānanda and Epigraphical Evidence", to be published in *Dr. H.V. Trivedi Felicitation Volume*, Bhopal. Its revised version will figure in the *Nirgrantha* 2, Ahmedabad, in 1997.
21. An epigraphical reference to Padmāvatyālaya at Kallili in the inscription of the Kadamba Ravivarmā (*c.* early 6th century) from Guḍanāpura is even earlier in time. (*See* in this volume A. Sundara's paper.)
22. The available archaeological evidence is for late tenth century as at the Mahāvīra temple at Ahāḍ near Udepur (Mevāḍ) in Rajasthan. The Śvetāmbara literature is totally silent on Padmāvatī till we come to early 11th century. Clearly, the Śvetāmbara Church (which essentially is western Indian) had adopted Padmāvatī from the southern Church where she meets with considerable frequency and where the antiquity of her worship and depiction goes back to the sixth century.
23. *Jainastotrasandoha*, pt. 2 (*Mantrādhirāja Cintāmaṇi*) (JSS2), Ed. Muni Caturvijaya, Ahmedabad 1936, pp. 75-76.
24. *Śrī Lalitastotrasandoha*, Ed. Hrīṅkāravijaya Gaṇi, Bangalore 1962, p. 103; also *Pañca Pratikramaṇa*, Ed. Pt. Sukhalalji, Agra 1921, "Pariśiṣṭa," p.45.
25. *Jainastotrasaṅgraha*, pt. 1 (JSS n1), Varanasi V.N.S. 2432/A.D. 1912, pp. 116-118; also JSS2, pp. 194-195,
26. *Jainastotrasandoha*, pt. 1 (JSS1), Ed. Muni Caturavijaya, Ahmedabad 1932, pp. 195, 196.
27. *Ibid.*, p. 94.
28. *Ibid.*, p. 204.

29. JSS2, p. 189.
30. JSS1, pp. 125, 128, 132, 142, 143, 146, and 161.
31. JSS2, p. 193.
32. JSS1, p. 244.
33. *Stutitaraṅgiṇī* [Sanskrit, pt. 2] (St. 2), Ed. Vijayabhadraṅkara Sūri, Madras V.S. 2043 (A.D. 1987), p. 117.
34. *Stutitaraṅgiṇī*, pt. 3 (St 3), Ed. Vijayabhadrankara Sūri, V.S. 2039 (A.D. 1983), p. 139.
35. *Kāvyamālā*, pt. VII, Ed. Mm. Pt. Durgāprasāda and V.L. Śastrī Panśikar, Bombay 1926, p. 107
36. JSS2, p. 176.
37. St. 3. p. 307.
38. JSS2, p. 147.
39. *Śrī Svādhyāya-dohanam*, Ed. Vijaya Kanakachandrasūri, Patan 1986, p. 161.
40. JSS2, p. 147.
41. *Ibid.*, p. 95.
42. St. 3, p. 239.
43. *Ibid.*, p. 13.
44. JSS n1, p. 5.
45. *Śrī Jaina Stotrasaṅgraha*, pt. 2, sec. edn., Varanasi V.S. 2439/A.D. 1883, pp. 46, 80 and 87.
46. JSS2, p. 155.
47. JSS2, pp. 108, 109.
48. *Stotrasamuccaya*, (SS), Ed. Muni Caturavijaya, Bombay 1928, pp. 112, 113.
49. JSS2, pp. 104-106.
50. SS. 104.
51. JSS2, p. 98.
52. *Ibid.*, p. 186.
53. St. 3, p. 270.
54. JSS2, p. 177.
55. JSS1, p. 86
56. St. 3, p. 373; and St. 3, p. 385.
57. JSS2, p. 227.
58. JSS1, p. 383, 384, and 390.
59. SS., p. 43.

पार्श्वनाथ प्रतिमाएं

: उत्तर प्रदेश से पूर्व कुणाल काल से लेकर बारहवीं सदी तक :

शैलेन्द्र कुमार रस्तोगी

जैन शासनधर्म का मूल तो अर्हत् चिन्तन ही है। वह भी उनसे किसी प्रतिफल की इच्छा से नहीं अपितु अपने अन्दर उनके गुणों को लाना है। अर्हतों को अतीत उत्सर्पिणी और अनागत उत्सर्पिणी में हुये और होने वाले २४, २४ तीर्थंकरों की सूची जैन ग्रन्थों में मिलती है।[१] वर्तमान अवसर्पिणी के २४ तीर्थंकरों को जोड़कर ७२ तीर्थंकर (पार कराने वाला) होते हैं। प्रथम तीर्थंकर ऋषभनाथ और अंतिम महावीर है। किन्तु २३वें तीर्थंकर भगवान् पार्श्वनाथ हैं।

पार्श्व का अर्थ समीपे सप्पंसयणे जणणी, तं पासइतमसि तेण पास जिणों. १०६९। पश्यति सर्वभावानितति निरूक्रात्पार्श्वः ।तथा गर्भस्थे भगवति जनन्या निशि शयनीयस्य पार्श्वे अन्धकारे सपों दृष्टं इति गर्भानुभावोऽयमिति पश्यतीति पार्श्वः। अस्यामवसर्पिण्यां भरतक्षेत्रे त्रयोविंशे तीर्थंकरे ।[२]

तीर्थंकर पार्श्व : ईसा० पू० ८७७, ७७७: को ऐतिहासिक पुरुष माना जाता है।[३]

भगवान् पार्श्वनाथ काशी के राजा अश्वसेन के पुत्र थे उनकी माता का नाम वामा था । इन्होंने तप की तुष्टि के अर्थ राजकीय विलासी जीवन को त्याग दिया था। इनकी चित्तवृत्ति आरंभ से ही वैराग्य की ओर विशेष थी । विवाह का प्रस्ताव हँसकर टाल दिया। एक बार ये वाराणसी में गंगा किनारे घूम रहे थे । वहाँ पर कुछ तापसी व माता-पिता विहीन ब्राह्मण कुमार कमठ आग जलाकर तपस्या कर रहे थे। ये इनके पास जाकर बोले "इन लक्कड़ों को जलाकर क्यों जीव हिंसा करते हो।" कुमार की बात सुनकर तापसी बड़े झल्लाये और बोले "कहाँ है जीव।" तब कुमार ने तापसी के पास से कुल्हाड़ी उठाकर ज्यों ही जलती हुई लकड़ी को चीरा तो उसमें से नाग-नागिन का जलता हुआ जोड़ा निकला। कुमार ने उन्हें मरणोन्मुख जानकर उनके कान में मूलमंत्र दिया और दुःखी होकर चले गये। इस घटना से कुमार उदास रहने लगे और राजसुख को तिलांजलि देकर प्रव्रजित हो गये। एक बार ये अहिक्षेत्र के वन में ध्यानस्थ थे। ऊपर से उनके पूर्व जन्म का वैरी कमठ कहीं जा रहा था। देखते ही उसका पूर्व संचित वैरभाव भड़क उठा। वह उनके ऊपर ईंट और पत्थरों की वर्षा करने लगा। जब उससे भी उसने भगवान् के ध्यान में विघ्न पड़ता न देखा तो मूसलाधार वर्षा करने लगा। आकाश में मेघों ने भयानक रूप धारण कर लिया, उनके गर्जन-तर्जन से दिल दहलने लगा। पृथ्वी पर चारों ओर पानी ही पानी उमड़ पड़ा। ऐसे घोर उपसर्ग के समय नाग-नागिन मर पाताल लोक में धरणेन्द्र और पद्मावती हुए थे, वे अपने उपकारी के ऊपर उपसर्ग हुआ जानकर तुरन्त आए । धरणेन्द्र ने सहस्त्रफण वाले सर्प का रूप धारण करके भगवान् के ऊपर अपना फण फैला दिया और इस तरह उपद्रव से उनकी रक्षा की। सुप्रभात स्तोत्र में इन्हें "घोर उपसर्ग विजयिन, जिन पार्श्वनाथ" कहा गया है। इसी समय पार्श्वनाथ को केवलज्ञान की प्राप्ति हुई और उस वैरीदेव ने उनके चरणों में सीस नवाकर उनसे क्षमा मांगी। इनकी जो मूर्तियां पाई जाती हैं, उनमें उक्त घटना की स्मृति

में सर पर सर्पफण बना हुआ होता है। जैनेतर जनता में इनकी विशेष ख्याति है। कहीं-कहीं तो जैनों का मतलब ही पार्श्वनाथ का पूजक समझा जाता है।

भगवान् पार्श्वनाथ की मूर्तियां सम्पूर्ण भारत में प्रस्तर, धातु एवं बहुमूल्य रत्नों आदि पर बनी पर्याप्त संख्या में उपलब्ध होती हैं। भारत का हृदय उत्तर प्रदेश है और इस उत्तर प्रदेश से जैन धर्म का बहुत ही निकट का संबंध है। क्योंकि ये भूमि कितने ही तीर्थंकरों के गर्भ, जन्म, तप, ज्ञान एवं निर्वाण कल्याणकों से पवित्र हुई है । प्रस्तुत निबंध में इसी भूमि से उपलब्ध प्रस्तर की पूर्व-कुषाण काल से लेकर १२वीं सदी तक की मूर्तियों को मात्र समाहित करने का प्रयास किया गया है। इनमें अधिकांश प्रतिमाएं लेखरहित और कुछ लेखयुक्त, बैठी, खड़ी, सर्वतोभद्र पर, मानस्तम्भों आदि पर पाई जाती हैं।

पार्श्व का आयागपट्ट पर सर्व प्राचीन निदर्शन

जैन धर्म में पूजा के निमित्त चौकोर पट्ट बनाये जाते थे जिन्हें मंदिरों के भीतर, चौराहों पर लोगों को पूजा करने के निमित्त उन्हें स्थापित किया जाता था इसलिये इन्हें आर्यकपट्ट या आयागपट्ट कहते थे। ऐसे आयागपट्ट ईसा पूर्व कंकाली टीला मथुरा से प्राप्त हुए हैं। कुछ आयागपट्ट कौशाम्बी से भी पाए जाते हैं।

राज्य संग्रहालय, लखनऊ को एक ही आयागपट्ट कंकाली टीला मथुरा से प्राप्त हुआ है जिस पर अंकित रचे हुए अक्षरों की लिपि के आधार पर लगभग सोडास शकक्षत्रप के द्वितीय शती का चतुर्थांश अर्थात् पूर्व कुषाण काल का है।[६] इस पर लेख नमो अर्हतान ..... शिवधो:षसका: ...... भर्याय .... आयाग प ....। अर्थात् शिवघोषा की पत्नी ने इसे स्थापित करवाया था। इस पट्ट के चारों ओर कमल, व अंगूर की बेलों व चारों कोनों को ईहामृगों व श्रीवत्स चिह्न से सजाया गया है। बीज में चार नन्दीपदों के मध्य तीन सोपानों वाली चौकी पर भगवान् पार्श्वनाथ को ध्यानस्थ दर्शाया गया है। इनके सिर पर सात सर्पफण का छत्र बनाया गया है। फणों के ऊपर स्तम्भ में लगी पताका फहरा रही है। भगवान् पार्श्व के दायें-बायें नमस्कार मुद्रा में एक-एक दिगम्बर मुनि खड़े हुए हैं।

पार्श्व अंकित चरण-चौकी : संग्रह में यह पार्श्व भगवान् की बैठी मूर्ति की चरण-चौकी बड़ी रोचक है। मूल मूर्ति दुर्भाग्य से प्राप्त नहीं है। इस पर लेख इस प्रकार है :

....स्थ निकियेकुलेगनिस्थ उग्गहिनियशिषो, वाचको घोषको

अर्हतोपश्वस्य प्रतिमा अस्तु, अर्हन्त पार्श्व की प्रतिमा से सुस्पष्ट है। लिपि के आधार पर जब हम अन्य प्रतिमा लेखों के अक्षरों से तुलना करते हैं तो ५८ कनिष्क प्रथम से पूर्व हुविष्क अर्थात् हुविष्क से पूर्व की यह चरण-चौकी स्वयंसिद्ध हो जाती है।

पार्श्व मस्तक : संग्रह में खंडित फणों से नीचे मुंडित मस्तकयुत पार्श्व का मस्तक है। इसकी आंखें गोल व आधी खुली हैं तथा माथे पर बिन्दी है। यह मस्तक हुविष्क व वासुदेव के शासन काल के मध्य बनाया गया प्रतीत होता है।[७]

लखनऊ के संग्रह में तीन अन्य पार्श्व मस्तक हैं[८] इन मस्तकों पर प्राय: मांगलिक यथा चक्र, नन्दीपाद, त्रिरत्न, पुष्पगुच्छ व घट आदि का अंकन पाते हैं। इनमें एक में सप्तफण के छत्र के नीचे पार्श्वमुख सुरक्षित पाते हैं किन्तु शेष दो के नीचे पार्श्वमुख का अभाव है। मथुरा संग्रहालय में एक सर्पफण के नीचे पार्श्वमस्तक का अंकन है और सर्पफणों पर स्वस्तिक, सरावसम्पुट, श्रीवत्स, त्रिरत्न, पूर्णघट व मत्स्य युग्म बने हैं[९]।

कुषाणकाल की पार्श्वनाथ की बैठी मूर्तियाँ[१०] : भगवान् पार्श्व की एक बैठी प्रतिमा कंकाली टीला मथुरा से कुषाणकाल पाई गई है। पहले प्रतिमा सिरहीन पाई गई थी बाद में उसके मस्तक को ढूंढ़कर उस पर लगा दिया गया। चरण चौकी पर हुविष्क संवत् सरे अष्टापन ....अंकित पाते हैं। इसे हुविष्क व वासुदेव के वर्ष ५८ से सम्बद्ध किया गया है। सर्पफण के भीतर की ओर बाईं ओर हवा में उड़ते एक देव का अंकन है तथा पीछे अशोक वृक्ष का मनोहारी अंकन है।[११] लेख में अष्ठापन अर्थात् ५८ अंकों में न लिखकर शब्दों में लिखे गये हैं। मूर्ति के मस्तक पर घुंघराले बाल हैं।

स्तूप के साथ पार्श्व[१२] : संग्रह में एक पार्श्व का अंकन भी स्तूप के साथ बड़ा ही महत्वपूर्ण है। पटिया पर ऊपर की ओर दाईं ओर छूट गया है मूल पृष्ठ ४ देखें । दो स्तूप हैं। बाईं ओर के अंतिम तीर्थंकर के पूर्व सप्तफणों के छत्र के नीचे पार्श्वनाथ शोभायमान हैं । इस पर लेख ९९ वर्ष नहीं है जो कि वासुदेव के समय का बैठता है।

कुषाणकाल की एक अन्य बैठी मूर्ति[१३] : पार्श्वनाथ सर्पफणों के नीचे विराजमान हैं। इनका सर मुंडित है। नीचे की चरण-चौकी पूरी घिस चुकी है और सर्पफणों पर स्वस्तिक, त्रिरत्न, चक्र व पुष्पगुच्छ अंकित हैं। यह हुविष्क वासुदेव के समय की प्रतीत होती है।

कुषाणकालीन सर्वतोभद्र प्रतिमाएं[१४] : संग्रह में पांच कुषाणयुगीन सर्वतोभद्र प्रतिमाओं पर तीर्थंकर पार्श्वनाथ को अंकित पाते हैं। इनमें जे० २३० प्रतिमा उल्लेखनीय है जो कि कनिष्क द्वितीय के समय की अर्थात् २५७ ई० की प्रतीत होती है। इस पर सन् १५ अंकित है। दाईं ओर अधपालक का भी अंकन है जिसका मुँह खंडित है और दूसरी अन्य प्रतिमा पर भी पार्श्व कायोत्सर्ग मुद्रा में खड़े हुए हैं। मथुरा संग्रहालय में भी ऐसी पांच तीर्थंकर प्रतिमाएँ हैं।[१५] ये सभी लाल चित्तीदार बलुए पत्थर की हैं।

संक्रान्तिकाल की पार्श्व प्रतिमा[१६] : संकलन में पार्श्व की एक ऐसी कायोत्सर्ग मुद्रा में मूर्ति उपलब्ध होती है जो कि ढलते कुषाणकाल व उगते गुप्तकाल की प्रतीत होती है क्योंकि तीर्थंकर की शरीर रचना व उनके उपासक का मुकुट व बाईं ओर खड़ी स्त्री मूर्ति जिसके ऊपर सर्पफण का आभास मिलता है। पद्मावती प्रतीत होती हैं। मूल मूर्ति का मुँह, हाथ व पैर खंडित हो चुके हैं। सर्पफण भी घिस चुके हैं। एक फण पर चक्र बचा है।

गुप्तकाल : पार्श्व प्रतिमा[१७] : संग्रह में मात्र एक लगभग पाँचवीं शती की पार्श्व प्रतिमा है। इसकी शारीरिक गठन, तलुओं की मांसलता, श्रीवत्स की संरचना आदि के आधार पर इसे पाँचवीं शताब्दी का माना जा सकता है। मथुरा संग्रहालय से कोई भी गुप्तकाल की पार्श्व प्रतिमा का उल्लेख उपलब्ध नहीं होता है। मध्यकाल में इस मूर्ति के मस्तक पर तिलक बनाना व आँखों को बड़ा व नाक को खंडित किया गया प्रतीत होता है।

शैल स्तम्भ, गुप्तकाल कहायूं, देवरिया[१८] : गुप्तकाल में पार्श्व प्रतिमाएँ कम मिलती हैं जिसका कारण कुछ भी रहा हो किन्तु इसी काल का अभिलिखित गुप्त संवत् १४१+३१९ = ४६० ई० का कहाऊं ग्राम जनपद देवरिया का सम्राट स्कन्दगुप्त के पाँचवें राज्य वर्ष का अपना ही महत्व है। इसके विषय में सर्वप्रथम १९वीं सदी में आरम्भ में बुचानन ने ध्यान इस ओर दिलवाया था। १८३९ में लिस्टननेहस स्थान का परिचय प्रकाशित किया और १८६१-६२ मे कनिघंम ने सर्वेक्षण कर इसका पूरा लेख प्रकाशित किया। लेख से विदित होता है कि मद्र ने : आदिकर्तृन : ऋषभ, शान्ति, नेमि, महावीर व पार्श्व की प्रतिमाएँ इस स्तम्भ पर नव उत्कीर्ण करवाई। चार तीर्थंकरों की खड़ी प्रतिमाएँ व पार्श्व की बैठी प्रतिमा है।

मध्यकालीन पार्श्व प्रतिमा[१९] : मथुरा संग्रहालय में चार बैठी प्रतिमाएँ हैं। प्रथम प्रतिमा में सर्पफणों के नीचे गद्दी पर पार्श्व भगवान् ध्यानस्थ बैठे हैं। सिंहों द्वारा सिंहासन उठाया हुआ है। दूसरी प्रतिमा की चरण-चौकी पर धर्म-चक्र बना है। पार्श्व सर्पफणों के नीचे ध्यानस्थ हैं। यह प्रतिमा नन्दी आनंदी बलदेव से आई थी। तथा पूर्व मध्यकाल की है। दूसरी प्रतिमा पार्श्वनाथ के मध्यकाल की है। इसमें एक मालाधारी विद्याधर सुरक्षित बचा है। इस प्रतिमा को कोसीकलां मथुरा से पाया गया था। इसके अतिरिक्त आगरे के कगरूल नामक स्थान से भी एक बैठी प्रतिमा संग्रह में है।

खड़ी मूर्तियां[२०] : एक मूर्ति काले पत्थर की खड़ी सप्तफणों के नीचे पार्श्व की कहाऊं देवरिया में है। लखनऊ संग्रहालय में राजघाट वाराणसी से एक अति ही मोहक प्रतिमा आई है यह सुरमई रंग की त्रितीर्थी है।[२१] मूलनायक पार्श्व के मस्तक पर सप्त सर्पफण चरण चौकी के दोनों ओर एक-एक सिंह तथा मध्य में धर्म-चक्र बना है। बाईं ओर वंदन मुद्रा में उपासिका तथा इसी ओर एक सर्पफण वेष्टित दोभुजी पद्मावती का अंकन है और दाईं ओर एक सर्पमंडित धरणेन्द्र खड़े हैं। मूल प्रतिमा के दाएं-बाएं एक-एक तीर्थंकर कमल की सजावटयुत गद्दी पर ध्यानस्थ बैठे हैं। सर्प को पार्श्व के पैरों के पीछे की ओर से बनाया गया है। इसकी कुंडली दिखलाई देती है। सर्पफण सात हैं, इनमें एक टूटा है। दोनों ओर मालाधारी विद्याधर तथा मध्य में सर्पफणों पर त्रिछत्र के ऊपर देवदुंदुभिवादक का अंकन है।[२२]

मध्यकालीन चौमुखी प्रतिमाएं[२३] : मथुरा संग्रहालय में मध्ययुगीन बैठी हुई सर्वतोभद्र प्रतिमा है जिस पर सप्तफणों के नीचे भगवान् पार्श्वनाथ बैठे हुये हैं। लखनऊ के संग्रहालय में इस काल की तीन प्रतिमाएँ हैं। एक मटीले पत्थर की शौरीपुर : बटेश्वर : आगरा[२४] और दूसरी अतिसुन्दर नवीं सदी की भूरे पत्थर की सराय अघत एटा जनपद[२५] की है (चित्र ४)। जिसमें पार्श्वनाथ दोहरे कमल की गद्दी पर खड़े हुए हैं और नीचे चारों तरफ चौमुखी के दो-दो ग्रह अर्थात् सूर्य, चन्द्र, मंगल, बुध, बृहस्पति, शुक्र, शनि व राहु आदि बने हुए हैं। तीसरी लगभग दसवीं सदी की फैजाबाद की है[२६]। यह घुटनों के नीचे से टूटी है। सर्पफण खंडित है किन्तु चौमुखी के ऊपर कमल-दल का अलंकरण बना हुआ है।

मानस्तम्भ पर पार्श्वनाथ का अंकन[२७] : संग्रह में एक भूरे रंग का मानस्तंभ है जिस पर आठ जिनेन्द्रों का अंकन है। यह स्तम्भ इलाहाबाद से आज से लगभग ६४ वर्ष पूर्व लाया गया था। स्तम्भ पर चार तीर्थंकर नीचे बैठे हैं और चार ऊपर कायोत्सर्ग मुद्रा में दिखाए गये हैं उनमें नीचे की ओर भगवान् पार्श्व को दो खम्भों के द्वारा बने लघु मंदिर के भीतर में बैठे ध्यानस्थ दर्शाया गया है। इनके ऊपर सप्तफण का छत्र है तथा सांप की दुम दाईं ओर चरण-चौकी पर सुस्पष्ट है।

मध्यकालीन खड़ा पार्श्व-आवक्ष[२८] : भूरे रंग के पत्थर का सप्तसर्पफणों के छत्र के नीचे पार्श्व मूर्ति का आवक्ष है। यह मूर्ति काफी घिस चुकी है और श्रावस्ती की है।

पंच तीर्थी[२९] : एक अन्य पंचतीर्थी भी संग्रह में है (चित्र ३)। सिंहासन के दोनों ओर एक-एक सिंह तथा मध्य में एक चक्र बना है। तदुपरान्त अलंकृत आसन पर पद्मासन में ध्यान लगाए पार्श्व भगवान् बैठे हैं। इन पर सप्तसर्पफणों का छत्र बना है। सर्प की कुंडली दोनों ओर बनी है। घुटनों के पास दोनों तरफ एक-एक चंवरधारी तथा दोनों ओर दो-दो ध्यानस्थ चार तीर्थंकर बने हैं । इनके ऊपर विद्याधर दम्पत्ति बने थे जो अब घिस चुके हैं। यह मूर्ति लेखरहित है किन्तु शैली के आधार पर लगभग दसवीं शती की है । ये जैन-पंचतीर्थी श्रावस्ती से आई थी और प्रथम बार प्रकाशन में आ रही है।

दीर्घकाय बैठी श्वेताम्बर संघ की पार्श्व प्रतिमा[30] : एक गहरे कलछऊ पत्थर की पार्श्व प्रतिमा भी बड़ी रोचक है। तीर्थंकर ध्यानस्थ बैठे हैं। उनकी दोनों बगलों के बीच में सर्प की कुंडली सुस्पष्ट है। चरण-चौकी पर सिंह नहीं बने हैं बल्कि आसन को पाँच फूलों से सजाया गया है। तीन फूल बीच में हैं जो पूर्ण है और दाएं-बाएं के फूल आधे-आधे हैं। मस्तक पर घुंघराले बाल व उष्णीष बनी है, गर्दन में रेखाएं हैं। वक्षस्थल पर गोल चक्र जैसा श्रीवत्स है तथा दोनों ओर बगलों के भीतर से सर्प की कुंडली दिखलाई देती है भगवान् पार्श्व का यह अति मनोज्ञ अंकन है। इस पर अंकित लेख में इसे 'देवविनिर्मित' कहा गया है जो ठीक ही प्रतीत होता है। इस प्रतिमा की चरण-चौकी पर लेख इस प्रकार है :

संवत् १०३६ कार्तिक शुक्ल एकादस्यां श्री श्वेताम्बर मूल संघेन पंचिभ चतु : स्थी : कायां श्री देव विनिर्मित प्रतिमा प्रतिष्ठापिता।

अर्थात् इसे संवत १०३६-५७ = ९७९ ई० में ''श्री श्वेताम्बर मूल संघ'' ने कार्तिक शुक्ल एकादशी को स्थापित कराया था। यह कंकाली टीला मथुरा से प्राप्त हुई है । (पार्श्वनाथ की श्रावस्ती से मिली सं० ११३४/ ई० १०७७ की प्रतिमा चित्र ५ में निदर्शित है ।)

पद्मावती व धरणेन्द्र सहित पार्श्व[31] : संग्रह की अति रोचक मूर्ति भूरे पत्थर की पार्श्व प्रतिमा है। यहाँ पार्श्व की प्रतिमा अति सजीव है। ये सिंहासन पर ध्यानस्थ हैं। बाईं ओर यक्षी पद्मावती खड़ी है। इन पर तीन फणों का छत्र है और दाईं ओर धरणेन्द्र चंवर लिये खड़े हैं और उन पर सर्प के तीन फणों वाला छत्र बना है। सप्तसर्पफणों के छत्र के नीचे भगवान् पार्श्व विराजमान हैं सर्पछत्र के ऊपर त्रिछल बना है और उसके ऊपर देवदुंदुभिवादक बना है तथा दाएं-बांए हवा में उड़ते माला लिये एक-एक आकाशचारी देव बने हुए हैं। चरण-चौकी के बाईं ओर नीचे कोने की ओर पीछी लिए मुनि तथा दायीं ओर उपासक दम्पत्ति बने हैं। यह प्रतिमा लगभग ११-१२वीं सदी की है। इस मूर्ति को देखते हुए कुमुदचन्द्र के कल्याण मंदिर स्त्रोत्र का श्लोक स्मरण हो आता है-

> **तदबिम्ब निर्मल मुखाम्बुज बद्धलक्ष्या,**
> **ये संस्तवंतव पिभोरचयन्ति भव्या : ॥ ४३**[32] **॥**

यह मूर्ति महोबा से आई है।

मध्यकाल की पार्श्व की खड़ी प्रतिमा[33] : यह श्वेत संगमरमर पर बनी दिगम्बर पार्श्व प्रतिमा भी बड़ी रोचक है। पार्श्व भगवान् की नासाग्र दृष्टि है और चरण-चौकी पर बने कमल पर खड़े हैं। बाएं-दाएं क्रमश: उपासिका-उपासक हैं। तदुपरान्त चंवरधारी दोनों ओर बने हैं। सर्प को पार्श्व के पैर से ही पीछे की ओर बनाया गया है जिसकी कुंडली उनके दोनों ओर दीख पड़ती है। सर्पफण नहीं बनाए गए हैं। इस प्रतिमा की एक अपनी ही विशेषता है कि जरा-सा भी थपकी देने पर झंकृत हो उठती है। इस विषय में **प्रतिष्ठा सारोद्धार** में उल्लेख है कि प्रतिमा बनाने के लिए शिला का चयन करते समय वही शिला उत्तम है जो चिकनी सुगन्ध, सुस्वर, और कठिन हो। यह प्रतिमा १२वीं या ११वीं शती की शैली के आधार पर लगती है। यह मूर्ति महोबा हमीरपुर जनपद की है (चित्र ६) ।

पद्मावती व धरणेन्द्र के साथ खड़ी पार्श्व मूर्ति[34] : भगवान् पार्श्व की कायोत्सर्ग मुद्रा में सर्प के सप्तफणों

के छत्र के नीचे वाली भूरे पत्थर की है। नीचे चरण-चौकी में दो खम्भों के मंदिर के भीतर सर्प के सप्तफणों के छत्र के नीचे चतुर्भुजी पद्मावती बैठी हैं। उसके ऊपर १/२ चौड़ी पट्टी है और उसके ऊपर भगवान् पार्श्व कायोत्सर्ग खड़े हैं। इनके सर्पफण टूटे हैं। मुँह भी टूटा है। ऊपर त्रिछत्र के नीचे उपासक व उपासिका व चंवरधारी बने हैं। आगे बाईं ओर सर्पफणों के नीचे धरणेन्द्र चतुर्भुजी तथा ऊपर चतुर्भुजी यक्षी परन्तु पता नहीं क्यों और किस हेतु बनाये गए हैं। इसके ऊपर ईहामृग अलंकृत है । प्रतिमा शौरीपुर : बटेश्वर : आगरे की है।

धरणेन्द्र व पद्मावती रहित बैठी पार्श्व मूर्ति[३५] : संग्रह में भूरे रंग के पत्थर की एक अति ही सजीव बैठी सुपार्श्वनाथ की मूर्ति है। चरण-चौकी पर दोनों ओर सिंह हैं। बीच में चक्र तथा दाएं-बाएं उपासक-उपासिकाएं बनी हैं। आसन के ऊपर वस्त्र बिछा है जिसका कोना सामने को लटका हुआ है। इसके ऊपर ध्यानस्थ तीर्थंकर पार्श्व बैठे हैं । संयोग से यह मूर्ति पूर्ण पाई गई है : पार्श्व के वक्षस्थल पर सकरपारे के आकार का श्रीवत्स उभरा बना है तथा कान इसके काफी लम्बे हैं। घुंघराले बालों के ऊपर छोटी-सी उष्णीष भी दीख पड़ती है। जो निःसंदेह बौद्ध प्रभाव प्रतीत होता है। पार्श्व के बाएं-दाएं एक-एक चंवरधारी खड़े हैं उनके ऊपर दोनों ओर हवा में उड़ते देवदम्पत्ति बने हैं। दोनों के ही बाएं देवियाँ बनी हैं जो क्रमशः बांसुरी व वीणा लिये हैं। तत्पश्चात् दोनों ओर एक-एक हाथी : ऐरावत : बने हैं ओर इनमें बाईं ओर हाथी के ऊपर बैठा सवार भी सौभाग्य से बच गया है दोनों हाथियों के बीच में व सर्पफण के मध्य में त्रिछत्र व आमलक बना है। इस मूर्ति पर लेख है। इसके अनुसार संवत् ११२० (ईस्वी १०६४) में इसको बनाया गया था। यह मूर्ति श्रावस्ती बहराइच जनपद की देन है।

पद्मावती के मस्तक पर पार्श्व का अंकन[३६] : पद्मावती की बड़ी ही मनोज्ञ मूर्ति है। ये अर्द्धपर्यंकासन में बैठी हैं। देवी के आसन को कमल की पंखुड़ियों से सजाया गया है। दायां घुटना कुछ टूटा है। दोनों ओर एक-एक उपासक व चंवरधारिण कमल पर खड़ी बनी है। देवी का नाम एक चरण-कमल पर रखा है। देवी चतुर्भुजी हैं। इनके ऊपर सर्प के सप्तफणों का छत्र बना है जिसके दो फणों को छोड़कर सभी टूट चुके हैं। सर्पफण के ठीक ऊपर आसन पर पार्श्वनाथ ध्यानासीन हैं। इनके दाएं-बाएं चंवरधारी तथा दाएं-बाएं देवदम्पत्ति माला लिये हुए दिखलाए गए हैं। यह मूर्ति महोबा कलातीर्थ की देन है।

इनके अतिरिक्त जनपद ललितपुर स्थित देवगढ़[३७] प्रतिमाओं का उल्लेख भी समीचीन रहेगा। यहाँ के मंदिरों में पार्श्वनाथ की मूर्तियाँ सुशोभित हैं। इनका समय लगभग ९वीं से १२वीं शती तक का बैठता है। यहाँ के कुल सात चित्र लिए गए हैं। इनमें एक मूर्ति देवगढ़ के मंदिर संख्या २ के परकोटे पर बनी है जिसकी चरण-चौकी पर गरुड़ या चकुवा भी बना है।[३८] यह मूर्ति १२वीं शती की है। पार्श्व प्रतिमाएँ प्रायः सर्प के सप्तफणों के छत्र के नीचे बनाई जाती हैं किन्तु कुछ प्रतिमाओं में इनकी संख्या तीन, नौ या ११ भी पाते हैं। कहीं-कहीं प्रतिमाओं पर सर्पफण नहीं पाते हैं किन्तु पीछे देह के उनकी सर्पकुंडली दिखलाई देती है या चरण-चौकी पर सर्प का लांछन या पार्श्व का नामोल्लेख भी पाते हैं।[३९]

जैन-साहित्य में कमठ के पार्श्व पर उत्सर्ग का वर्णन तो पाते हैं किन्तु इस कथानक को अभिव्यक्त करने वाली कोई भी प्रस्तर की मूर्ति उत्तर प्रदेश में उपलब्ध नहीं होती है किन्तु दक्षिण में एलौरा की गुफा संख्या ३२ व तिरुकोळानाथ आर्कट से ऐसी मूर्तियां मिलती हैं।[४०]

पार्श्व भगवान् के जन्म, तप एवं उपदेशों से पूत उत्तर प्रदेश की पावन धरती से प्राप्त ईसा पूर्व से १२वीं

शती तक के उनके अकाट्य अभिलेखीय साक्ष्यों एवं सुललित बिम्बों के प्रति

नरेन्द्रंफणीन्द्रं सुरेन्द्रं अधीशं शतेन्द्रं सुपूजे भजेनायशीशं।
मुनीन्द्रं गणेन्द्र नमोजोडिहाथं नमो देवदेवं सदा पार्श्वनाथं॥ [४१]

नमन करते हुए इस निबंध को यहीं विश्राम देने की अनुमति चाहूंगा।
शुभमऽस्तु ।

कृतज्ञताज्ञापन

इस निबन्ध के तैयार करते समय तिथि के सम्बन्ध में लेखक जर्मन विदुषी प्राध्यापिका जी० बी० मिटरवारनर, म्युनिख यूनिवर्सिटी का हार्दिक आभार व्यक्त करता है।

श्री लाल चंद जैन, श्री अजीत प्रसाद जैन, मंत्री, तीर्थंकर महावीर स्मृति केन्द्र, शोध पुस्तकालय, चारबाग, लखनऊ का भी हार्दिक आभार व्यक्त करता है।

संदर्भ-सूची

१. **तिलोयपण्णाती** महाधिकार ४, **प्रवचन सारोद्धार,** सात गाथा २९०. ९२, २९५, ९७ तथा अन्य ग्रन्थ, बालचन्द्र जैन, **प्रतिमा विज्ञान** पृ० ३२, जबलपुर १९७४ ।

२. **अभिधान राजेन्द्र** पृ० ८९६ पंचमोभाग, **आवश्यक चूर्णि** । रतलाम् १९२१ ।

३. **भगवान् महावीर स्मृति ग्रन्थ,** सं० ज्योतिप्रसाद जैन, पृ० ३८ खन्ड ६, लखनऊ १९७५ ।

४. कैलाशचन्द्र शास्त्री, **जैन धर्म** पृ० १७, १८ वाराणसी १९७६ ।

५. राज्य संग्रहालय संख्यक जे० २५३, आकार ८६, ९२, १० से० मी० लाल चित्तीदार पत्थर १. *U.P. Shah, Studies in Jaina Art,* p. 12, वाराणसी १९५५ Vincent Smith, *Jaina Stūpa at Mathura,* ५, Plate 8, व V.S. Agrawal, *Guide to Lucknow Museum,* p. 4.

५. राज्य सग्रहालय, लखनऊ, सं० जे० ६७ आकार ३८, ५५ से० मी० लाल चित्तीदार पत्थर ।

७. रा० सं० ल० सं० जे० ११४ आ० ४४ ६५ से० मी सफेद-रंग भूरे रंग का बलुआ पत्थर ।

८. रा० सं० ल० संख्या जे० ७७, आ० १, २०, ८७ से० मी० लाल पत्थर जे० ९०, ८०, ३० से० मी०. लाल चित्तीदार पत्थर' व जे० ९६, आ० ४५, ३० से० मी० लाल चित्तीदार पत्थर ।

९. रा० सं० मथुरा बी० ६२, R.C. Sharma, *Mathura Museum and Art, p. 37, Mathura,* १९७६, ५६० वी० एस० अग्रवाल **यू० पी० हिस्टोरिकल सोसायटी** २३, पार्ट १.२, पृ० ६२ ।

१०. जे० २५ व जे० ११३ आ० ८६ से० मी० देह भाग हैं और ४० से० मी० शिर ।

११. उद्गच्छता तव शिति दुति मंडलेन लुप्तच्छुदच्छविशशकैकेतरुबभूव ॥२४॥ श्लो २४ **कल्याणमंदिर स्तोत्र, ज्ञानपीठ पूजाञ्जलि,** दिल्ली १९८२, पृ० ४९६ से ५०४ तक ।

१२. रा० सं० सं० जे० ६२३ आ० ५६, ४८ से० मी० ।

१३. रा० सं० सं० जे० ३९ आ० १. ०४ से ५७ से० मी० लाल चित्तीदार पत्थर ।

१४. ,, जे० २३० आ ६०, १९, जे० २३४, आ० ७६, २९ से० मी०
,, जे० २३५ आ ५४, २३, जे० २३७, आ ६० २४ से० मी०
,, जे० २४४ आ० ६१, २७

१५. राज संग्र० मथुरा बी० ६७ आ० २ फु० १० इंच, बी० ७९, आ १ फु० ११ इंच, बी० ७०, बी ७१, बी० ७२, १ फुट ३ इंच। तीर्थंकर मूर्तियाँ, *U.P. Historical Society of Uttar Pradesh*, Vol. 23. भाग १, २, पृ० ६३, ६४, १९५०।

१६. रा० सं० ल० सं० जे० १०० आ० ४५, २८ से० मी० लाल चित्तीदार पत्थर ।

१७. ,, जे० ७७ आ १.२० से० मी, ६७ से० मी० ।

१८. २४ फुट ऊँचा स्तम्भ १.१० वर्गाकार स्तम्भ के नीचे चौपहलमध्य अठपहल और ऊपर से १६ पहल आकार है। पश्चिम दिशा में सतह से २. ६ भगवान् पार्श्व की २.३ ऊँची बैठी प्रतिमा बनी है।

१९. १. रा०सं० म० सं०बी० २६ आ० १" ८" रमेशचन्द्र शर्मा, *Mathura Museum and Archaeology* ।

२. ,, ,, ,, ,, २५१ आ० ३'-0 V.S. Agarwal, *JUPH.S,*. Vol. 23, pts. 1-2, पृ० ६३, लखनऊ १९५० ।

३. तीर्थंकर मूर्तियाँ मध्यकाल की पृ० ६३ आ० तीन फुट।

४. रा० सं० म० सं० १५०५ वही, पृ० ६४, २.७ इंच।

५. ,, ,, सं० ४०. २८७४। २ बी० एन० श्रीवास्तव व शिवाधार मिश्र *Inventory of Mathura Museum from1939 to date, Museum Archaeologial Bulletin* सं० ११.१२, पृ० ९८ ।

२०. मेरे पास चित्र है।

२१. रां० सं० सं० ४८, १८२ *Annual Report of Provincial Museum, Lucknow*, १९५०, p. 11 ।

२२. एतनिन्वेदतिदेव जगतत्रयाय, मन्ये नद ननभिनमः सुरदुन्दुभिस्तै **कल्याण मन्दिरस्तोत्र** श्लोक संख्या २ ५ ।

२३. बी ६५, आकार २.१० इंच आर०सी० शर्मा *Mathura.*, पृ० ?

२४. जे० ८१३, आ० २५, २६ से० मी० ।

२५. जे० १४१, आ० ५८, ३० से० मी०, भूरा पत्थर ।

२६. छ ५२.७४ ए, आ० ८०, ३५ से० मी० भूरा पत्थर ।

२७. ओ० ७२, आ०- ५"x१'-८", चौड़ा. ४' चौकोर देखिए मेरा लेख, ''जिन बिम्बों से सुशोभित राज्य संग्रहालय का एक विशिष्ट मानस्तम्भ'' पृ० ६५ खण्ड-२ **भग० महा० जय० स्मा०** जयपुर १९७२ ।

२८. जे० ८७७ आ० ३०, ३१ से० मी० भूरा पत्थर ।

२९. रा० सं० ल० सं० जे० ८५९, आ० ५७, ४४ से० मी०, भूरा रंग का रेतीला पत्थर ।

३०. रा० सं० ल० जे० १४३ आ० १.७० से० मी, १.३३ से० मी० ७७ से० मी० मेरा लेख ''श्वेताम्बर कलारत्न कंकालीर्क मणिभद्र'' पृ० ३७ जयपुर १९८० ।

३१. रा० सं० ल० जी० ३१० आ० ४३, २५ से० मी०। मेरा लेख ''महोबा की जैन मूर्तियाँ'', **कैलाश चन्द्र शास्त्री अभिनंदन ग्रन्थ**, पृ० ३३ रीवां १९८०।

३२. कल्याण मंदिर स्तोत्र सं० ४३ **ज्ञानपीठ पुजांजलि,** दिल्ली १९८२ ।

३३. जे०, ३१३ आकार ७८.२, २७ से० मी०। वही **प्रतिष्ठा सरोद्धार** आ० ३ श्लोक ७८ ।

३४. रा० सं० ल० सं० जे० ७९४ आ० ६९, २४ से० मी० काले गहरे भूरे रंग का पत्थर ।

३५. रा० सं० ल० सं० जे० ८७९ आ० ६४, ३३ से० मी० मटीला सफेद पत्थर ।

३६. रा० सं० ल० सं० जी० ३१६ आ० ६०, ३६ से० मी० भूरा पत्थर ।

३७. Klaus Bruhn, *Jaina Images of Devagadh Vana*, Leiden 1969, चित्र सं० १९८, २०४, १२६, ४०४, व २३१ अर्थात् मंदिर संख्या ३, ४, १७ व २० तथा दीवाल में ।

३८. मंदिर सं० २ के परकोटे की दीवाल पर मेरे संग्रह का चित्र ।

३९. ज्योदि प्रसाद जैन, **रूहेलखंड कूमायूं और जैन धर्म**, पृ० १३.१४ लखनऊ १९७० व **पद्मानन्द महाकाव्य** १। २६ तथा बी० सी० भट्टाचार्य *Jaina Iconography* ।

४०. C. Sivaramamurti, *Panorama of Jaina Art*, नई दिल्ली १९८३, चित्र ५४६ व १४२ ।

४१. कवि वृन्दावनदास-**पार्श्वस्तुति** ।

चित्र-सूची

IMAGES AND TEMPLES OF PĀRŚVA IN CENTRAL INDIA

Amar Singh

Pārśvanātha, the 23rd *Tīrthaṅkara*, whose historicity has been fully established, is regarded by many modern writers of history as the real founder of Jainism. In this paper I intend to deal with the studies of images and temples of Pārśva in Central India (Madhya Pradesh and Bundelkhaṇḍ region of Uttar Pradesh), which were built in the territories where Gupta, post-Gupta, Pratīhāra, Cedi, Ca ıdella, Kacchapaghāta and Paramāra dynasties had ruled within their temporal brackets from *c.* fourth century A.D. to *c.* 13th century A.D. In ancient and medieval periods, several temples for Pārśvanātha had been built. The buildings in course of time had disappeared leaving only stray remains; so the still standing temples for the Jina are somewhat rare to meet with while loose images abound in number.

The earliest images of Pārśvanātha are reported from Mathurā (U.P.);[1] but no image of the Jina of comparable antiquity has so far been found in Central India. In point of fact, it does not appear there before the fifth century A.D. In the Gupta, but more frequently from post-Gupta and Pratīhāra periods, Pārśvanātha's images are met with in fair abundance. These have been reported from Udaigiri, Vidiśā, Nacanā-Kuṭhārā, Gyāraspura, Gwalior, Amrol, Deogarh, Sirā-Pahārī, Kuṇḍalpur, Baḍoh-Paṭhārī, Tu-Main and the neighbouring regions of Jabalpur and Tevar (ancient Tripurī).

Gupta and post-Gupta Periods

The Udaigiri cave 20 (Plate 7) near Vidiśā, excavated according to the inscription in the Gupta year 106 (A.D. 425-426) and hence in the reign of Kumāragupta I, was meant for an image of Pārśvanātha. However, the loose image now present in the cave is of a much later date. A badly mutilated relief of a seated Pārśva in *dhyāna-mudrā*, which, as suggested by U.P. Shah, is the image referred to in the inscription.[2]

One other, and an excellently fashioned image of Pārśvanatha which was originally enshrined in a Jaina temple at Gyāraspur near Bhilsā (Vidiśā), currently in the Victoria and Albert Museum, London, shows Pārśvanātha seated below the Dhātaki tree practising the "exposure to all weathers" austerity when Meghamālī attacked him by creating a terrible storm. The serpent-king Dharaṇendra spreads his hoods above the head of the Jina and his companion Padmāvatī holds an umbrella over him. On either side of the cobra-hoods are the *mālādhara*-celestials hovering in the sky and at the top are shown hands beating the *duṁdubhi*-drum. The base in front shows a *gaṇa*-dwarf holding *cakra* in his hands. The image can be dated to *c.* seventh century A.D.[3]

In a sandstone *sarvatobhadrikā* image from Vidiśā (Vidisha State Museum No. 357/1295), Pārśvanātha (Plate 8) is seated on the coils of a snake in *dhyāna-mudrā* with a seven-hooded canopy over his head. On the face of the *siṁhāsana*, the *dharmacakra* is shown between the two lions and the *cāmara*-bearers. Above the serpent-hoods, on either side, celestial beings carrying garlands glide in air and flank the *devaduṁdubhi*; the *trichatra* also is depicted atop the Nāgarāja Dharaṇendra. Stylistically, this image may also be assigned to *c.* seventh century.

Another *sarvatobhadrikā* image (Plate 9), reported from Karaitalai (Jabalpur District), currently in the Mahant Ghasidas Memorial Museum, has on one of its faces a seated Pārśvanātha with a seven-hooded canopy over his head. Two lions are depicted on the pedestal sitting back to back with a *dharmacakra* in the centre, flanked by two standing *cāmara*-bearers. A part of the plain carpet decorated with a beaded border is shown suspended from the seat. The serpent-canopy is flanked by two flying garland-bearers, the Jina's head below shows closed meditative eyes, elongated ears, combed-back hair with central *uṣṇīṣa*, and the posture of the hands making a triangle with the body are features favouring a date in the sixth-seventh century.

In an image reported from Nacanā-Kuṭhārā (District Panna) (Plate 10) and now preserved in the Tulsi Ashram Sangrahalaya at Ramban in District Satna, Pārśvanātha is shown seated on the coils of a snake in the *dhyāna-mudrā*, protected by a seven-hooded canopy over his head. He is flanked by Indra and Upendra, standing in *tribhaṅga*-posture, each carrying a *cāmara* in his hand. Well-proportioned body, half-closed eyes in trance, and an effulgence of subtle mystical luminescence on the face of the image show the characteristics of the classical art of the Gupta period still continuing, thus suggesting a date not later than the seventh century.

A group of Jaina sculptures from Sirā Pahārī, a hill near Nacanā, Panna District, has an image of Pārśvanātha of about the seventh-eighth century A.D. It stands in the *kāyotsarga-mudrā* without any drapery and has a huge serpent coiled behind the whole figure making a canopy of seven hoods over the Jina's head.

A very interesting image (Plate 11) of Pārśvanātha in the Indian Museum Calcutta (No. A 2541) and originally from some site possibly in Madhya Pradesh, is remarkable in that it portrays, with due elaboration, the *upasarga* of Śaṁbara or Meghamālī. The central figure of Pārśvanātha in *kāyotsargā-mudrā* is being attacked by the demon Meghamālī from both sides with the help of the *bhūtas, vetālas* and other evil spirits, while Dharaṇendra is shown protecting the Jina, adjusting as he does his coiled body from the back and seven-hooded canopy over his head. On the right side of the Pārśva, Yakṣī Padmāvatī, the companion in this context of Dharaṇendra, is standing on a snake with a serpent canopy over her head and holding a *chatra*-parasol in her hands. On stylistic grounds, the date of the image has been fixed to *c.* sixth or early seventh century A.D. but possibly it is later.

Gopagiri-Maurya

According to the medieval Śvetāmbara (quasi-historical) biographical narratives on Bhadrakīrtti *alias* Bappabhaṭṭi Sūri (active *c.* A.D. 770-839), a king Āma, the son and successor of Maurya Yaśovarmā of Kanauj (A.D. 725-752), is said to have built temples to Jinas at Gopagiri and Kānyakubja under the influence of the Sūri.[5] Thus, during the late eighth and early ninth century, Jainism had some weight in the Gwalior territory.

Gwalior Fort, famous for the rock-cut Jaina images of the Tomara period, has also a remarkable early sculpture of Pārśvanātha (Plate 12) now set up at the north-eastern corner on the gate of the open theatre of Scindia School in the Fort. The head of the Jina bears the character of earlier art; the elongated eyes, however, mark the beginnings of the medieval period. Above the serpent-hood, *nāgas* in half-human form bearing water-pots in their hands, pour libations over the deity. Two garland-bearing *vidyādharas* float in the air at the top-flanks. Taking in view the anatomical features, hair style, *ekāvalī* of the celestial beings and the form of the *nāgas* — all these reflecting the persistence of some of the classical characteristics of the Gupta art. Meister dates the image to *c.* eighth century.[6]

An image of Pārśva (Plate 13) from Amrol (a village south-east of Gwalior), assign-able to ninth century, shows a seven-hooded *nāga* protecting the Jina and also has an umbrella above. Two elephants standing on lotus flowers are also shown pouring water from pots by way of *abhiṣeka* to the Jina. Below this, on either side, the *nāgīs* sitting on lotus flowers pass water up from their positions to the elephants above for the lustration of the Jina. Garand-bearers are also present on either side of the *nāga* hood.[7]

Pratīhāra-Period

An image of Pārśvanātha from Vidiśā (Vidisha State Museum) (Plate 14), standing in *kāyotsarga*-posture, depicts a large serpent coiled behind the Jina's body and making a canopy of hoods over his head. The *nāgīs*, interestingly, are depicted on both sides of the Jina with folded hands. The *siṁhāsana*-front shows a male and a female figure, each seated on a lotus flower and holding lotuses in their hands and flanking an unidentified object. Nāgarāja Dharaṇendra and Yakṣī Padmāvatī having three-hooded serpent canopy over their heads are present, standing as they do on either side of the Lord. The image may be assigned to *c*. ninth century.

A mutilated image of Pārśvanātha belonging to *c*. ninth century from Badoh-Paṭhārī (Vidisha District) is at present in a bad state of preservation. Its head and legs are broken. Pārśvanātha is shown seated on a lotus seat in *dhyāna-mudrā*. Padmāvatī holding the rod-umbrella in her hands is depicted on the right side of the Jina. The serpent-coils are also seen covering the entire back side of the Lord.

In an image reported from Tu-Main in District Guṇā, Madhya Pradesh, now in the Sagar University H.G. Museum (No. 72.1), Pārśvanātha is shown seated in *dhyāna-mudrā* with a seven-hooded canopy over his head. The *dharmacakra* is shown in the centre of the lion-throne. Elephants standing on the lotus flowers and grasping stalked lotuses in their trunks are present on both sides of the Jina whose chest is marked by *śrīvatsa*. Half closed eyes, serene face, elongated ears, curly hair, and well built broad chest of the *Tīrthaṅkara* bears the characteristics of the classical age of Gupta period and may be dated to *c*. ninth century.

In a *sarvatobhadrikā* image (Plate 15) from Cirainti village (District Śāhḍol), Pārśvanātha is shown seated cross-legged in the *dhyāna-mudrā* on a *masūraka*-cushion placed upon a carpet decorated with lotus petals motif. The *siṁhāsana* shows a four-armed sitting Padmāvatī in the centre. On both sides of the throne, also come to view a seated and a standing attendant. The head of the Jina is covered with a seven-hooded canopy. The representation of the triple umbrella flanked by flying garland-bearers and *devaduṁdubhi* (two hands grasping a drum) above the umbrella is likewise noteworthy. On the chest of the Jina is the *Śrīvatsa* mark. Curly hairs with a short *uṣṇīṣa*, elongated ears touching broad shoulders of the Jina, and bow-shaped eye-brows show progression towards the medieval idiom, suggesting thus the date of the image in *c*. ninth century.

In three other images (Plates 16-18) from two temples, No. 12 and 15, in the Jaina group at Deogarh (District Lalitpur, U.P.), Pārśvanātha is shown seated in *dhyāna*-

mudrā on a *siṁhāsana* and with the seven-hooded serpent-canopy over his head. A *dharmacakra* is present between the lions of the throne. Above the seat a decorated carpet is also seen suspended. In the first image (Plate 16) Pārśvanātha is seated on a decorated *masūraka* placed on the carpet. In the second image (Plate 17) he is seated on the serpent coils with a horizontal lay on the carpet and in the third image (Plate 18) he is shown simply seated on a decorated carpet. In all the three examples he is flanked by a pair of *cāmara*-bearers. Above the serpent-hoods is the *chatratraya* flanked by celestial beings carrying garlands. On stylistic grounds these images may be dated to the *c.* ninth century.

Mention may also be made of some Pārśvanātha images belonging to the ninth century standing in the *kāyotsarga-mudrā* with a seven-hooded serpent canopy over their heads, embedded as they are in the western compound wall of the temple No. 12 and as part of the *sarvatobhadrikā* images housed in the Sahu Jain Sangrahalaya, both in Deogarh.

In Central India, after the Pratīhāras, the Cedis or Kalacūris ruled over the eastern part (Ḍāhala and Mahākośala), the Candellās over the northern part (Jejākabhukti, currently Bundelakhaṇḍ) and the Paramāras over the western part (Mālavadeśa, Mālvā); while the central part was ruled over for some time by the Kacchapaghātas.

Kalacūri Territory

The Cedis or Kalacūris extended their liberal patronage to the Nirgrantha religion as evident by several images of Pārśvanātha, dating from the 10th to the 12th century, found in District Jabalpur and the site of Tevar (Tripurī), the ancient Cedi capital. Pārśvanātha sculptures are also known from Sirpur, Singhanpur, Śāhḍol, Garhā and many other places in the former Rewā State in Baghelkhaṇḍ region where the art developed under the patronage of Kalacūris had prevailed.

Kāritalāi (District Jabalpur) was an important centre of the medieval Nirgranthism during the Kalacūri period. The five images of Pārśvanātha in the Mahant Ghasidas Memorial Museum at Raipur are from Kāritalāi and belong to the tenth and the 11th century. Of these two are in point of fact *caturviṁśati-paṭṭas* with Pārśvanātha as the *mūlanāyaka*. The first image (Plate 19) shows him seated in *padmāsana* in *dhyāna-mudrā* on a serpent which is shown in the act of canopying Pārśvanātha with his seven hoods. The image has miniature representations of nine other *Tīrthaṅkaras* to the right and eight to the left, the remaining six originally represented on the top row above the *chatra* are now missing. The pedestal of the image has miniature representations of seated Dharaṇendra and Padmāvatī. On the pedestal, the carpet is decorated with *kīrttimukha* and the cushion with three lotus flowers. Indra and Upendra are presented in the *tribhaṅga*-posture at the flanks of Pārśva, turning as they do toward the Lord. Elephants flanking the *trichatra* and the *devaduṁdubhi* as usual figure in the top section.

The other two, but partly mutilated images, betray almost the same characteristics, the tail here shown hanging on the carpet through the cushion. The remaining two images are badly damaged.

In one other image housed in the Rani Durgavati Museum, Jabalpur, Pārśvanātha (Plate 20) is shown seated in *dhyāna-mudrā* protected by a serpent-hood canopy and flanked by Indra and Upendra standing in the *tribhaṅga*-posture. Above, the usual garland bearers, the two elephants, and the triple umbrella are depicted. On both sides of the pedestal, seated figures of Dharaṇendra and Padmāvatī with serpent hoods over their heads are shown. The *siṁhāsana* shows the *ārādhakas* (devotees) in the centre. Serpent tail as a *lāñchana* of the Jina is presented on the carpet, hanging as it does from the seat, and above it, the *nava-grahas* beginning with Āditya are shown sitting in a panel. The image belongs to *c.* 11th century A.D.

A Pārśvanātha sculpture from Sirpur housed in the Mahant Ghasidas Memorial Museum at Raipur, too, represents the art of the Cedis. The Jina is seated in *padmāsana* under the seven-hooded canopy of the serpent king Dharaṇa whose body is rendered into a couple of parallel coils and seemingly serves as a cushion at the back of the *Tīrthaṅkara*. At the extremities, *makaras* forming the back-seat of the Jina are also discernible. The face, hands, and knees of the figure are damaged. The Jina has the *śrīvatsa* mark at the centre of his chest and the *cakra* mark is impressed on the palm. His curly hair is adorned with *uṣṇīṣa* in the centre. The pedestal of the image is much mutilated.

In an image from Singhanpur in Śāhḍol District (Plate 21), Pārśvanātha is shown standing on a conventional lotus placed upon the tail of a serpent coiled behind the Jina, covering his head with hooded canopy flanked by celestial beings. Above the canopy the *chatratraya* is shown with elephants standing on lotuses. By the sides of the legs of the standing Jina, Indra and Upendra are presented semi-profile-wise looking towards the Jina. (Almost the same type of image, reported from Śāhḍol belonging to the 10th-11th century, was kept at Collector's bungalow in the year 1968.)

In another image (Plate 22) from Pañcamaṭh temple, Singhanpur, (Śāhaḍol District), Pārśvanātha is seen seated in *dhyāna-mudrā* with a seven-hooded serpent canopy over his head. He is flanked by the customary *cāmara*-bearers standing in *tribhaṅga*-

posture and looking toward the Jina. The *siṁhāsana* is topped by a lotus seat and a carpet with decorated fringes is seen partly hanging down. The tail of the serpent is also presented on the carpet. Celestial beings carrying offerings in their hands and elephants as usual are depicted on both sides of the triple umbrella. The curls of Jina's hair are schematically rendered, *uṣṇīṣa* is low and compressed, ears are elongated, and the face bears a smile. The image may be dated to *c.* 10th century.

On a *sarvatobhadrikā* image belonging to the 10th century from Śāhaḍol, lying besides the Durgā temple (in 1968), Pārśva is shown sitting on a lotus-seat in turn placed upon a *siṁhāsana* that has the *dharmacakra* in the centre. Pārśvanātha is flanked by two *cāmara*-bearers.

The images of Pārśvanātha in the collection of the State Museum in Dhubela Palace near Nowgong (District Chatarpur) in the style of the Kalacūri region were collected from various places in the former Rewā State in Baghelkhaṇḍ. Among them are two seated and three standing representations. One of them is shown in *dhyāna-mudrā* (with a serpent-canopy over his head), on a *siṁhāsana* flanked by Indra and Upendra, and the usual garland-bearers, elephants and the *chatratraya* on the top. On the pedestal, devotees are shown (Plate 23). Another image represents Pārśvanātha seated in *padmāsana*, the *śrīvatsa* symbol, however, is absent in this image.

The three standing images of Pārśvanātha are of red sandstone, while two show miniature representations of the four seated Jinas besides the main image of Pārśvanātha in *kāyotsarga*-posture.

In a standing image from Garhā, Rewā District, and housed in the Tulsi Sangrahalaya, Ramban, Pārśvanātha is shown with a serpent canopy over his head, a *cāmaradhara* and a *mālādhara* on the Jina's right flank. The portion on the left side of the image is broken. *Srīvatsa*-mark is present on the chest. The image may be assigned to *c.* 11th century A.D.

Candellā Territory

In the Bundelkhaṇḍ or Jejākabhukti region of the Candellās, Khajurāho, Mahobā, Deogarh, Bānpur, Canderi, Buḍhī-Canderi, Siron, Khurd, Cāndpur, Dudhai, and Madanpur were important sites of Jaina art and architecture.

At least 20 images of Pārśvanātha are reported from Khajurāho (District Chatarpur) alone, ranging in date from the tenth to the 12th century A.D.[8] They are either shown sitting in *dhyāna-mudrā* or standing in *kāyotsarga-mudrā*.

A remarkable Pārśvanātha image reported from a field near the Ghaṇṭāi temple at Khajurāho is now in the Jaina collection. The tail of the serpent, the *lāñchana* of the Jina, dangles over the carpet of throne. Its coils form the seat of Pārśvanātha and hoods form the canopy over his head. Dharaṇendra in human form and Padmāvatī, both crowned over by snake-hood canopies, are shown seated in *padmāsana* on Pārśvanātha's main seat, on either side of which is an Indra with lotus in one hand and flywhisk in the other. The *parikara* is decorated with elephants, *vyālas* and *makaras,* etc. On either side of the canopy, above the *yakṣas,* are elephants; whereas the parasol is flanked by *gandharvas* and *vidyādharas* with musical instruments and garlands. The limbs of the *Tīrthaṅkara* are in good proportion. The head shows *uṣṇīṣa.*[9]

An important Pārśvanātha image in the Khajuraho Museum (No. 1654), in the standing-posture, is with the usual attendant *Yakṣa* and *Yakṣī.* The depiction of the nine *grahas* in this image is remarkable.[10]

In another Pārśvanātha image from Khajurāho (Plate 24), housed in the selfsame Museum (No. 1618), he is shown seated in *dhyāna-mudrā* flanked by the *cāmara*-holding Indra and Upendra. The *siṁhāsana* has the *dharmacakra* in the centre but with rim shown frontwise. On the corners of the pedestal are the seated pair of *Yakṣa* and *Yakṣī* with the snake-canopy over their heads. A carpet decorated with fringes is seen suspended from the seat and above the seat is a decorated cushion. On both sides of the Pārśva's head, two seated mini-Jina figures are depicted. The cobra-canopy is flanked by elephants, also two standing tiny figures of Jinas and the *vidyādhara* couples holding garlands. *Vyālas* and *makaras* are also shown in the *parikara. Śrīvatsa* mark is present on the chest. Curly hair are shown with *uṣṇīṣa.* The image may be assigned to *c.* tenth century.

Deogarh, District Lalitpur, U.P., has a group of Jaina temples and sculptures on the eastern sector of the fort dating from the ninth to the 12h century. About 30 standing or seated images of Pārśvanātha are reported from this site, kept either in the temples or in the open area in the fort. In the early images, of the ninth century, Pārśvanātha is flanked by Dharaṇendra with *cāmara* and Padmāvatī holding a large umbrella in her hands, as already mentioned above.

In other Pārśvanātha images represented on the temples Nos. 1, 4, 6, 9 and 12 and belonging to the 10th and 11th century A.D., he is simply shown seated in *dhyāna-mudrā* or standing in *khaḍgāsana,* the back fully covered by the coils of the snake. He is generally flanked by *cāmara*-bearers shown front-wise. Sometimes seated or standing smaller figures of *Tīrthaṅkaras* are also depicted on both sides.

Above the serpent-hoods, a *chatratraya* is flanked by garland-bearers and elephants are also present with *devaduṁdubhi* on the top.

On the western wall of temple No. 1, there are two Pārśvanātha images standing in *kāyotsarga*-posture flanked by *cāmara*-bearers, Indra and Upendra. By the sides of the feet, two worshippers are shown with folded hands. *Dharmacakra* is depicted between the two seated lions on the pedestal. Above, the serpent-canopy and the *chatratraya* are flanked by *mālādhara-vidyādharas* and on the top the *devaduṁdubhi* is represented.

In temple No. 4, Pārśvanātha (Plate 25) is shown standing as usual but the pedestal is flanked by seated *Yakṣa* and *Yakṣī* with triple-hooded canopy over their heads. On both sides of Pārśva are shown four standing tiny Jina figures. Garland-bearers and elephants flanking the umbrella are also depicted as usual with *devaduṁdubhi* on the top.

In another image, fixed on the boundary wall of temple No. 12, Pārśvanātha is standing as usual but here his *lāñchana*, the snake, is present on the carpet of the seat, while at the other place *kukuṭa* is shown on the carpet as his *lāñchana*.

Eight Pārśvanātha images (six standing and two seated) from Siron, District Lalitpur in U.P., are housed in the sculpture-shed of the Jaina group of modern temples. In the standing images Pārśvanātha (Plate 26) is generally shown in *khaḍgāsana* on a *siṁhāsana* flanked by *cāmara*-bearers standing in *dvibhaṅga*-posture facing front side and two seated worshippers with folded hands. A snake is coiled behind the Jina covering the whole of his back, while seven-hooded canopy is present over Pārśva's head. The *trichatra* is flanked by garland-bearers and elephants. *Devaduṁdubhi* is also seen on the top. Excepting for one image, the *Śrīvatsa* mark is generally present on the chest. Curly hair with *uṣṇīṣa* as usual is present. In the two images the Lord is flanked by four seated miniature Jinas and in one case by such six seated Jinas. Generally, the *Yakṣas* and *Yakṣīs* are shown facing front. The *lāñchana* is not depicted. Usually, the Jina stands on a lotus seat. In one example he is flanked by the standing Dharaṇendra holding *cāmara* and *Yakṣī* Padmāvatī carrying the parasol; both have five-hooded canopy over the head. In this image the pedestal as well as Indra and Upendra are absent.

An image similar to a standing image from Siron-Khurd of the 10th century, is housed in the State Museum, Lucknow (J. 882) and another image, of about the 11th century from the same place, is in the collection of Jhansi Museum (No. 80.24).

In the seated images from Siron, Pārśvanātha (Plate 27) is shown on a decorated cushion in *dhyāna-mudrā* under a seven-hooded serpent canopy flanked by *cāmara*-

bearers facing front. Above the hoods on both sides of the *trichatra* and the *devaduṁdubhi*, four seated miniature Jinas, *mālādhārī vidyādhara* couples, and elephants are depicted. On the pedestal a carpet decorated with *kīrttimukha* is seen suspended between the two lions flanked by seated *Yakṣa* and *Yakṣī* at the corners. *Śrīvatsa*-mark is present on the chest. The image may be dated to 11th century. In another seated image from the same place, Pārśvanātha is flanked by two standing and two seated mini Jinas.

Two standing Pārśvanātha images belonging to *c.* 11th century have been reported from Dudhai, District Lalitpur, where he is shown on a *siṁhāsana* flanked by Indra and Upendra bearing *cāmaras.* His back is fully covered by the coils of the cobra whose seven hoods are above the head of the Jina. *Trichatra* and *devaduṁdubhi* are flanked by elephants. On one side of the Pārśva ten miniature Jinas are also depicted, thus resulting in the *caturviṁśati-paṭṭa* as a slab.

Two images of Pārśvanātha reported from Mahobā (District Hamīrpur), U.P., and of the 12th century, are housed in the Jhansi Museum (Nos. 80.18 and 80.83). In one image he is standing in the *kāyotsarga*-posture on a pedestal with seven-hooded canopy above his head. A *cāmara*-bearer attendant is flanked on either side of the Jina. On the pedestal donors are incised with folded hands. The *lāñchana* of the Pārśva—two coiled snakes—is also depicted. It has a two-line inscription on the pedestal bearing the date *saṁvat* 1253 (A.D. 1196). In another image of about the 12th century, Pārśvanātha is shown standing with Dharaṇendra of the same dimensions bearing the *cāmara* on the right side of the Jina.[11]

Kacchapaghāta Territory

Pārśvanātha images are also met with in the territory ruled by the Kacchapaghātas in and around Gwalior and Paḍhāvalī. Two sculptures of about the tenth-11th century are housed in the Central Archaeological Museum, Gwalior. They were acquired from Paḍhāvalī and Gwalior Fort. The Paḍhāvalī image represents Pārśvanātha seated in *padmāsana.* He has a *śrīvatsa*-mark on his chest. Behind his head, the *prabhāmaṇḍala*-halo is also depicted. Above the head of the Jina, *trichatra* flanked by the elephants and the *devaduṁdubhi* are, as in most examples, present on the top. The attendant Nāgendras flanking the *Tīrthaṅkara* are shown standing on elephants and with serpent-hoods on their heads. The pedestal shows a *dharmacakra* and the devotees have been assigned a place between the two lions.

The second image of Pārśvanātha from Gwalior Fort is inscribed and can be attributed to the 11th century. The small figures of the Jinas in the *parikara* suggest that the image was meant to be of *caturviṁśati* specification. A small figure of *kṣetrapāla* with his *vāhana*, dog, is also seen on the pedestal.

In two *sarvatobhadrikā* images from the Gwalior Fort, one housed in the Central Archaeological Museum, Gwalior, and another in a private collection of Mr. H.N. Dwivedi from Murar (Gwalior), are of the period about the tenth century. Pārśvanātha is depicted simply standing on a lotus seat with a serpent-canopy over his head. Mention may also be made of a *sarvatobhadrikā* from Amrol, in District Gwalior where a mutilated Pārśvanātha image is present on a pedestal. On the Fort wall at Gwalior between the Lakṣmaṇa Gate and the Hāthiā Gate, there is a relief showing Mother and Child in a rectangular niche. It shows a mutilated lady figure in reclining posture with a child by her side, accompanied by attendants and a meditating *Tīrthaṅkara* seated above the niche. This panel seems the representation of a Jina's mother, assignable to *c.* 10th century (as was also agreed by Dr. N.P. Joshi in a Seminar on the Art of Khajurāho). Above the head of Mother there is a standing male figure having seven-hooded canopy over his head, though not in *kāyotsarga*-posture. If we identify this image with *Yakṣa* Dharaṇendra, then this would lead to the conclusion that the panel depicts the birth of Pārśvanātha.

Paramāra Territory

The Paramāras of Mālvadeśa were perhaps even more liberal patrons of Jainism than the Candellās. While the extant Nirgrantha temples in this region are not considerable, Jina images are found scattered almost everywhere. However, mention may be made of a Pārśvanātha temple at Dhār, where the Digambara Jaina author Devasena wrote the *Darśanasāra* in A.D. 933: And Prabhācandra wrote his several commentaries on earlier Digambara Jaina works as also composed two works on *darśana*, namely the *Prameya-kamala-mārtaṇḍa* and the *Nyāya-kumudacandra*. Besides these, many Pārśvanātha images, either individually or in groups, are reported from this region.

In an image (Plate 28) from Hiṅgalājagarh (District Mandasore), now housed in Bhānpura State Museum (No. 290), Pārśvanātha is shown seated in *dhyāna-mudrā* on a decorated cushion over the *siṁhāsana* with the *dharmacakra* having the rim facing and flanked by Dharaṇendra and Padmāvatī. The carpet above the pedestal is decorated, as oftener, with *kīrttimukha*. The back of the Jina is fully covered with the coils of Nāgendra whose hoods are now in broken state. Two seated attendants standing on stalked lotuses are also seen on both the sides of Pārśva. *Śrīvatsa* mark is present on the chest. His half closed eyes, elongated ears, serene face, broad shoulders, and the beaded necklace (*ekāvalī*) of the attendants suggest the date of the image *c*. tenth century.

A seated tenth-century image of Pārśvanātha flanked by attendants with mutilated pedestal, head and serpent-hoods from Bujgaḍh (Mandasore District) is housed in Bhānpur State Museum (No. 36).

A head of Pārśvanātha, protected by seven-hooded cobra, hailing from Hiṅgalājagaṛh, is in the collection of the Central Museum, Indore. His curly hair, smiling face, elongated ears, suppressed *uṣṇīṣa* and attentiveness of the cobra-god are remarkable. The image may be dated to the 10th century.

In one other image from Bujgarh, (Bhanapur State Museum No. 42), standing and of about the tenth-century, though in a very bad state of preservation, Pārśvanātha is shown on a lotus seat fully backed by the serpent coils flanked by Indra and Upendra. Padmāvatī is on Jina's left side, the portion on the right side is broken.

Another tenth century image from Hiṅgalājgarh in the Indore Central Museum (Pārśva standing) (Plate 29) is shown on a lotus seat flanked by Indra and Upendra holding *cāmaras*. The serpent coils are shown behind the back of the Jina and a canopy of seven hoods over his head.

In one more image from the same place and in the same Museum, Pārśva is depicted simply with a seven-hooded canopy over his head.

Gandharvapurī (District Dewās) has yielded a colossal standing Pārśvanātha with a seven-hooded canopy over his head flanked by Indra and Upendra as *cāmara*-bearers, the *vidyādhara* couples hold garlands; four seated Jinas, the *trichatra* and the *devaduṁdubhi* figure above the canopy. *Śrīvatsa* mark and *uṣṇīṣa* are present. The image may be assigned to the 11th century. It is housed in the State Museum, Gandharvapurī (No. GOP 81).

In another seated image from the same place and housed in the same Museum (No. 230.89), Pārśvanātha is shown with Indra and Upendra. His back is shown fully covered with coils of the snake making canopy of seven hoods over his head. *Vidyādhara* couples, triple umbrella, elephants and *devaduṁdubhi* are shown as usual. The image is mutilated and may be dated to *c*. tenth century.

On the north wall of a modern Śāntinātha temple at Burhi Canderī (District Guna), M.P., a Pārśvanātha image assignable to the tenth century A.D. is shown to be flanked by *Yakṣa* and *Yakṣī* standing on a *siṁhāsana*.

A remarkable seated image of Pārśvanātha (Plate 30) from Bhojpur (Raisen District) is enshrined in the *garbhagṛha* of the Śāntinātha temple, dated *c*. 11th century. Here the pedestal is absent. Pārśvanātha is shown seated on the serpent coils on a decorated cushion. He is flanked by the *Yakṣa* and the *Yakṣī* with five-hooded canopy over their heads. Four seated Jinas are depicted flanking the *chatra* above the canopy. A seated Jina in a *rathikā* is also shown on the top above the *devaduṁdubhi*. A standing image of Pārśva from the same place dated *c.* 11th century is also noteworthy. Another standing image bearing the usual features is also reported from Rajendra Udyan in Pannā District, datable to *c.* 10th century.

In an interesting image of Pārśvanātha from Guna in the collection of Jaina Archaeological Museum, Ujjain, the Jina is shown seated in *padmāsana* under the canopy of a seven-hooded serpent. *Yakṣa* Dharaṇendra and *Yakṣī* Padmāvatī are present on his left and right.

A standing image of Pārśvanātha, dated *c.* tenth-11th century, housed in the Vidisha State Museum (No. 349/1287) is fully covered at the back with the serpent coils and is flanked by the seated devotees, Indra and Upendra, and two standing and two seated Jinas. Above the canopy on both sides of the *trichatra* and *devaduṁdubhi*, *mālādhārī-vidyādharas* and elephants are present. *Śrīvatsa* mark is also present on the chest.

In Bare Bābā, Kuṇḍalpur, District Damoh, which is not far from Vidiśā, there are a large number of loose sculptures representing *Tīrthaṅkaras* as well as the *Yakṣīs*. In one image, Pārśvanātha is shown standing in *kāyotsarga* on a *siṁhāsana* flanked by the *cāmara*-bearing Indra and Upendra facing front. The full back of the Jina is covered with the coils of a serpent whose seven-hooded canopy is shown over his head and the tail passes on the carpet spread over the *siṁhāsana*. Above the serpent-hoods, the ubiquitous *trichatra*, *devaduṁdubhi*, and *mālādhārī-vidyādharas* occur. The features, regrettably, are rather heavy and inelegant for the tenth century bracket.[12]

Inside the Udaigiri cave 20, near Vidiśā, a loose image of Pārśvanātha is shown seated (Plate 31) on a decorated cushion with a seven-hooded canopy over his head. He is flanked by the *cauri*-bearing Indra and Upendra standing on elephants. Above the canopy on both sides of the *trichatra* and *devaduṁdubhi*, *mālādhārī-vidyādhara* couples, elephants and four miniature Jinas are depicted. On the pedestal a *dharmacakra* between the two lions facing front is flanked by seated *Yakṣa* and *Yakṣī* on the corners. *Śrīvatsa* mark on the chest of the Jina is also present. The date of the image may be *c.* 11th century.

Pārśvanātha is also represented in an image reported from Ahmedpur (Vidiśā) dated about the 11th century and now housed in the Central Archaeological Museum, Gwalior. In this image he is simply shown standing in *kāyotsarga*-pose protected by a serpent-canopy over his head.

Conclusion

From the foregoing discussion we may conclude that, from the ancient through pre-medieval to the medieval period, scores and scores of images of Jina Pārśva were carved and, inferably, many temples for that Jina had been built in Central India. While extant buildings in this vast province are rare to meet with, the images are found scattered all over the region. In Central India, these begin to appear from the fifth century.

The images of Pārśvanātha belonging to the Gupta, post-Gupta and Pratīhāra periods show that the generalities of the classical art of the Mathurā tradition were followed in Central India also. In these images the Jina is shown seated in *dhyāna-mudrā* or standing in the *kāyotsarga-mudrā* with seven-hooded canopy of Nāgarāja over his head. On the *siṁhāsana* is generally shown the *dharmacakra* between the two end-lions. Sometimes he is also depicted seated on the coils of the snake or on a decorated cushion kept upon an ornamented piece of cloth dangling downwards from the seat. He is customarily flanked by Dharaṇendra bearing the *cāmara* and Padmāvatī holding the umbrella in her hands. Above the snake-canopy, *chatratraya*, *devaduṁdubhi* flanked by elephants standing on lotus flowers, and garland-bearing *vidyādharas* also began to appear. The *śrīvatsa* mark on the chest of the Pārśva is generally absent in the beginning, which was a common feature of the Mathurā Jina images in the Kuṣāṇa and Gupta periods. The *lāñchana* of Pārśva is also not depicted up to the Pratīhāra period.

Pārśvanātha images of the tenth and 11th centuries represent a fully developed phase of the sculpture in almost whole of Central India. He is depicted in seated and standing postures of all sizes with simple and elaborate *parikaras* usually accompanied with demi-gods and sometimes with smaller figures of *Tīrthaṅkaras* and the surround adorned by *vyālas*, *makaras*, etc. He is oftener shown flanked by *cāmara*-bearing Indra and Upendra. Dharaṇendra and Padmāvatī are depicted on the corners of the *siṁhāsana*. *Śrīvatsa* mark is usually present on the chest of the Jina but the distinguishing *lāñchana* and the *prabhāmaṇḍala* are not depicted excepting in a few cases. The later subsidiary images suffer from pronounced angularity, and stiffness is in evidence in the treatment of Jina's body. Also, the eyes are now elongated and eye-brows become bow-shaped. Moreover, the earlobes touch the shoulders, hair mostly curly with low and compressed *uṣṇīṣa*.

In the images from the Kalacūri territory, Pārśvanātha is usually shown seated on the coil or coils of the serpent whose tail is depicted hanging on the carpet through the cushion. The *cāmara*-bearers are generally shown standing in the *tribhaṅga*-posture, turning and looking toward the Jina. In the images of the Paramāra zone, Jina's back is shown fully covered with the coils of the snake and the *cāmara*-bearing attendants are depicted looking frontwise. The images of the Candellā and the Kacchapaghāta territory appear to be highly influenced by, or show the same details as in the Paramāra Art of the Mālava country.

NOTES AND REFERENCES

1. U.P. Shah, *Studies in Jaina Art,* Banaras 1955, pp. 77-78, plate IV, fig. 12.
2. *Ibid.*, pp. 14-15.
3. B.N. Sharma, "Art-objects in Museums: Victoria and Albert Museum, London", *Jaina Art and Architecture,* Vol. III, New Delhi 1975, p. 544.
4. Niraj Jain, *Anekanta* (Hindi), Delhi, XV, 19, pp. 222-223; also U.P. Shah, *Jaina Art.*, Vol. I, Bhartiya Jnanpith, New Delhi 1974, p. 129, plate 64.
5. R.C. Majumdar and A.D. Pusalkar, *The Age of Imperial Kanauj (History and Culture of the Indian People 4),* Bombay 1955, p. 289.
6. Michael W. Meister, "Āma, Amrol and Jainism in Gwalior Fort", *Journal of the Oriental Institute, Baroda,* XXII (No. 3, March 1973), pp. 354-58.
7. *Ibid.*
8. Marutinandan Prasad Tiwari, *Khajurāho kā Jaina Purātattva* (Hindi), Khajurāho 1987, p. 48.
9. Niraj Jain, "Chapter 38: Collections at Khajurāho", *Jaina Art and Architecture,* Vol. III, Bharatiya Jnanpith, New Delhi 1975, p. 594, plate 376 B.
10. *Ibid.*, plate 377 A.
11. S.D. Trivedi, *Sculptures in the Jhansi Museum,* Jhansi 1983, p. 87, fig. 84.
12. Krishna Deva, "Chapter 16: Central India: Examples of Early Medieval Art in Central India", *Jaina Art and Architecture,* Vol. I, Bharatiya Jnanpith, New Delhi 1974, p. 168, plate 94 B.

LIST OF ILLUSTRATIONS

(All illustrations are published here by the courtesy and kindness, American Institute of Indian Studies, Center for Art & Archaeology, Ramnagar, Varanasi.)

PĀRŚVANĀTHA IMAGES IN ORISSA AND BENGAL

D.R. Das

Orissa and Bengal, the two contiguous states of Eastern India, witnessed a brisk activity of the Nirgrantha missionaries for long centuries. Interestingly, their activity was very intense in remoter and inaccessible areas. While the history of this activity in Orissa is known to us, albeit inadequately, our knowledge of the spread of Nirgranthism in Bengal, on the other hand, is not extensive.

I. ORISSA

A literary reference seems to suggest that the Nirgrantha religion had entered Orissa before the birth of Mahāvīra. According to a legend, recorded in the late Nirgrantha texts, Karakaṇḍu, the king of Kaliṅga, was a disciple of Pārśvanātha.[1] If this tradition has any historical value, Nirgrantha became the royal religion of Orissa through the influence of Pārśvanātha. Jainism continued to enjoy royal patronage even after Karakaṇḍu. Nandarāja of Magadha is reported in the Hāthigumphā inscription (*c.* 50-25 B.C.) at Udayagiri to have carried away a Jina image from Kaliṅga obviously after defeating its ruler. When Khāravela of the Mahāmeghavāhana family became the king of Kaliṅga, he not only recovered the said Jina image ('Kaliṅga Jina' of the Hāthigumphā inscription) but also turned Bhubanesvar into a great centre of Nirgrantha religion.[2] Archaeological exacavation has laid bare the foundation of an apsidal temple on the summit of the Udayagiri at the outskirts of Bhubanesvar. It is generally believed that this temple was built by Khāravela or one of his successors to house a Jaina divinity (Kaliṅga Jina?). After the fall of the Mahāmeghavāhanas, the history of Nirgranthism in Orissa becomes obscure. However, the Nirgrantha religion apparently had continued to flourish. Hiüen Tsang, during the second quarter of the 7th century, saw many Nirgranthas in Kaliṅga and more than ten thousand temples of *Tīrthaṅkaras* in Kaliṅga.[4] The Śailodbhavas, who at that time were ruling in Koṅgoda and its adjoining territories in southern Orissa, were known to have extended support to the Nirgrantha establishments in their kingdom.[5] Since Nirgranthism *alim* Jainism never failed to enjoy patronage of different ruling houses of Orissa, a phenomenal growth, as a result, of that religion took place in this region and its centres sprouted in almost every part of that country.[6] Simultaneously, there was a proliferation in the production of images of Jaina divinities and building of temples to house these images. Most of these images are now lying scattered around the ruins of their original places of worship.

Among the *Tīrthaṅkaras*, images of Ṛṣabha and Pārśva outnumber those of the other Jinas. Images of Pārśvanātha have been found in places like Martasol, Pundal, Ayodhyā (Plate 32) and Charampā in the Balasore District, Ānandpur, Khiching, Bāripāḍā, Koisali and Khuntapāla in the Mayūrbhañj District, Vaidakhiā, Gaḍacaṇḍi, Podasiṅgiḍi (Plate 33), and Sainkul in the Keonjhar District, and Cuttack, Byre, Pratāpanagarī (Plate 34) and Bhānpur in the Cuttack District; next Kākaṭpur, Śiśupālgarh, Khaṇḍagiri (Cave Nos. 7, 8, 9 and 11) and Bāgalpur in the Purī District, and Bhairavasiṅgpur, Jeypore, Cārmūlā, Nandapur and Jāmuṇḍā in the Korapūṭ District. In the Indian Museum, Calcutta, is preserved an image of Pārśvanātha (Plate 38) which was collected from the Circuit House, Purī. These images have been generally executed in stone and, occasionally, in bronze. From the bank of the river Kuakhai near Bhānpur, bronze images of several Jinas were recovered. (Of these images only that of Pārśvanātha escaped the hands of thieves.) Three Pārśvanātha images in metal have been found at Khuntapāla and one each at Byre and Kākaṭpur. Also, one metal image of this *Tīrthaṅkara* from an unknown locality is preserved in the Orissa State Museum at Bhubanesvar.

The images of Pārśvanātha, discovered in Orissa, display certain common characteristics. In most cases, the *Tīrthaṅkara* is represented as standing in *kāyotsarga* posture. His seated images are invariably in *yogāsana*. With a few exceptions, a lotus seat on a lion throne is provided for the seated Jina. As his principal cognizance, a snake rises from behind him and spreads its seven hoods over his head. A canopy of three-tiered umbrella (*chatratraya*) is placed above the snake hood. Below the pedestal appears a *nāga* couple. Entwining their tails with each other, they are shown as *ārādhakas* or devotees of the *Tīrthaṅkara*. From the standpoint of the position assigned, they plausibly are Nāgarāja Dharaṇendra and his consort. Sometimes various offerings are depicted at the base of the pedestal. A constant attendant of Pārśvanātha is a *cāmara*-bearer who stands on his either flank. The *devadāru*, the *caitya-vṛkṣa* of the *Tīrthaṅkara*, is usually shown on the stele. Garland-bearing *vidyādharas* (*mālādharas*) occur on the two corners of the upper end of the stele. Presence of the *gandharvas* is indicated by two pairs of hands, one pair beating a drum and the other sounding cymbals. Thus, about five out of the eight *mahāprātihāryas* are shown in association with the Jina figures.

In addition to the above-mentioned characteristics, some images are endowed with certain individual iconographic traits. For instance, a snake is present on the pedestal of the Kākaṭpur bronze image. Beneath the lotus seat of the seated image of Pārśvanātha on the right wall of Cave No. 7 on the Khaṇḍagiri is carved a pot (Plate 35). On the pedestal of his other image in the same cave is shown a lotus (Plate 36). At Bhānpur, the image bears the *śrīvatsa* mark on the chest. In some cases, the *Tīrthaṅkara* was accompanied by eight planetary divinities. One such image was found at Pundal, one at Ayodhyā (Plate 32), and Jeypore and two are preserved in the Chaudhuri Bazar Jaina temple at Cuttack. Excepting Rāhu, the personified planets are in *yogāsana*. The attributes in their two hands are as follows:

Sūrya	-	two lotuses;
Soma	-	staff and pitcher;
Maṅgala	-	rosary and book;
Budha	-	rosary and club (?);
Bṛhaspati	-	rosary and pitcher;
Śukra	-	bow and arrow;
Śani	-	rosary and pitcher

At Ayodhyā, minute figures of demonic and animal-headed creatures, aggressively advancing from either side of the upper part of the stele towards Pārśvanātha, probably illustrate the famous *upasarga*-tormentation inflicted on the Jina by Kamaṭha and his retinue.

Pārśvanātha, as *mūlanāyaka,* is shown on a *caturviṁśati-paṭṭa* or stele showing 24 Jinas from Gaḍacaṇḍi near Podasiṅgiḍi. Also in Cave No. 8 on the Khaṇḍagiri, he occupies the position of *mūlanāyaka* among the group of 24 *Tīrthaṅkaras*. At Khiching he has on his either side three *Tīrthaṅkaras* standing one above another in a vertical row. An image, kept in the Chaudhuri Bazar Jaina temple at Cuttack, the Jina is accompanied by four *Tīrthaṅkaras* in *yogāsana* who cannot be identified. His image from Purī (Plate 38) is flanked on the right by Śāntinātha and Ṛṣabhanātha and on the left by two unidentified Jinas, all seated in *yogāsana*. An image of Pārśvanātha at Vaidakhiā has on its left the standing figures of Śāntinātha and Mahāvīra and on its right Candraprabha and Ṛṣabhanātha.

Pārśvanātha also appears on *caumukha* votive shrines. Thus a *caumukha,* in the Cuttack Caudhuri Bazar Jaina temple, has on its four faces Jina Ṛṣabha, Śāntinātha, Pārśvanātha, and Vardhamāna.

In order to suggest an emaciated body, resulting from the severity of their ascetic life, deep concave indents were produced on the sculptured figures of the

Tīrthaṅkaras found at Chārampa. One of these *Tīrthaṅkara* images represent Pārśvanātha in *yogāsana*.

A feature of the iconography of Pārśvanātha images of Orissa is that the *Tīrthaṅkara* is seldom accompanied by Padmāvatī, his *śāsanadevī*. At Jāmuṇḍā, however, in his seated image, she is present under the lotus seat. Here the goddess is sitting in *yogāsana* under the canopy of a three-hooded serpent. She has four arms, the attributes of which are indistinct. On the left corner of the pedestal of the standing image of Pārśvanātha in the Khiching Museum, occurs a tiny figure of his *śāsanadevī*. She sits in *yogāsana* under a five-hooded snake canopy. The attributes in her two hands are indistinct. In Cave No. 7 on the Khaṇḍagiri, Padmāvatī appears under Pārśvanātha who is in *yogāsana* (Plate 36). Sitting in *lalitāsana* on a lotus throne, the goddess is endowed with three eyes and two arms. Her right hand is held in *varada* while the left carries a lotus. Under her lotus seat is also carved a lotus flower. In Cave No. 8 on the same hill, Padmāvatī is shown under the seated figure of Pārśvanātha (Plate 37). The goddess here is seated in *lalitāsana*, under the canopy of a five-hooded snake. She has eight arms which, clockwise from the lower right hand, show the *mudrā* and attributes as follows: *varada*, arrow, sword, flower (?disc), lotus, shield, bow, and lotus. Unlike the Jāmuṇḍā example, Pārśvanātha and Padmāvatī in the Khaṇḍagiri caves are placed in two separate compartments. At Nandapur was found an independent image of Padmāvatī sitting in *lalitāsana* on a double-petalled lotus (Plate 39). Over her head were spread five hoods of a snake. Her four arms displayed clockwise from the lower right hand, the following: *varada*, flower, radish(?) and axe. A miniature figure of Pārśvanātha occurred on the crest of the stele while an elephant was carved on the pedestal.

From the foregoing discussion, it is evident that the images of Pārśvanātha were carved in Orissa in accordance with a set formula, which had remained unchanged. Iconography, therefore, is of very little help in establishing the chronological order of these images. In some instances, Pārśvanātha as well as his attendants are provided with *bhāmaṇḍala*. Such examples are found at Jāmuṇḍā, Bhairavsingpur and Pratāpanagarī (Plate 34). On the stele from Purī (Plate 38) haloed *Tīrthaṅkaras* occur on either side of Pārśvanātha. Again, the group of planets when represented on the stele, includes eight planets only. In Orissa, halo seems to have ceased to characterize the divine images from about the tenth century. Similarly, the number of planets was increased to nine with the inclusion of Ketu in their group towards the close of the ninth century. Therefore, the images of Pārśvanātha, associated with these two features, may be assigned to a period before the tenth century. His seated image at Podasiṅgiḍi (Plate 33), which seems to belong to the eighth/ninth century on stylistic ground, is one of the earliest of Jina images discovered in Orissa. Most of the images of Pārśvanātha and those of other Jaina divinities, however, seem to have been produced during the Somavaṁśī period which began towards the close of the ninth century. Epigraphic evidence suggests that the Somavaṁśīs encouraged the spread of the Nirgrantha religion in their kingdom.[7] Some of the old Nirgrantha caves on the Khaṇḍagiri were converted into Jina shrines during this period.[8] Apparently, Pārśvanātha and other images of the creed, carved on the walls of these caves, were the result of this conversion which in turn was due to a continual memory that the caves belonged to the Nirgrantha creed. Reference in this connection may be made to an inscription on the wall of Cave No. 11. It announces: "In the year 549, in the victorious reign of Śrī Udyotakeśarī, the decayed wells and decayed tanks were shown (i.e. cleansed) for bathing and drinking and (the images of) 24 *Tīrthaṅkaras* were established (i.e., carved on the walls of the caves) on the auspicious Kumāra Parvata. If any heretic causes even damage (to them), such a cheat (will) by his act, excite the anger of Śrī Pārśvanātha."[9] The Nirgrantha religion lingered on in Orissa even after the fall of the Somavaṁśīs towards the close of the 11th century. However, the Jagannātha cult, with its rising popularity since the beginning of the Gaṅga rule, was destined to overwhelm Orissa in the near future when the religion of the Buddha as well as of the Jina were to be obscured.

II. BENGAL

Association of Bengal with Nirgrantha religion seems to have begun from the time of its inception. Mahāvīra is reported to have travelled in the pathless countries of the Lāḍha (Rāḍha in West Bengal), as narrated in the "*Uvadhāna-sutta*" (*c.* third/second cent. B.C.) inside the *Ācārāṅga* Book I, before he attained enlightenment.[10] According to a tradition, recorded in the *Bṛhat-kathākoṣa* of Hariṣeṇa (A.D. 933), the patriarch Bhadrabāhu, who was the preceptor of Candragupta Maurya, was born at Devīkoṭa (i.e. Koṭivarṣa, modern Bangarh in the West Dinajpur District, West Bengal).[11] The same source reports that he was initiated in the order of friars in Puṇḍravardhana. According to the second section of the *Sthavīrāvali* (*c.* 100 A.D.) of the *Paryuṣanā-kalpa* (compiled *c.* A.D.503/516), from Godāsa, a disciple of Ārya Bhadrabāhu, emanated a branch of friars, Godāsa-gaṇa, which had in course of time split into four branches, Koṭivarṣīyā, Puṇḍravardhanīyā, Tāmraliptikā and Dāsī-Kharvaṭikā.[12] Of these four sub-orders, the first two represent the well-known places in north Bengal, the third in lower Bengal and the fourth probably in West Bengal.[13]

It is thus evident that Nirgrantha was a popular religion in Bengal from a very early period. The discovery of the vestiges of the Nirgrantha establishments and divinities in different parts of Bengal, therefore, is not surprising. However, the abundance of such antiquities in the Chotā Nāgpur-plateau region of the three neighbouring districts of Midnapore, Bankura, and Purulia is significant. Deserted temples and mounds caused by ruined temples and scattered images in their vicinity and also at other places bear ample testimony to the fact that Nirgrantha creed or Jainism once became the religion of the masses and continued to be so for a long time in these three south-western districts of West Bengal. This is further evident from the place names of undoubted Jaina inspiration. Reference in this connection may be made to Pārśvanātha which is the appellation of a village on the river Kansai in the Bankura District, indicative as it is of the eminence of Pārśvanātha in this locality. The immense popularity of the 23rd *Tīrthaṅkara* is also suggested by the large number of his images found in Bengal. Obviously, these images were enshrined exclusively and, in certain instances, together with images of other Jinas and attendant divinities in temples. All these temples are either deserted or are in ruins. The remains of a temple, which definitely housed an image of Pārśvanātha, has been traced at Pāresnāth.[14] Built in red sandstone, it was a structure of dry masonry. Iron dowels and cramps were used to keep the masonry blocks of the structure together. The foundation of another temple of Pārśvanātha was discovered at Kendua in the Bāṅkurā District.[15] Once a building of ashlar masonry, it consisted of a deula (*prāsāda*) and a *mukhaśālā* (*maṇḍapa*). The *deula* was built on a *triratha* (*dvi-aṅga*) plan and oriented toward east. Another recognisable element of the structure is the *khurā* (*khura*) moulding in its *pābhāga* (*kaṭi*). Pārśvanātha may once have been the presiding deity also of the two deserted temples, one at Harmaśrā and the second at Deulbhirā, in the Bāṅkurā District. Not far away from the temple at Harmaśrā, a partially damaged image of Pārśvanātha is lying. His image (Plate 40), discovered near the temple at Deulbhirā, was shifted to the Indian Museum, Calcutta. Both temples are of the *rekhā* (Latina) order and made of laterite. At Harmaśrā, the temple had a *mukhaśālā* (*mukhamaṇḍapa*) which has disappeared long since. *Pañcaratha* (*tri-aṅga*) on plan, bereft of any decorative embellishments and facing east, these two temples seem to belong to a period not earlier than the 12th century.

While it is difficult to locate or identify the buildings which enshrined Pārśvanātha, his images are encountered at many sites of Bengal. So far, such images have been discovered at Kantaberia,[16] Raidighi[17] and Dakṣiṇa Barasāt[18] in the South 24-Parganas District, Beharasai (Plates 41 and 42) Rājjpara,[19] and Ayodhyābād, Nepura Bandhar and Dumurtod[20] in the Midnāpore District, Bahulārā (Plate 43), Kenduā, Pāresnāth,

Harmaśrā, Deulbhirā (Plate 40), Dharapat, Biharinath and Barjorā (Plate 51) and an unspecified locality (Plate 13)[21] in the Bāṅkurā District, Sat Deuliyā (Plate 52) in the Burdwān District, and Pakbirrā (Plates 14, 15, 16, and 18),[22] Anai-Jambad (Plate 48), Charrā and Puruliā (Plate 50)[23] in the Purulia District.

Images of Pārśvanātha, found in Bengal, are known either as seated in *yogāsana* or standing in *kāyotsarga*. In both versions, the Jina has a lotus placed above the *siṁhāsana*. On the pedestal occur a worshipful *nāga* couple whose coils are often entwined with each other. With rare exceptions, they rise on their tails to flank the legs of the *Tīrthaṅkara*. The *nāga* holds a jar with his hands and the *nāgī* a staff-like object which may be a musical instrument. By the sides of the *nāga* couple stand two *cāmara*-bearers on lotus pedestals. On the stele of the Indian Museum image (Plate 44), collected from somewhere in the Bānkurā District, the *nāga* is kneeling but the *nāgī* is standing. The *cāmara*-bearers appear above them. Again, above the *cāmara*-bearers are placed two seated worshipful figures. As in other areas, a serpent, with its coils carved on the back-slab, spreads its seven hoods over the head of every specimen of Pārśvanātha image in Bengal. Above the serpent hood is a canopy of tri-linear *chatra*. On one side of the *chatra* is depicted a pair of hands beating a drum and on the other another pair sounding cymbals. The corners of the upper part of the stele are occupied by garland-bearing *vidyādharas*. The stele is also marked with the *caityadruma* and flowers. Sometimes a halo is shown behind the head of the Jina as well as those of his attendants. His image (Plate 40), discovered at Deulbhirā, is shown in *yogāsana* on a pedestal which has a lotus marked in its centre. Apart from the two *cāmara*-bearers and the seven-hooded serpent, the Jina is not accompanied by anything else. An unusual image, found at Dakśin Barasāt, shows four snakes issuing out of the left and right shoulders of Pārśvanātha. The Jina is further adorned with a *vanamālā*. At Pakbirrā, a standing image of Pārśvanātha has on its either side two standing *Tīrthaṅkaras*. Placed one above the other, the *Tīrthaṅkaras* remain unidentified on account of their indistinct cognizances. Occasionally, the planetary divinities were shown on the stele. Reference in this connection may be made to the image-stele (Plate 43) in the Siddheśvara temple at Bahulārā. Two examples, one from Pakbirrā (Plate 47) and the other from Beharasai (Plate 41), also give indications of the presence of the planets at the sides of Pārśvanātha. *Cauviśi*-stelae with Pārśvanātha as the *mūlanāyaka* were also produced in Bengal. On three such stelae, one at Anai-Jambad (Plate 48), the second at Suisā, and the third, lying in three fragments, at Pāresnāth, the miniature figures of the standing *Tīrthaṅkaras* are arranged in two parallel rows on either side of the *mūlanāyaka*. At Suisā, the image of Pārśvanātha has an elaborately carved stele. Some of the details of this badly abraded carving may have a connection with the *upasarga*-legend associated with Pārśvanātha. Apart from the representation either independently or as *mūlanāyaka*, Pārśvanātha also figures on several *caumukha* votive shrines. Such votive shrines have been noticed at Pakbirrā (Plate 49), Puruliā (Plate 50), Charrā, Barjorā (Plate 51)[24] and Sāt Deuliyā (Plate 52). Another votive shrine is kept in the Haripada Sahitya Mandir Museum at Puruliā (Plate 50). A *caumukha* as *devacchandaka* or *gandha-kuṭi* having the crowning *śikhara* of the Latina class at Pakbirrā, while showing Pārśvanātha, Candraprabha, Ṛṣabhadeva, and Śantinātha in *kāyotsarga* on its four sides, exhibits on every face of its spire five Jinas in three vertically aligned niches and thus completes the figure 24 of the Jinas. *Caumukha* shrines from Puruliā and Barjorā are also of this type. (Do they represent Aṣṭāpada-prāsāda?)

On several *pañcatīrthika* stele, Pārśvanātha appears as one of the four Jinas around the *mūlanāyaka*. Thus at Pakbirrā, he occurs by the side of Candraprabha and Mahāvīra. In another interesting example, again from Pakbirrā, the seated images of Ṛṣabhanātha, Pārśvanātha, Padmaprabha and two other unidentified Jinas are placed in a row above the standing figure of Ambikā.

Wide distribution and the occurrence of a large number of Pārśvanātha images indicate that the Jina enjoyed a position of considerable importance in Bengal. The sculptors, who had executed these images, seem to have sufficient familiarity with the rules of Nirgrantha iconography. Commonality in the general details of all the images of the Jina in different districts and decades in Bengal may suggest that the convention which guided the sculptors did not vary with the changes of time and locale. It is, therefore, not possible to arrange these images in a strict chronological order on the basis of their iconography. What is, however, certain is that most of these images should be dated after the ninth century since none of the Jaina temples, now extant in Bengal, can be assigned to a date prior to the tenth century.[25] Gauḍa Saṁgha, to which Somadeva of the *Yaśastilaka-campū* (tenth century) belonged, apparently had originated in Bengal.

III. APPENDIX

In different parts of Bengal, images of a multi-armed male deity under a hooded snake-canopy have been found (Plate 53). Some of the emblems, held in the hands of the deity, assert his Vaiṣṇava affiliation. As such the god is taken to be a representation of Viṣṇu. Over the snake-hood canopy is shown a tiny figure in *yogāsana*.

This tiny figure generally has been identified with Amitābha. Therefore, the most common view is that the images of this class suggest a syncretism between Vaiṣṇavism and Buddhism and as such these images should be described as Viṣṇu-Lokeśvara.[26] But this identification does not explain why the majority of these images hail from areas which were once strongholds of the Jainas. Sometimes images of Jaina divinities and the so-called Viṣṇu-Lokeśvara were found side by side. In view of this fact, the snake-hood canopy of the deity assumes some significance. As on the head of Pārśvanātha, here also the snake often spreads seven hoods. Moreover, crest-figure is not unknown to Nirgranthist iconography. Under the circumstances, the possibility of these images being the result of syncretism between the Nirgrantha and the *Bhāgvat* cults cannot be ignored.

NOTES AND REFERENCES

1. For legends relating to Karakaṇḍu, *see* Jagannath Patnaik, "Jainism in Orissa", in *Sidelights on History and Culture of Orissa*, ed. M.N. Das, Cuttack 1978, p. 308 f. The story of Karakaṇḍu makes it not very unlikely that Pārśvanātha visited Orissa and played a definite role in the spread of the Nirgrantha-darśana in this region. This possibility notwithstanding, the reading in the panels of the upper storey of the Rānīgumphā on the Udayagiri some episodes of the life of Pārśvanātha, related by the *Pārśvanāthacarita*, is not justified (*see* R.P. Mohapatra, *Jaina Monuments of Orissa*, Delhi 1984, p. 15f.).
2. D.C. Sircar, *Select Inscriptions bearing on Indian History and Civilization*, Vol. I, Calcutta 1965, p. 213 ff.
3. Debala Mitra, *Udayagiri and Khandagiri*, New Delhi 1975, p. 43 f.
4. T. Watters, *On Yuan Chwang's Travel in India*, ed. F.W. Rhys Davids and S.W. Bushell, Vol. II, London 1905, p. 196 ff. (The figure, of course, seems highly inflated.)
5. Sarat Chandra Behera, *Rise and Fall of the Sailodbhavas*, Calcutta 1982, p. 178.
6. For a discussion on Jaina antiquities of Orissa, *see* Mohapatra, *Jaina Monuments., passim.*
7. Debala Mitra, "Glimpses of Jaina Relics in Orissa", *Orissa Review* (Monumental Special), 1976, p. 16.
8. *Ibid.*
9. K.C. Panigrahi, *Chronology of the Bhauma-Karas and Somavaṁśīs of Orissa*, Bhopal 1961, p. 53. According to a different view, the inscription was engraved in the year 5 of Udyotakeśarī's reign (*see* Mitra, *Udayagiri and Khandagiri*, pp. 6 and 68).
10. *History of Bengal*, Vol. I, ed. R.C. Majumdar, Dacca 1943, p. 36.
11. Pramode Lal Paul, "Jainism in Bengal", *Indian Culture*, Vol. III (No. 3), 1937, p. 525.
12. R.C. Majumdar, "Jainism in Ancient Bengal", *Jain Journal*, Vol. XVIII (1984), p. 126 f.
13. Koṭivarṣa, Puṇḍravardhana, and Tāmraliptī have been identified respectively with Bangarh in

West Dinajpur District (West Bengal), Mahāsthāngarh in the Bagura District (Bangladesh), and Tamluk in the Midnapore District (West Bengal).

14. Debala Mitra, "Some Jaina Antiquities from Bankura, West Bengal", *Journal of the Asiatic Society*, Vol. XXIX (1958), p. 133 f.
15. *Ibid.*, p. 134.
16. Gaurisankar De, "The Jaina Background of 24 Parganas," *Jain Journal*, Vol. XVII (1983), p. 143.
17. Kalidas Dutt, "The Antiquities of Khari", *Varendra Research Society Monograph*, No. 3 (1929), p. 5 and fig. 3.
18. *Idem*, "Antiquities of North-west Sundarbans", *ibid.*, No. 4 (1930), p. 7 and fig.3.
19. D.K. Chakravarty, "A Survey of Jaina Antiquarian Remains in West Bengal", *Jain Journal*, Vol. XVIII (1984), p. 145.
20. Information regarding the last two sites in the Midnapore District was kindly supplied by Shri Gaurisankar De.
21. Find spot of this image is not mentioned in the Accession Register of the Indian Museum where it is now preserved. Its accession number is 72/6.
22. For an account of the sculptures found at Pakbirrā, *see* Krishnajivan Bhattacharyya, Pratip Kumar Mitra and Atul Chandra Bhowmick, "Jain Sculptures at Pakbirra", *ibid.*, Vol. XX (1986), p. 127ff.
23. This piece of sculpture, collected from elsewhere, is now kept in the Haripada Sahitya Mandir Museum, Puruliā.
24. This *caumukha* votive shrine is preserved in the Vangiya Sahitya Parishad Museum at Vishnupur.
25. Puran Chand Nahar (*Jaina Inscriptions*, Calcutta 1918, Pt. 1, p. 1) brings to our notice an epigraph on the back of an image of Pārśvanātha dated in Saṁvat 1100. The image is installed in a temple at Azimganj (Murshidabad District). Roma Chatterjee (*Religion in Bengal*, Calcutta 1985, p. 358) takes this epigraph as an evidence of the revival of Jainism in Bengal during the 12th century. Nahar, however, indicates that the image was brought from Chitor.
26. J.N. Banerjea, *The Development of Hindu Iconography*, New Delhi 1974, p. 554.

LIST OF ILLUSTRATIONS

(The author wishes to thank all individuals and institutions for providing the illustrative material for this paper.)

PĀRŚVANĀTHA IMAGES IN ELLORĀ

Maruti Nandan Prasad Tiwari

I

Pārśvanātha, the 23rd *Tīrthaṅkara,* was accorded a specially favoured position in visual representations at the Southern Nirgrantha or Digambara rock-cut shrines. The Northern Nirgrantha sites reveal that, in terms of popularity, Jina Pārśvanātha was next only to Ṛṣabhanātha; while in the images from south India, Pārśvanātha and Mahāvīra enjoyed the position of veneration to the same degree. Of all the 24 Jinas, the chief distinguishing feature of Pārśvanātha in having the snake-canopy overhead first appeared in *c.* first or second century A.D.[1] Up to *c.* the sixth century A.D., Pārśvanātha was shown both with five[2] as well as seven-hooded[3] snake-canopy. The Pārśvanātha images of the Nirgrantha-Śvetāmbara sites usually show the *aṣṭa-mahāprātihāryas* in the *parikara,* as well as the figures of the Śāsanadevatās at the two extremities of the throne. Barring a few examples from Osiāñ, Kumbhāriā, and Delvāḍā (Mt. Ābū),[4] the Pārśvanātha images at the Śvetāmbara sites invariably contain the figures of Sarvānubhūti and Ambikā as Śāsanadevatās, in place of the conventional Dharaṇendra Yakṣa and Yakṣī Padmāvatī. Sarvānubhūti and Ambikā, the most popular Yakṣa-Yakṣī pair in the Śvetāmbara examples, was otherwise traditionally associated with the 22nd Jina Ariṣṭanemi. However, in a few instances, the cobra-canopy has been provided over the heads of Sarvānubhūti and Ambikā for emphasizing their association with Pārśvanātha. The Pārśvanātha images from the Digambara sites of North India usually contain the figures of Dharaṇendra and Padmāvatī, either standing formally at the right and left flanks with the snake-canopy, or seated near Jina's throne-ends. In former examples, Padmāvatī invariably holds a long parasol above the head of Jina; while Dharaṇendra is shown either with folded hands or as bearing a fly-whisk. The images from north India, in some instances, show the figures of Dharaṇendra and Padmāvatī both at the Jina's throne ends and on the two sides of the *mūlanāyaka* figure. The Pārśva images from south India usually show the figures of Dharaṇendra and Padmāvatī standing on the two flanks of the *mūlanāyaka* which, however, are sometimes substituted by the *cāmaradharas.*

II

Ellorā in Aurangabad district of Maharashtra occupy a singular position in respect of history of architecture for its prolonged rock-cut shrine activities and the high quality of its figural and decorative art from *c.* middle of the sixth to about mid-tenth century A.D. and perhaps a little beyond. The site is all the more important due to its being the confluence of the three principal Indian sects, the Vaidika, the Buddhist, and the Nirgrantha. A series of five principal Nirgrantha caves (Nos. 30-34), occupying the northern horn of the Ellorā ridge, are important from the standpoint of the study of Nirgrantha iconography and architecture of the southern school of pre-medieval and the early phase of the medieval times. These rock-cut hall-shrines, belonging exclusively to the Digambara sect, are datable to the ninth and tenth centuries A.D. The earliest Jaina caves apparently were carved during the reign of the Rāṣṭrakūṭa emperor Amoghavarṣa I (A.D. 815-881), the great patron of the Nirgrantha religion. These caves, among other Jina and subsidiary figures, contain several rock-cut images of Jina Pārśvanātha.[5]

In Ellorā, Pārśvanātha is represented by over 31 examples, this being the highest number met with at any single Jaina site. The figures of Pārśvanātha in Ellorā, however, never occupy the position of a principal image, and is thus not found in the sanctum proper. Of the 31 figures, nine show Pārśvanātha in *dhyāna-mudrā*, the remaining in the *kāyotsarga* posture. The Pārśva figures are all carved either in the *gūḍhamaṇḍapa* or in the *vīthikā* or fore-lobby. They show almost identical features, with a few definite peculiarities. The placement of the figures of Pārśvanātha, mostly facing Bāhubalī (in the corresponding position on the opposite wall) may have some underlying meaning. Such a placement may have been actuated by the commonality of the fact of *upasarga* (though of a different nature) in both cases.[6]

Pārśvanātha in Ellorā, when seated, is usually accompanied by a triple parasol, fly-whisk bearing attendants, lion-throne, the hovering *mālādhara*-angels and the drum-beater suggestive of some of the *aṣṭa-mahāprātihāryas*, an invariate feature of the *arhat* images (Plate 56). On the contrary, the images in the *kāyotsarga-mudrā* show no *prātihārya* with Pārśva. This may be suggestive of Pārśvanātha yet not attained to Jinahood. The seated figures of Pārśvanātha in one case is, surprisingly, joined by the figures of Yakṣa Sarvāhṇa and Yakṣī Ambikā.[7] The rendering of Sarvāhṇa and Ambikā in the present instance reminds us of their invariate association with Pārśvanātha at the Śvetāmbara sites of western India. In a single instance, a seated figure of Pārśvanātha (cave 30) is carved at the *lalāṭa* of the lintel as well.

Pārśvanātha figures at Ellorā, seated or standing, invariably have been provided with seven-hooded snake-canopy. The largest number of figures are carved in cave 32 where occur as many as 12, three of which are in the *dhyāna-mudrā*. The caves 30, 31, 33 and 34 are having in order five, two, ten, and two figures.

The Pārśvanātha images from Ellorā are specially significant for elaborate rendering, in the *parikara*, of the *upasarga* or tirade of tormentations inflicted on Pārśva by the evil spirit Śaṁbara. The earliest known examples, illustrating the *upasargas* of Pārśvanātha are in Bādāmī (Cave IV) and Aihoḷe (Jaina Cave), both datable to *c.* A.D. 600, wherein the figures of Śaṁbara are shown attacking Pārśva with a boulder or with some weapon (Plate 54). However, the figures of Padmāvatī, in both instances, holds a long obliquely laid parasol and is joined by the figure of Dharaṇendra, both standing on the right flank of Pārśvanātha. Close to the figure of Pārśva with five-hooded snake-canopy, sits at his left the figure of Śaṁbara bowing in humility with folded hands. The most elaborate representations of such scenes depicting the onslaught of Śaṁbara to dissuade Pārśva from his *tapas* are met with at Ellorā. Barring a few examples known from the Mālādevī temple at Gyāraspur (Vidisha, M.P.), Indian Museum, Calcutta[8] (provenance probably Bihar), and Huṁca (Dist. Shimoga, Karnataka, two examples),[9] such elaborate representations are rarely encountered. In the rendering of the *upasarga*, at Ellorā are noticed three, four, five, six, seven or eight figural manifestations of Śaṁbara, each one engaged in the act of causing a different type of assault to Pārśvanātha. In about 20 images, all in the *kāyotsarga-mudrā,* the *upasarga* scenes are carved, this being the highest number for such images at any site. Surprisingly, the available Pārśva images belonging to the Nirgrantha-Śvetāmbara tradition do not show the *upasarga* episode. Instead, in the ceiling each of the Mahāvīra and the Śāntinātha temple at Kumbhāriā (*c.* A.D. 1062 and 1082, Banaskantha District, Gujarat), we come across the detailed renderings pertaining to the enmities of Kamaṭha (Meghamālī or Śaṁbara) and of Marubhūti (Pārśvanātha in his previous existence).

The earliest literary reference to the *upasarga* of Pārśva is inside the *Pārśvābhyudaya kāvya* of Jinasena of Pañcastūpānaya of the Southern Church (before A.D. 784 or more probably *c.* 825),[10] wherein only two *upasargas* posed by the devil Kamaṭha are described; they are the *apsarases* or the beautiful damsels and the hurling of huge rock-boulders at Pārśva.[11] Another work, the *Uttarapurāṇa* of Guṇabhadra (*c.* mid-ninth century A.D.) deals with the life of Pārśva in detail; but that pertains mainly to the enmity between Marubhūti and Kamaṭha or Pārśva and Śaṁbara in their previous existences. As to the *upasargas* of Śaṁbara during the course of *tapas* of Pārśva, it merely mentions that the devil Śaṁbara had caused different *upasargas* continuously for seven days. It further mentions that, in course of the onslaught, Śaṁbara lifted and threw hillocks at Pārśva.[12] Both works also refer to the manifestation of Dharaṇendra along with his consort (the name Padmāvatī not mentioned) for protecting Pārśva from the *upasargas* of Śaṁbara. Dharaṇendra covered Pārśva with his hoods forming the canopy over his head while his consort raised a *vajramaya chatra*—adamantine-parasol—over the snake-canopy.

The detailed account of the different *upasargas* of Śaṁbara to Pārśva is found perhaps for the first time in the *Pāsanāhacariü* (A.D. 1077) of the Digambara author Padmakīrtti which gives a telling description of how Śaṁbara himself took different forms and used fatal weapons such as thunderbolt, arrow, spear, *mudgara*, axe, parasol etc. to shake Pārśva from his *tapas*. He also made abortive attempts through ferocious animals namely, *śārdūla* (tiger), lion, monkey, dog, bear, snake, boar, buffalo, elephant, ox, etc. to shake up Pārśva from his meditation. He also caused *upasargas* by the horrendous goblins such as the *vaitāla*-monster, *piśāca*-demon, *ḍākinī*-ogress and by *grahas* or obscuring planetary divinities, also snakes, eagles, and *kumbhāṇḍa*-monster with their terrifying cries to frighten Pārśva. An *upasarga* by the bewitching *apsarases* was also conjured up to lure away Pārśva from his trance. After failing in his efforts to shake Pārśva, Śaṁbara next caused non-stop rains. When the rain water crossed the shoulder of Pārśva, Dharaṇendra came to his rescue along with the *nāga*-ladies. The king of snakes next raised his seven hoods over the head of Pārśva for providing full cover and rested Jina's feet in the folds acting as lap. As usual, Padmāvatī raised a parasol over the snake-hoods of Dharaṇendra. Śaṁbara, finding his efforts going futile, was incensed and attacked even *nāgarāja* Dharaṇendra with the weapons such as thunderbolt, *vajra-daṇḍa* and mountain boulders, in which too he failed.[13] Filled, then, with remorse, Śaṁbara bowed to Pārśva asking for forgiveness. The details of the various *upasargas* in the figures of Pārśva from Ellorā almost fully correspond with the details in the *Pāsanāhacariü*. Since the figures of Ellorā in point of time are earlier than the text, it may be presumed that an identical but earlier tradition was before the artists at Ellorā, the textual source of which is now lost. Some general as well as the individual features of the images of Pārśvanātha from Ellorā showing elaborate rendering of the *upasarga* may now be looked into. In such scenes, Śaṁbara has been shown in different forms, either riding on buffalo or lion or hovering in air and as throwing spear, dagger, trident, mace, thunderbolt, snake, and boulders at Pārśvanātha. In all instances, the target of the fierce attack of the devil Śaṁbara, in his different manifestations carved on two sides, is Pārśva who stands unshaken by the onslaughts and is absorbed in deep trance. Barring an exception (cave 31) where Dharaṇendra is shown in human form (Plate 55), in all other instances from Ellorā he appears in the snake form with seven-hooded canopy over the head of Pārśva and its coils running all over his body down to the feet. On the contrary, the north Indian images from the northern Nirgrantha (Acela-kṣapaṇaka) sites invariably show the figure of Dharaṇendra in human form who stands on the right flank of Pārśva, while the corresponding left flank is occupied by Padmāvatī who holds a long parasol. Padmāvatī, in the images from Ellorā, on the other hand, has always been depicted on the right flank of Pārśvanātha. She stands mostly on lotus and holds a long obliquely laid parasol seen above the cobra hoods and ultimately providing shade above the head of Pārśva as a mark of his greatness and also for protecting Pārśva and Dharaṇendra from the heavy shower due to Śaṁbara's sorcery. Sometimes Padmāvatī is joined by one or two *nāgī* figures which, however, conforms to the tradition of the *Pāsanāhacariū* referring to the presence of *nāgakanyās*. The shaft of the parasol held by Padmāvatī is delineated with such tenderness that it looks like a lotus stalk.

The compositional scheme in the Pārśvanātha images from Ellorā showing the *upasargas* is superb. It graphically blends different moods and depiction-modes of details. Pārśvanātha in deep meditation appears as a symbol of total austerity and self-sacrifice, while the hostile devils in terrifying forms represent demonic fury. The tenderly modelled figures of Padmāvatī, on the other hand, is suggestive of divine beauty and beneficence. In consonance with the literary injunctions, Śaṁbara, wearing *mukuṭa* and other ornaments, appears along with his consort in humility with folded hands as if asking forgiveness. It is surprising that, despite a variety of representations of different *upasargas*, that caused by the charming *apsarases* is not carved in any of the examples at Ellorā. The slender and motionless figures of Pārśvanātha at Ellorā shows tranquillity and weightlessness. The face of the *mūlanāyaka* is always calm and benign with a faint smile which suggests that, unshaken by the *upasargas*, the Jina is aware of what is going around despite his being in deep trance. The body of Padmāvatī, though slim and tenderly flexioned, is slightly fleshy but not without the feminine grace and elegance. The figures of Śaṁbara in its different formal emanations show different modellings, sometimes meaty and plumpish, sometimes dwarfish and evil-looking. The facial features and expressions of the host of figures of the demon Śaṁbara are in all instances terrifying.

The figure in cave No. 30 shows Śaṁbara in different forms, in the act of attacking Pārśvanātha with a huge rock-boulder, and also with the sword and shield. In one of the examples, however, Dharaṇendra also stands close to Padmāvatī on the right flank of Pārśvanātha.

Of the five figures of Śaṁbara in an example from cave 31, one is interestingly shown with a lion face carved on its belly which was a usual convention of showing one of the form of the *gaṇas* but more specifically *kumbhāṇḍa*, the early examples of which are known from Bādāmī (Plate 56). The figure of Padmāvatī here is adorned with jewellery and is gracefully modelled.

The representations of Pārśva in cave no. 32 are most elaborate in respect of the rendering of the *upasargas*. In one of the figures, Śaṁbara, kneeling at the feet of Pārśva with folded hands, has a terrifying appearance with bulging eyes and protruding fangs. In one case figure of Śaṁbara is shown only as bust after the manner of Rāhu. In an elaborate example (Plate 57), the seated figures of Śaṁbara and his consort are shown at the feet of Pārśva and the *chatradhāriṇī* Padmāvatī are finely executed. The dynamic figures of Śaṁbara, eight in number, in differing forms, make a realistic depiction of the severe inflictions cast by Śaṁbara toward Pārśva. Three figures ride on lion and buffalo and hold snake and dagger. The figure carved very close to Pārśva apparently fail to shake Pārśva from his *tapas* which is suggested by his calm and benign face. This undoubtedly is the best of all figures of Pārśva at Ellorā both in terms of details and the enactment of the legend which appears ethereal. In some of the examples, the compositional scheme is not so elegant and it appears crowded as well as lack in vitality. In one of the instances, a monster is shown only by his head with his hands being closed to its mouth. In all examples, different emanatory forms of Śaṁbara attacking Pārśva are carved on both sides as hovering, so as to suggest that the inflictions originated from the sky. In an example in cave No. 32 a figure of *ḍākinī* with snake garland and twisted snake in arm is also carved (Plate 58). The image also contains two diminutive figures of Jinas standing at the two extremities. However, a bearded monk with hands raised in *tapas* stands close to Padmāvatī; he may be identified with Kamaṭha or Kaṭha performing penance. Another detailed representation in cave No. 32 showing eight devilish figures of Śaṁbara is not so fine in terms of its compositional setting. The carver, however, has here paid considerable attention to the details of *upasargas* with forceful elaboration (Plate 57). But the weird power of Śaṁbara seems ridiculous before the spiritual luminosity of Pārśva. Of the eight figures, two ride on buffalo and lion, while one is shown blowing a conch. The figure hovering in the air and hurling a huge boulder at Pārśva is the most forceful of all such depictions. In one of the examples in cave No. 32, two figures riding respectively a lion and buffalo attack Pārśva with trident and thunderbolt (Plate 59).

In one of the examples in cave No. 33, an unbearded monk wearing *kaupīna* and standing with folded hands with a begging bowl hanging from his arm, is shown in close proximity of Pārśva on the left (Plate 61). The figure may be identified with Kamaṭha, though this mode of depiction finds no parallel textual explanation. In one of the examples at cave No. 33, a vigorous depiction of a devil attacking Pārśva with trident is worth noting (Plate 62). The image, though mutilated, contains beautifully modelled figure of Padmāvatī in *atibhaṅga*. Likewise, the figure in cave No. 34 shows the demon riding a buffalo and making a bid to attack Pārśva with *mudgara*-dumbbell (Plate 63).

Thus the sculptors at Ellorā worked with a deep sense of imagination and had avoided the monotony in the details for representing the episode of Pārśva's *upasarga* (which repeatedly figures) and also in integrating different aspects represented by the figures of Pārśva, Padmāvatī, and Śaṁbara. The variety revealed in forms and postures of different figures and their elaboration as well as expressiveness in such representations are unparalleled in the rendering of *upasargas* of Pārśva. Perhaps the scale of the composition on cave-walls provided the space for, and the textual tradition before the patrons and the carvers supplied the necessary details for the dramatic elaboration of the episode. (A smaller image of seated Pārśva but without the *upsarga* episode is shown in Plate 60).

NOTES AND REFERENCES

1. Bronze image in the Prince of Wales Museum, Bombay and an *āyāgapaṭa* from Mathurā with the seated figure of Pārśva in the centre, now in the collection of State Museum, Lucknow. Acc. No. J253.
2. The bronze image (*c.* first century A.D.) in the Prince of Wales Museum, Bombay and the two figures at Bādāmī and Aihoḷe (*c.* A.D. 600) show five-hooded snake-canopy with Pārśva.
3. Images from Kaṅkālī Tīlā, Mathurā.
4. Vimala Vasahī, Dilwara, Mt. Ābū.
5. For details, consult R.S. Gupte and B.D. Mahajan, *Ajanta, Ellora and Aurangabad Caves*, Bombay 1962, pp. 218-24; also the *Jaina Art and Architecture*, (ed. A. Ghosh), Vol. I, New Delhi 1975, pp. 188-91; K.V. Soundara Rajan, 'Ellorā', *Encyclopaedia of Indian Temple Architecture*, Vol. I, Pt. II (eds. Michael W. Meister and M.A. Dhaky), Delhi 1986, pp. 129-30.
6. Bāhubalī (the son of the first Jina Ṛṣabhanātha), as a result of his rigorous *tapas* and deep trance, became a powerful symbol as well as a material image evocative of the ethos of self-sacrifice and of *ahiṁsā* preached by the Jinas. The same idea of rigorous *tapas* and deep trance are met

with in the example of Pārśva standing likewise in the *kāyotsarga* for attaining the *kevala-jñāna*. He had to encounter with terrible *upasargas* caused by Meghamālī or Śaṁbara (the soul of devilish Kamaṭha). Despite the *upasargas*, Pārśva remained completely unaffected and stayed stable in *tapas* because of his inexhaustible inner spiritual strength. The probable source of the mythology of *upasargas* of Pārśva was the legends of Buddha's *Māravijaya* and Kṛṣṇa's uplifting of Govardhana mountain.

7. Cave No. 33.
8. U.P. Shah, "A Pārśvanātha Sculpture in Cleveland", *The Bulletin of the Cleveland Museum of Art*, December 1970, pp. 303-11.
9. M.A. Dhaky, "Śāntara Sculpture", *Journal of the Indian Society of Oriental Art*, New Series, Vol. IV, 1971-72, pp. 78-96.
10. *See* the recent article in Hindi by M.A. Dhaky, "Dakṣiṇātya Nirgrantha Paramparā ke Kucha Granthoñ kī Aitihāsika Samasyāeñ," *Sandhāna*, Vol. V, 1992, pp. 17, 18.
11. *Pārśvābhyudaya kāvya* of Jinasena, ed. M.G. Kothari, Bombay 1965, IV *sarga*, verses 45-48.
12. *Uttarapurāṇa* of Guṇabhadra, ed. Pannalal Jain, Bharatiya Gyana Pith, Varanasi 1954, *sarga* 73, verses 136-140.
13. *Pāsanāhacariü* of Padmakīrtti, ed. Prafulla Kumar Modi, Varanasi 1965, *sarga* 14, veres 4-30.

LIST OF ILLUSTRATIONS

(All illustrations are published here by the courtesy and kindness, American Institute of Indian Studies, Center for Art & Archaeology, Ramnagar, Varanasi.)

JINA PĀRŚVA AND HIS TEMPLES IN INSCRIPTIONS: SOUTHERN INDIA (C. 5TH TO 11TH CENT. A.D.) ANDHRA PRADESH, KERALA, AND TAMIL NADU

K.V. Ramesh

The topic originally assigned to me included only Andhra Pradesh and Kerala, two diagonally placed states in which epigraphical references even to Jainism in general, let alone 'Pārśvanātha and his temples' in particular, are hard to come by. Shri K.G. Krishnan's pre-occupations elsewhere, which came in the way of his participating in this Seminar, and his affection for me led him to hand over Tamil Nadu to me and made available some more material which enabled me to add a couple of pages to the paper which, in any case, is a brief affair because of the paucity of epigraphical information. This is not to say that Pārśvanātha finds no place in the religious records of the three States under reference. What is meant is that, although the sculptural representations of Pārśva and his attendant deities are met with fairly frequently in the context of ancient and medieval rock-cut reliefs and structural temples in several past and present Jaina centres in these States, not many of them are backed by the presence of direct or even indirect epigraphical records or references. I have included in this paper only those sites which have sculptures of Pārśva and his attendant deities side by side with inscriptions referring to them, directly or indirectly. While speaking of Jainism in South India, an historical fact of sterling significance which we keep in mind is that Karnataka and Tamil Nadu, which lie to the west and east of Andhra Pradesh and Kerala, had more or less completely overshadowed the two latter States in the matter of receiving and playing host to Jainism. Of the three regions of my concern, the ancient Āndhra country, which had maintained very close alliance with the Magadhan power nucleus from very early times, had played host to Buddhism in a big way. The meeker in numerical strength because of its sterner ascetic discipline and consequent austerity and hence less attractive Jaina religion followed the line of least resistance and entered Karnataka, thence waded its way further south into Tamil Nadu and Kerala and was, in early and later historical times, also carried sporadically to places here and there in Andhra Pradesh. We must recognize the fact that in Āndhradēśa, the patrons of Jainism were mostly rulers and people who were either invaders or migrants from Karnataka who got almost all Jaina inscriptions written in the Kannaḍa language though by then Telugu also had come to be used as a major epigraphical medium. So also, even in Tamil Nadu where Tamiḻ, Tamilians and Jainism had interacted significantly and to a considerable all-pervading benefit, the continuing influence of the Kannaḍigas is sufficiently attested to by epigraphical sources.

To the best of my knowledge, there is only one pre-Telugu early historical Jaina site in Andhra Pradesh, Dānavulapāḍu in Cuddapah District. Though about a dozen Jaina inscriptions, most of them in Kannaḍa, unearthed during excavations conducted in that village, they belong to a period as late as the eighth-ninth centuries. Later, a brick chamber revealed there and an image of Pārśvanātha enshrined therein have been attributed to *c.* third century A.D.[1] The inscriptions, however, do not contain any reference to Pārśvanātha.

In point of fact, there are only a couple of references to Pārśvanātha in inscriptions from Andhra Pradesh, and these too are of a period as late as the 11th and 12th centuries A.D.

Of these the Cilūr (Hyderabad District) pillar inscription[2] of the Kalyāṇa-Cālukya ruler Vikramāditya V, in Kannaḍa language and dated in A.D. 1012, records a grant of lands made by the king's *daṇḍanāyaka* Padmanābhayya to the Arhat Pārśvadeva of Indra-Jinālaya attached to the Antara-vasadi of Cilakūru. From the name of the temple, Indra-Jinālaya, we may reasonably infer that it was built in the reign of, or in memory of one of the three Rāṣṭrakūṭa emperors bearing that name. It is noteworthy that Pārśvadeva is mentioned herein as Aṇṇal-Atiśaya-Pārśvadēva. Aṇṇal, among other things, also stands for the *Arhat*, more so in Tamiḻ. From the adjective *atiśaya* we must surmise that the image had miraculous potency, for *atiśayas* of the Jina in Nirgrantha terminology imply extraordinary physical characteristics and attendant glory phenomena and images or *tīrthas* which are qualified as '*sad-atiśaya-yukta*' are supposed to possess the curative or benign influence or power.

A Kannaḍa inscription[3] from Ujjili (Mahbubnagar District), engraved in the 11th century characters, is dated in Śaka 888 (current), Prabhava (=966-67 A.D.) and registers grants made to the Jaina *Tīrthaṅkara* Cenna-Pārśvadeva installed in the Baddi-Jinālaya in the town of Ujjivoḷol. The name of the temple, Baddi-Jinālaya, tempts me to conclude that it was probably built by, or during the reign of and named after the Rāṣṭrakūṭa emperor Baddega Amōghavarṣa who ruled during A.D. 936-39. The gift was received, on behalf of the temple, by its *ācārya* Indrasēna-paṇḍita.

On the reverse of the slab is engraved another Kannaḍa inscription[4] of A.D. 1097 recording the gift of a tank to Pārśvanātha of the same temple, Baddi-Jinālaya, by *daṇḍanāyaka* Bhānudevarasa, an officer of the then reigning Kalyāṇa-Cāḷukya king Vikramāditya VI. This gift was also received by Indrasēna-paṇḍita, the *ācārya* of the temple.

The fact that the name of the *ācārya* of the Pārśvanātha temple was the same in A.D. 966-67 and in A.D. 1097 can be explained away in two ways; either that the abbatial *ācāryas* of that temple were hereditarily called Indrasēna-paṇḍitas or that the earlier grant of A.D. 966-67 had to be renewed in A.D. 1097 and was received on behalf of the deity by the then *ācārya*. In any case, it is clear that Baddi-Jinālaya enjoyed the patronatge of the royalty in sufficient measure for at least a century and a half. Taking it for granted that I will be allowed to break the time-barrier of the fifth to the 11th century marginally, I will refer here to the Gōvindapuram (Warangal District) Kannaḍa inscription of A.D. 1122.[5] According to this inscription, Nāgarāja, the minister of Guṇḍarāja, constructed a temple for Pārśva-Jineśvara:

Ratn-aṁbōdhi-viyac-chaśāṅka-gata-
Śāk-ābde Plave vatsare
rājat-Phālguṇa-māsa-nirmmala-tṛitīyā
Śauri-vāre vare I
lagne Pārśva-Jineśvarasya bhavan-
ārādhya-pratiṣṭām śubhaṁ
udyad-bhakti-vidhāna-pūrvvam-akarōt
śrī-Nāgadēva-prabhuḥ II

With the permission of Mēḍarāja, the elder brother of Guṇḍarāja, he also gifted four tanks to the temples:

tad-dēvasya nivēdya-dīpa-vara-pūj
-ārthaṁ gaṇ-āmbōnidhiḥ
Toppa-śrēṣṭhi-bṛihat-taṭāka-puratas-
sāṁbraṁ taṭākaṁ mudā I
Pārśv-āgra-tri-taṭāka-saṁyutam-adāc-
chrī-Nāgadevō vibhuḥ
śrī-Mēḍa-kṣitipāla-saṁmata-paraś-
candr-ārkka-tāraṁ śubham II

A guild of horse-dealers chimed in with grants of cloth pieces (*cīrṇṇa*) at the rate of two per horse for the worship of Pārśvanātha:

praty-aśvam Pārśvadēvasya ghōṭaka-vyavahāribhiḥ I
pūj-ārthaṁ cīrṇṇa-yugaḷaṁ dattam-ā-candra-tārakam II

Pedda-Kaḍumūru (Mahbubnagar District) has also yielded a Jaina inscription[6] dated in A.D. 1119, referring as it does to the reign of Kalyāṇa-Cālukya Vikramāditya VI. This Kannaḍa inscription records a grant of 12 *mattars* of land and a tank to the god Parissadeva (Pārśvadeva) installed in the *basadi* of Śaṅkara-seṭṭi in Piriya-Kaḍambūru.

From these scanty epigraphical references, one thing becomes clear that Jainism never became a popular religion in Andhra Pradesh among the local Āndhrans, and that whatever patronage it received over there was more or less confined to rulers and people from Karnataka.

Jainism did not fare any better in Kerala and epigraphical references to Pārśvanātha and his temples there are few and far between. Significantly, these few available inscriptions are located in places which have been either subsequently transferred to Tamil Nadu as a sequel to States' reorganization or are situated on the Kerala-Tamil Nadu border. Hence, I propose to discuss those inscriptions along with those of Tamil Nadu.

Tiruccāraṇattu-malai near Citral and Nāgarkovil, both of them now in Kanyakumari District in Tamil Nadu but not long ago were included in the erstwhile Travancore state, and Kallil in Koṭṭayam District, Kerala, had flourished as important Jaina centres in which Pārśvanātha and his *śāsana-devatā* Padmāvatī had occupied the pride of place. We, however, have no inscriptions specifically referring to these deities from those places.

In point of fact, the earliest direct epigraphical mention of Pārśvanātha occurs in the Aivarmalai inscription[7] of Pāṇḍya Varaguṇa II dated Śaka 792/A.D. 870-71. This is an important inscription from our point of view. It is engraved on a neatly dressed portion of the rock above a natural cave on the Aivarmalai hills in the village of Aiyampāḷaiyam, Madurai District. What concerns us here is the statement contained in the inscription that Śāntivīrakkuravar, the disciple (*māṇākkan*) of Guṇavīrakkuravaḍigaḷ, renovated the image of Pārśvanātha and his Yakṣī at Tiruvayirai (*Tiruvayirai Pārisva-paṭāraraiyum=Iyakki-avvaigaḷaiyum pudukki*) and also endowed 502 *kāṇam* (gold coins) for food offerings to the two deities (*iraṇḍakku-muṭṭāv-avi*) and for feeding, probably daily, one ascetic (*aḍigaḷ*). The reference here is obviously to the reliefs of Pārśvanātha and Padmāvatī engraved inside the cave. Since they had to be renovated in A.D. 870-71, we may reasonably suppose that they must have been originally carved long before that date, perhaps a few centuries earlier.

Some three decades ago, on a hillock at Ālattūr (Palghat District) was discovered a Jaina temple site in ruins.[8] Amidst the ruins were found the images of Mahāvīra, Pārśvanātha, and a partially damaged Vaṭṭeluttu inscription[9] of about the tenth century A.D. The inscription refers to one main Jaina temple or shrine as Nalañjiyar-palli and to an unknown number of subsidiary temples or shrines as *vali-ppaḻḻigaḷ*. We also gather from the inscription that the main Jaina deity of that place was called Tirukkuṇavāyttēvar, but we have no means of knowing whether this local name was conferred on Mahāvīra or Pārśvanātha.

Cōḻavāṇḍipuram (South Arcot District, Tamil Nadu) flourished as an important Jaina centre in the 10th-11th centuries as evidenced by sculptures carved on the groups of boulders on the hillock called Āṇḍimalai at that place.[10] Of particular interest here is a pair of huge boulders leaning against each other; in the recess between these boulders is found a loose slab, about 4 feet high, with a fairly ancient sculpture of the Jaina goddess Padmāvatī cut on it in high relief. On the sides of the boulders facing each other on either side of the goddess are two panels, one containing in bold relief the figure of Gommaṭa or Bāhubali and the other, that of Pārśvanātha. Near the Gommaṭa figure is engraved a small inscription[11] in Tamiḻ characters of about the tenth century recording the erection of a *Tevāram* (=*Dehāra*), a divine abode, the divinities meant here obviously being Pārśvanātha, his *Yakṣī* Padmāvatī, and Gommaṭa, by a private individual named Vēli Koṅgaraiyar Puttaḍigaḷ. The goddess Padmāvatī is today locally known as Kāḷiyamman, thus shorn of her original Jaina association.

Nāgarkovil is now in the Kanyakumari District, Tamil Nadu, but formerly formed part of the Travancore State. The place name is derived from Nāgar + kōil which literally means the temple of the Nāga deity. The temple, originally a Jaina one, has a long history of being earlier mistaken for a Brahmanical fane, of Anantālvār, on the erroneous premise (or argument of convenience) that the hooded serpent, the characteristic emblem of Pārśvanātha, was Ādiśeṣa! A number of inscriptions[12] in this temple, all belonging to the early years of the 16th century, mention the Nāga deities and the god Nāgarāja of Kōṭṭaru *alias* Mummuḍiśōḷapuram and also refers to the Jaina supervisors of the temple, Guṇavīra-paṇḍita and Kamalavāhana-paṇḍita. What is more, images of Jina Mahāvīra and Arhat Pārśva are found sculptured on the pillars of the *maṇḍapa* in front of the Nāgarāja shrine. From this it is apparent that the Nāgarkoil was a Jaina temple, that the Jaina deity Pārśvanātha had come to be called Nāgarāja after his Nāga emblem, and that the effective conversion of the temple into the Brahmanical fold occurred sometime late in the 16th century or thereafter.[13]

NOTES AND REFERENCES

1. *Archaeological Survey of India Annual Report*, 1905-06, pp. 120-27; P.B. Desai, *Jainism in South India*, Sholapur 1957, pp. 17 and 22.
2. *Epigraphia Andhrica*, Vol. II, pp. 50 ff.
3. *Andhra Pradesh Government Archaeological Series*, No. 3, Inscription No. MN 61.
4. *Telaṁgaṇa-śāsanamula*, p. 67, No. 35.
5. *Andhra Pradesh Government Epigraphical Series*, No. 6, *Inscriptions of Andhra Pradesh, Warangal District*, No. 26, pp. 71 ff.
6. *Ibid*., p. 62, No. 32.
7. *Epigraphia Indica*, Vol. XXXII, pp. 337-38; *South Indian Inscriptions*, Vol. XIV, No. 22.
8. *Journal of Indian History*, Vol. 44, pp. 536 ff.
9. *Annual Report on Indian Epigraphy*, 1959-60, No. B 238.
10. *Annual Report on South Indian Epigraphy*, 1936-37, pp. 60-61.
11. *Ibid*., No. 251.
12. *Travancore Archaeological Series*, Vol. VI, pp. 153 ff.
13. I am thankful to my colleague, Dr. M.D. Sampath, Superintending Epigraphist in the Directorate of Epigraphy, for his help in preparing this paper.

JINA PĀRSVA AND HIS TEMPLES IN INSCRIPTIONS: SOUTHERN INDIA (KARNATAKA) (c. 5th to 11th century A.D.)

Madhav N. Katti

Karnataka, ancient and medieval Karṇāṭadēśa, was for long a stronghold of Jainism. As a result, throughout the historical period, several Jaina temples and often inscriptions referring to the construction of, and endowments to the temples for various *tīrthaṅkaras* are known in fair number. Almost all the sub-territories of Karnataka can boast of temple-building activities connected with the Jaina deities for about one and a half millennium. However, as in the case of Śaivite and Vaiṣṇavite temples, many buildings, for which we have the testimony of inscriptions, have not survived. Nonetheless, these inscriptions amply reflect the prosperous times Jainism once had enjoyed in Karnataka.

All of the important ruling dynasties of Karnataka, commencing with the Kadambas, and their feudatories, supported different religions in their dominions. Scores and scores of temples for many different divinities, including those of the Jaina pantheon, were constructed. The rulers, their consorts, princes, feudatories and chieftains, and their generals or military governors made munificent donations to such temples for the daily worship of, and offerings to the deities as well as for the maintenance, repairs, and renovations of the temples, irrespective of their personal faith. Thus, during the reign of the Kadambas of Vanavāsī, the Cālukyas of Vātāpi, the Rāṣṭrakūṭas of Mānyakheṭaka, the Cālukyas of Kalyāṇa, and still later the Hoysaḷas, the Kaḷacūryas as also some minor dynasties to whose reign-period the subject of our discussion pertains, a number of Jaina temples came to be constructed. The élite of the society together with the laity, too, lent their share as patrons. Among the Jaina sects, the Śvetāmbara or Śvetapaṭa and the Nirgrantha (possibly the surviving remanant of the sect of Pārśvanātha) had been much less important compared to the Yāpanīya and the Digambara orders, the latter represented by the Mūla Saṅgha and the Drāviḍa Saṅgha had considerable following in Karnataka.

Amongst the Jaina deities, Pārśvanātha occupied a very prominent place as several inscriptions refer to the construction of the temples or *vasatīs*, called *basadis* in Kannaḍa, for this deity. The images of the Jina were in most examples shaped in stone in Karnataka. Today, in several cases, we come across the sculptures lying in different regions of the State on account of the dilapidated condition of the temples, and in a number of cases due to the original buildings' destruction. And yet, as a matter of delight, a good number of temples not only exist but are under worship even to this day.

The majority of inscriptions (which form the source material of the present paper), are in Kannaḍa language and script, while a few are in Sanskrit. Both Kannaḍa as well as Sanskrit languages are together employed for the rest of inscriptions. The script of the Sanskrit inscriptions is Southern Brāhmī in the early centuries of the Christian Era; while in the later centuries, it is Kannaḍa. The epigraphs highlight various socio-cultural and religious aspects of the contemporaneous times. In some cases the details of date are lost and for these the palaeographic dating is resorted to. I will discuss here some of the more important and interesting inscriptions as evidence for Pārśvanatha's shrines, and the grants made to them for conducting daily worship and offerings to the deities of such buildings and for buildings' repairs and refurbishment during different centuries.

There is a Pārśvanātha *basadi* in Śravaṇabeḷgoḷa (Hassan District), which traditionally is believed to preserve the memories of Maurya emperor Candragupta, Ārya Bhadrabāhu, and various other personages. However, there are no inscriptions referring to the construction of a *basadi*, installation of the deity, etc. at that age on this haloed hill. A number of epigraphs otherwise refer to the deity Pārśvanātha; but they all belong to the 11th and later centuries.[1] The rock-cut Jaina cave (No. IV) in Bādāmī, Bijapur District, possesses perhaps the earliest image of Pārśvanātha in its forelobby. This belongs to the early Cālukya period. While there are no contemporaneous epigraphs in the cave, on stylistic grounds the cave and its sculptures of the Calukya phase are believed to be of the period of Maṅgaleśa. Earlier than this, in the Kadamba period, there is an interesting reference to a Jaina deity in a copperplate charter belonging to the 4th regnal year of king Mṛgeśavarman[2] assignable to the late 5th century A.D. This charter refers to *bhagavat-arhat-mahājinendra*, without mentioning the name of the *tīrthaṅkara*. Further discoveries alone can shed light if Pārśvanātha was here intended or implied. The charter was granted combinely to the Śvetapaṭa-mahā-Śramaṇa *saṅgha* and the Nirgrantha order.

Though the inscriptions of the period of the Cālukyas, and following them of the Rāṣṭrakūṭas, mention about the erection of temples to the Jaina deities, there is no reference to Jina Pārśvanātha directly during those periods. There is, however, a figure of Pārśvanātha on the rocky hill of Ādōni near Bellary (presently in Kurnool

District) with an inscription on its side.[3] There are a few more sculptures in the area, without being associated with inscriptions.[4] They can be assigned to *c.* tenth century on stylistic grounds. However, further investigations are needed in that regard.

A Kannaḍa inscription from Kargudari [5] (Dharwar District), belonging to the reign of Jagadekamalla of the Kalyāṇa-Cālukya dynasty, refers to the construction of the temple of Vijaya-Pārśva-jinendra, by *mahā-vaḍḍavyavahāri* Kalliśeṭṭi, at Karegudure (the findspot of the record) and states that the śeṭṭi made over a number of grants to the temple for the purpose of worship and offerings to the deity and for the food-offerings to the preceptors dwelling therein, (*Karigudureyoḷ taṁma māḍisida Vijaya-Pārśva-jineṁdran-aṁga-bhoga, raṁga-bhogakam-alliya riṣiyar-āhāra-dānakkam*). The grants were made on the occasion of the *saṅkramaṇa*, as *sarvabādhā-parihāra*. The record is dated Prabhava, Pushya bahuḷa, pāḍiva, Monday, Dakshiṇāyana-saṅkramaṇa (A.D. 1027[6]). Jagadekamalla referred to in the inscription, very probably was Jayasiṁha II (Jagadekamalla I).

The inscription next in time belongs to the reign of Trailokyamalla (Someśvara I) of the Kalyāṇa-Cālukya dynasty.[7] The inscription, except for the part of its grant portion (including boundary details), is in Sanskrit language. The script is Kannaḍa. It mentions the king as *Trailokyamalla-deva*, whose epithets are given as follows: *Samasta-bhuvanāśraya-śrī-prithvī-vallabha-mahā-rājādhirāja-parameśvara-parama-bhaṭṭāraka-satyāśraya-kuḷa-tiḷaka-Cāḷukyābharaṇa*. The record is dated Śaka 976, Jaya, Vaiśākha, Amāvāsya, Somavāra, Sūrya-grahaṇa, which corresponds to A.D 1054 May 9, f.d.t. 26. Trailokyamalla's queen is mentioned as Ketaladevi, who is stated to be administering over the *agrahāra* Ponnavāḍa on the date of the record. Her feudatory Cāṁkirāja of Vāṇasa-vaṁśa, is referred to as the *pāda-kamala-bhramara* of *yogirāṭ* Mahāsena-muni and also as *paripūrṇa-cāru-vidyānidhi*. The inscription further states that he caused the construction of the *Jinendra-geha* and installed the images of the deities, Pārśvanātha, Śāntinātha, and Supārśvanātha. The *basadi* was known as 'Bhuvana-bhuṁbhuka'.

The three shrines of this *trikūṭa basadi* were in this order: Śāntinātha's shrine was in the middle, flanked by those of Pārśvanātha and Supārśvanātha (*Parama-Śānti-jinendra-gehaṁ-dvayonugata-Pārśva-Supārśva-vāsaṁ*). It is further stated that the image of Pārśvanātha together with the 'great serpent' was got sculptured (*mahānāgaṁ-racitaṁ Pārśvadaivataṁ*) by Jinavarma who is referred to as the *chatra* of Mahāsena-muni. The *basadi* is further described as 'Tribhuvanatilaka'. The grants were made on account of the *sūrya-grahaṇa* for the food-offerings to the *ṛṣis* (ascetics) and the *jīyas* (preceptors) as *śarvanamāsya* by the emperor Trailokamalla himself, at the request of (one of his consorts) Ketaladevi. The grants inciuded land, garden, house-site, shops, the sculptor's house (*kalkuṭigara mane*) and oil-mills. The recipient of the grant was evidently Mahāsena-muni of Mūla-saṅgha, Varasēna-gaṇa, and Pogari-gaccha.

An inscription from Guḍigere[8] (Dharwar District) which can be assigned to *c.* A.D 1075-76, records a number of gifts to the temple of Pārśvanātha at Dhvajataṭāka (i.e. Guḍigere the findspot of the record) by *aṣṭopavāsi-kantiyar*, at the instance of her teacher Śrīnandi. Here *aṣṭopavāsi-kantiyar* is the nun who performed eight fasts in continuity; Cālukya Someśvara II was on the throne on the date of this record. Another record from Soraṭūru[9] (Gadag Taluk, Dharwar District) engraved during the reign of the same emperor (Someśvara II) refers to a very interesting occasion when Huḷiyabbajjike, disciple of the same preceptor Śrīnandi (his *gaṇa* being mentioned as Sūrastha and *anvaya* as Citrakūṭa), received the grant made to the *basadi.* This hints to the fact that she was in charge of the management of the *basadi.* These instances reflect the important role played by the Jaina nuns or female preceptors during this period.

An inscription from Doṇi [10] (Dharwar District) belonging to the reign of Cālukya Vikramāditya VI, dated A.D. 1097, refers to the administration of the place Droṇīpura by Lakṣmī-mahādevī, Vikramāditya's senior queen (*piriyarasi*), states that Soviseṭṭi, a merchant of that place, caused the construction of the Jaina temple and made gift of a garden to Cārukīrti-paṇḍita of the Yāpanīya-saṅgha and Vṛkṣamūla-gaṇa. The temple no longer exists, the solitary image of Pārśvanatha from the place is the only indication of the deity in the *basadi* mentioned in the epigraph.

There are a number of Cālukya period inscriptions assignable on palaeographical grounds to the 11th-12th centuries A.D., which furnish some evidence about the Pārśvanātha temples; to these I shall presently turn. According to an inscription preserved in Gulbarga,[11] Āḍakki (the present-day Āḍaki in the vicinity of Gulbarga) which was a flourishing Jaina centre during this period, had a Jaina temple by name Koppa-Jinālaya, dedicated to Pārśvanātha. This temple is referred to as Cenna-Pārśva (also as Cenna-Pārśvanātha; *Cenna* meaning beautiful). An inscription from Koppal[12] (Raichur District) refers to Kuśa-Jinālaya and the deity Pārśvanātha. Baṁkur[13] (Gulbarga District) has preserved ruins of a number of Jaina temples. Of these, *bastiguḍi* has the images of Pārśvanātha and Padmāvatī, amongst other images like Ādinātha, Caturviṁśatī-Jinas, Vardhamāna, and others. On stylistic grounds, they can be assigned to the Kalyāṇa Cālukya period (11th-12th centuries A.D.). A thorough exploration may reveal many more sculptures and inscriptions of interest to us.

While the village Ciñcoli[14] has preserved a Pārśvanātha sculpture, Hagaragi[15] has a sculpture of Pārśvanātha attended by Padmāvatī and Dharaṇendra; Kāḷagi[16] and Maḷkheḍ[17] have again preserved images of Pārśvanātha amidst the temple ruins. At Huṇisi-Haḍaṅgili,[18] the medieval Jaina temple of the site is referred to as *Śrīkṣetra-Huṅasi-Haḍaṅgili-Pārśvanātha-Padmāvatī-basti,* in the official records. These all are in Kalyāṇa-Cālukya style and may be assigned to 11th-12th centuries A.D.

Two inscriptions from Haḷebīḍ[19] (Hassan District), of the Hoysaḷa period, are of considerable interest. The first refers to the construction of the temple of Pārśvanātha by Tippaṇa and Harideva, sons of Mallisețți, while the second record refers to *puṇise-jinālaya.* Since the latter record is also from the same place, the reference therein is obviously to the same Pārśvanātha-Jinālaya, which may have been referred to as such, because it may have been situated in the vicinity of a tamarind tree (*puṇise*).

The inscriptions of the 10th or 11th century, though mostly donative, furnish some important and interesting account of the temple-building activity for Jina Pārśva. However, in respect of the period prior to those centuries, a further epigraphical survey is needed. As earlier noticed, a number of sites have preserved ruins of Jaina temples and sculptures. A thorough examination of these may possibly bring to light some hitherto unknown epigraphs, some even referring to Jina Pārśva.

A comparison with the situation in other parts of India, particularly Southern, reveals similarity to a fair degree in the nature of inscriptions, temples, and sculptures pertaining to the Pārśvanātha cult. In Karnataka, as also in other parts of Southern India, the sculptures installed in the *sanctum sanctorum* are of stone. The uniqueness of Karnataka is that the worship of Pārśvanātha is attested to in all ages after Jainism had secured a firm foothold.

NOTES AND REFERENCES

1. B.R. Gopal (ed.), *Epigraphica Carnatica,* Vol. II (Rev.), pp. 3 ff.
2. *Ibid.*. *Corpus of Kadamba Inscriptions,* p. 35; *cf.* also P.B. Desai, *Jainism in South India and some Jaina Epigraphs,* Sholapur 1957, p. 97.
3. *Ibid.*, p. 149. At Bādāmī (Bijapur District), the rock cut cave IV of the Vātāpi-Calukya period (*c.* A.D. 600) contains Jaina sculptures of all *tīrthaṅkaras* seemingly added in the Hoysaḷa period. However, there is no contemporaneous epigraph in the cave.
4. Desai, *Jainism.*, p. 149.
5. N.L. Rao (ed.), *A.R. Ep.*, 1950-51, No. B. 67.

6. The details of date seem to correspond to December 18, A.D. 1027. The *tithi pāḍiva* ended on the previous day. Dakṣiṇāyanasaṁkramaṇa, however, occurred on December 24.
7. N.L. Rao (ed.), 1950-51, B.25. The findspot of the record (which is now in the Prince of Wales Museum, Bombay), is in all probability Honvāḍ, Bijapur District. References to *bhujaṅgarāja* and *mahānāga* in the paper read in this Seminar by Prof. M.A. Dhaky strengthens the point that the reference to *mahānāga* in this inscription is to the serpent king Dharaṇendra behind the image of Pārśvanātha.
8. Desai, p. 144. The Cālukya emperor mentioned in this record is Someśvara II.
9. *Cf.* J.F. Fleet and R.C. Temple (ed.), *Indian Antiquary,* Vol. XVIII, pp. 75 ff; also Desai, *ibid.*, p. 143.
10. Desai, *ibid.*, p. 144. *Cf. South Indian Inscriptions,* Vol. XI, Part II, Ins. No. 140. The place is also referred to as Droṇikāgrāma, Droṇīpura, Droṇikapura, and Doṇi.
11. Desai, *ibid.*, p. 321 ff.
12. *Ibid.*, p. 350, Text line 3.
13. *Ibid.*, pp. 183 ff.
14. *Ibid.*, p. 185.
15. *Ibid.*, p. 186.
16. *Ibid.*, p. 192.
17. *Ibid.*, pp. 192 ff.
18. *Ibid.*, pp. 241 ff.
19. G.S. Gai (ed.), *A.R. Ep.*, 1963-64, Nos. B 361-62. This place is situated in Hassan District.

PĀRŚVANĀTHA IN FIGURAL ART OF KARNATAKA

A. Sundara

Antiquity

Traditionally, Jainism is believed to have begun to be spread in Karnataka with the arrival of Śruta Kēvalin Bhadrabāhu along with Prabhācandra (*EC.* Vol.II; 1973: pp. xlii-iv) believed to be Candragupta, the Mauryan emperor (*c.* B.C. 325-301), together with a host of disciples in Śravaṇa Belgoḷa (Hassan District), the most sacred and prominent Jaina centre in South India even to this day. However, the interpretation of the concerned epigraphs and literary notices do not clearly lead to such conclusions. The earliest known references to the erection of temples, *basadis*, and consecration of Jina images in Karnataka are the early Kadamba records, copper plate as well as lithic charters, ranging from the period of Kakusthavarmā (*c.* A.D. 405-430) to Harivarmā (*c.* A.D. 519-530). They (Gopal 1985; Nos. 3, 8, 9, 13, 16, 22, 23, 24, 29, 36 & 37) state about either the construction of a Jinālaya or grants to them by the ruling monarchs, often at the request of their officers rather than on their own initiative.[1] In this context, excepting two records, all other invoke the *Tīrthaṅkara* usually as *bhagavān jinendra* and in the text as *bhagavadarhat.* The temples, too, are simply described as *arhadāyatana/ devālaya/ śālā* and *caityālaya.* In this context there is no specific mention of any of the 24 *Tīrthaṅkaras.* Even an attempt of contextual interpretations of the invocatory verses or the relevant expressions in the texts, does not seem to indicate any particular Jina as the descriptive attributes therein are common to all *Tīrthaṅkaras.*

Of the two records mentioning *Tīrthaṅkara's* names, that (No.3) of the Kākusthavarmā ends with "*Namo Namaḥ Ṛṣabhāya Namaḥ*". But the record registers a grant of land to the king's general Śrutakīrti from Kheṭa village belonging to holy Arhats. There is no mention of any specific *caityālaya.* However, it may be deduced that there were *caityālayas* for the Arhat Ṛṣabha also in this period in the Kadamba territory. For during the subsequent Vātāpi-Cālukya and Rāṣṭrakūṭa periods, depiction of the images of Ṛṣabha, Pārśva, and Vardhamāna Mahāvīra was frequent. Images relating to other *Tīrthaṅkaras,* of the Vātāpi-Cālukya period, however, have not so far come to light.

The other Kadamba copper-plate charter (No. 29), of Harivarmā, speaks of the grant of "Vasanta-vāṭikā" village in Suddi-Kundūru Viṣaya by the king to the

"Arhadāyatana" got built by Mṛgeśavarmā in Palāśikā, modern Halśi (Khanapur Taluk, Belgaum District). Mṛgeśavarmā caused to be built a Jinālaya in Palāśikā and granted 33 *nivartanas* of land extending from the river Mātṛsaṛt up to the Ingiṇi-saṁgama, to Dāmakīrti the Bhojaka (officiating priest) and Jiyanta the Āyuktaka for the Jaina ascetics of the Yāpanīya, Nirgrantha, and Kūrcaka sects. Harivarmā's record ends with salutation "*Namōrhate Vardhamānāya*" (No. 13). Possibly, therefore, Mṛgeśavarmā's *āyatana* was dedicated to Jina Vardhamāna.

If the frequency of occurrence of Jina Ṛṣabha and Vardhamāna in the Cālukyan and Rāṣṭrakūṭa periods may be taken as symptomatic of their probable still earlier representation in Karnataka, it may be expected that, in the early Kadamba period which was no less favourable to Jainism, these two Jinas may have been under warship as has been briefly discussed above. Depiction of Pārśvanātha during this period is also probable. There is, in point of fact, an indirect hint supporting this probability. Guḍnāpura inscription of Ravivarmā (pp. 81-91) refers to "Padmāvatyālaya" in Kallīli village. If Huṁca (ancient Pombuca, Shimoga Dist.), another important Jaina centre with several Jaina *basadis* (including that of Pārśvanātha) in Karnataka and celebrated for the Padmāvatī temple is any guide[2], in Kallīli also there must have been a Jinālaya dedicated to Pārśvanātha whose *śāsana-dēvatā* happens to be Padmāvatī. If this surmise is correct, then this is the earliest known indication regarding Pārśvanātha in sculpture. The village has not been correctly identified. During my exploration in Halśi, I found only one *basadi*, of *c.* 11th century A.D., but of a plan of an early tradition, consisting of a *garbhagṛha* and a *gūḍhamaṇḍapa* similar to a few of the early Cālukyan temples in Aihoḷe, such as for instance the *Tārābasappaguḍi*. It is likely that this temple was perhaps of the early Kadamba founding and originally may have been in brick. In the later period stone replaced the brick, more or less following the original plan. In a neighbouring later building is a well moulded stone *pīṭhikā* for a *Tīrthaṅkara* image, of rather an unusual type, perhaps of pre-Cālukyan period. Elsewhere in the village, in a Garuḍa temple, there is a *siṁhapīṭha* of a *Tīrthaṅkara* image. Roughly a kilometer east of the village is a large ancient site at the foot of a hill within a mud fortification, locally known as "Bōḍke Ṭembe" and identified as ancient Palāśikā by me. Traces of brick structures at this site indicate that it was a town with numerous brick buildings which possibly had included the Jinālayas referred to in the inscriptions. Further explorations and excavations at this site and Kallīli area may reveal the actual remains of Jinālayas with icons of *Tīrthaṅkaras* including probably Pārśvanātha of the early Kadamba period.

Pārśvanātha in Sculpture

From the Vātāpi-Cālukya period onwards, Jinālayas were erected in progressively larger number. *Tīrthaṅkaras* are shown exclusively in two forms; in *khaḍgāsana* (*kāyavyutsarga*) or in *padmāsana*. In the *khaḍgāsana* or *kāyavyutsarga* form, Jina Pārśva is usually flanked by the seated or standing Dharaṇa Yakṣa and Yakṣī Padmāvatī; and above the Nāga hoods is *mukkoḍe* or *chatratraya*, triple umbrella. Near the shoulders are depicted *cāmaras* on both the sides, though this is not an invariate feature. In Gulbarga region, on the central part of the chest may be delineated the *śrīvatsa* symbol; but this is a rare feature to meet with.

In the *padmāsana* form, usually the *Tīrthaṅkara* is shown as seated on a seat with pillow behind against the *makara-paṭṭikā* as the back. The image is flanked by Indras as *cāmara*-bearers. In this case, almost invariably, and occasionally in the other form, the Yakṣa and Yakṣī are separately installed on the sides of the doorway to the *garbhagṛha*, and thus in the *antarāla*-vestibule of the *caityālaya*. The images in these two forms are generally consecrated as cult-icons in the *garbhagṛhas*.

Images of Pārśvanātha in *padmāsana* are depicted as *lalāṭabimba* at the central block of the lintel of a doorframe, but generally without the Yakṣa and Yakṣī figures for lack of space. The Jina, in rather rare instances, is also shown in *khaḍgāsana* on the exterior wall (Hallūr temple of the Rāṣṭrakūṭa period, Nittūr temple of the Cālukya period, Śāntinātha-basadi in Jīnanāthapura near Śravaṇa Belgoḷa and of the Hoysaḷa period), and as one of the four *Tīrthaṅkaras* in the Caturmukha-Sahasrakūṭa representation in the Śaṅkha-basadi, Lakṣmeśvara (Shirahaṭṭi Taluk, Dharwad District). The *khaḍgāsana-mūrti* form also figures at the centre (or alternatively also the *padmāsana*) along with the other *Tīrthaṅkaras* in similar posture surrounding the central image in *caturviṁśati-paṭṭas*.

Very rarely indeed, the main episodes from the life of Pārśvanātha are carved in a narrative vein. The only one of its kind is probably a series of such panels in the columnar hall in front of the Pārśvanātha temple in Halebiḍu, known as "Vijaya Pāraśvanātha" (A.D. 1133) founded by Boppadeva in memory of his father Gaṅgarāja, a minister and general to the Hoysaḷa king Viṣṇuvardhana[3].

Images of Pārśvanātha in the two usual forms with some variations in regard to the auxiliary features, especially the first two, are most commonly found in the main Jaina centres: Bādāmī, Aihoḷe, Kambadahalli, Śravaṇa Belgoḷa, Huṁca, Shimoga area, and Mudabidre (Karkala) where there are numerous Jaina *basadis*. However, a few of the Pārśvanātha sculptures in Bādāmī-Aihoḷe, Huṁca, Śravaṇa Belgoḷa and in Bilicoḍu are endowed with some special features which render them more dramatic and interestingly significant. Excepting the Bādāmī-Aihoḷe sculptural forms in the rock-cut Jaina caves (*c.* A.D. 600), I am not aware if similar sculptures of the other forms are met outside Karnataka.

Pārśvanātha in Bādāmī - Aihoḷe

In Bādāmī in the *layana* (excavated rock temple) IV, are fine sculptures of Bāhubali and Pārśvanātha facing each other, carved as they are on the shorter walls of the *vīthikā* or *paṭṭaśālā*-forelobby. Generally, above Pārśvanātha's (and also Supārśvanātha's) head is the canopy of *nāga*'s five or seven hoods, one of the distinct features of identification of the respective *Tīrthaṅkaras*. In the Bādāmī instance (Plate 64) the canopy is depicted as having five hoods. A female attendant to the right of the *Tīrthaṅkara* is holding the parasol over the canopy, a feature occurring in the Cālukyan sculpture, but disappearing in later periods. She also has *nāga*-hood over the crown, and is therefore most probably an early form of Padmāvatī. To the left is seated a royal person in *rājalīlāsana*. Above the parasol are the *vidyādhara*-angels showering flowers. To the left is indistinctly carved Kamaṭha or Śaṁvara attempting to hit the meditating Jina. The image of Pārśvanātha in an identical position in the *paṭṭaśālā* of the Jaina Cave at Aihoḷe shows Śaṁbaraạ, Padmāvatī (having her own *nāga*-canopy), and five-hooded Dareṇendra. (*See* here M.N. Tiwari, Plate 54.)

The *nāga* hoods of the canopy are five; hence the *Tīrthaṅkara* has to be identified as Pārśvanātha in view of the accompanying Yakṣa and Yakṣī, indeed an indisputable criterion in determination. The presence of Kamaṭha further supports the identification. In the early sculptural depictions, there largely are sculptures of Vardhamāna Mahāvīra and Pārśvanātha better known to history. The delineation of the other traditionally known *Tīrthaṅkaras* in sculpture apparently is later.[4] In the Cālukya period, therefore, the need of standardizing the number of *nāga* hoods in connection with Pārśvanātha was not felt. It was in the wake of regular sculptural representation of Supārśvanātha in the subsequent period, who like Pārśvanātha, is characterised by *nāga*-canopy, there arose a need of distinguishing him from the other. This was met with by the depiction of a particular number of hoods, Supārśvanātha being an earlier *Tīrthaṅkara*, the number of hoods in his case is appropriately made seven in contrast to Pārśvanātha's five.

If these observations are acceptable, then in Bādāmī-Aihoḷe area are the earliest available representation of Pārśvanātha, radiating as they do a kind quiescent majesty.

The Pārśvanātha Sculpture, Humca

Pombuca or Humca is one of the greater Jaina centres in Karnataka, even now a pilgrim centre known for the Padmāvatī temple, worshipped by the non-Jaina communities as well. Historically, it was the capital of the Śāntaras from the eighth century onwards, who got built many *caityālayas* dedicated to Pārśvanātha, Bāhubali, and a Pañcakūṭa-basadi collectively during 9th-12th centuries A.D. (M.A. Dhaky has studied the sculptural wealth of this place that led him to identify the art as distinct and to describe it as "Śāntara school of art".[5])

In the first hall of the Pārśvanātha-basadi are two almost identical, large, sculptural steles (3.0 × 1.0 m. approximately) of Pārśvanātha. They exhibit a further elaboration of the *upasarga*-theme (Plate 65) first noticed at Bādāmī. The *Tīrthaṅkaras* are in *khaḍgāsana*. The *nāga* raising his body spirally behind him, spreads his hoods over the Jina's head. Demon Kamaṭha, with a host of his attendants with stones and sticks, is shown fiercely attacking the Jina from all sides. But Pārśvanātha remains unperturbed like the sea receiving roaring and rushing rivers only to be merged in it, loosing their identities, indeed an excellent composition and equally a masterly portrayal in which every figure appears distinctly in different mood and posture.

The Pārśvanātha - basadi, Śravaṇa Belgoḷa

On the summit of Candragiri, Pārśvanātha's is one of the several *basadis* standing to the south beside the "Kattale" and "Candragupta" basadis. The plan of the Pārśvanātha-basadi is somewhat unusual. Externally, the width of the *garbhagṛha* is as much as that of the *gūḍhamaṇḍapa*. (Generally, the width is kept to half of the *gūḍhamaṇḍapa* elsewhere. But rarely a *basadi* of the type of Pārśvanātha is found at Aihoḷe (i.e. Caranti Maṭh group), Ron (Dharwad District). In such cases it is found that there are two small chambers on the sides of the *garbhagṛha* meant for storing valuables, articles of worship, or the *Tīrthaṅkara* images made of precious stones such as crystal, jasper, lapis-lazuli, etc., accessible only from the *garbhagṛha* though a small opening in the side walls. But in the *basadi* in Śravaṇa Belgoḷa there are no such indications of the existence of side chambers. Whether in course of time the original openings were later permanently sealed is a matter to be investigated. But what is really noteworthy here is the colossal figure of Pārśvanātha as well as the mode of providing entry to the *garbhagṛha*. Here a severely plain and narrow doorway occurs, only a little wider than the maximum width of the image. Consequently, devotees in the *gūḍhamaṇḍapa* feel that the colossal image is set up as though in a tall niche, somewhat reminiscent of the colossal Buddha in the rock excavated niche in Bamiyan (Afghanistan). There is no doorframe as such consisting of various *śākhās* like the one in the neighbouring Cāmuṇḍarāya-basadi. Carving of the doorway with ornate *śākhās* has been deliberately avoided here so that the attention of the devotees is focused entirely on the Jina image. The *nāga*-hoods look both realistic and vivid (Plate 66). To the right, near the hoods, is a pedestal projected from the wall. With the help of a ladder the priest/devotees can get on it and perform the *abhiṣēka* rite. As mentioned above, usually the images of the respective Yakṣa and Yakṣī in the *basadis* are placed on the sides of the *garbhagṛha*-doorway in the *antarāla*. But here this feature has been eliminated. Instead, on the side walls of the entrance, are drawn in outline in red colour, the figures of the Yakṣa and Yakṣī; they were obviously not meant to be sculpted. Carving of the images along the lines in the walls would have created deep niches that would have weakened the walls. This mode of construction and image-placement had been resorted probably to make the Jina image as the sole focus of attention. Such mode of representing Pārśvanātha has not been noticed elsewhere.

A rare form of Pārśvanātha sculpture from Bilicoḍu

This is indeed a noteworthy sculpture from Bilicoḍu (Chitradurga District) of *c.* 11th century A.D., located in the outskirts of the village in a modern grave-yard. Obviously it is brought from some Jaina temple in the village and installed on a platform in the present place. (It is about 70 cm high and 30 cm broad.) It depicts the Jina in *khaḍgāsana.* On the sides are shown seated figures of Yakṣa and Yakṣī. The unique feature of the sculpture is the representation of two entwined *nāgas* like those in any other Nāga sculpture. In the single loop so formed by the Nāgas bodies and between the hoods are medallions showing fully blossomed lotuses. The *Tīrthaṅkara's* feet is in between the hoods just above the lotus and the Yakṣa and Yakṣī are represented right on the top of the hoods. Apparently, the sculpture has the combination of a *Tīrthaṅkara* and the Nāgas of the type of the Brahmanical sculptural representational tradition. The combination looks unusual, even strange ! A careful perusal of the Jaina *Purāṇas,* however, explains this mix up. In the *Pārśvanātha-purāṇa,* it is narrated that Pārśvanātha, born as he was in Kāśī, and though he was a prince, was uninterested in mundane life and was inclined more towards the quest of the Self. One day, while he was wandering about on the bank of the river Gaṅgā, saw some ascetics performing austerities in front of a burning hearth. They were feeding the hearth with fire-wood. Pārśvanātha questioned them why they were harming the creatures. Surprised and angered they asked him to show the creatures that were said to have been harmed. Pārśvanātha took out a burning fire-wood from the hearth and split it with an axe. Within the burrow of the wood were found two serpents male and female already partially roasted struggling for life. Realising that they would not survive, Pārśvanātha exhorted the *mantra* of *Pañcanamaskāra* (i.e. Reverence to *Arhats, Siddhas, Ācāryas, Upādhyāyas,* and *Sādhus*) and left the place grief-striken. Later, while he was engrossed deeply in meditation in the forest of Ahicchatrā, a semi-divine being Kamaṭha, his former enemy, saw him and remembering the enmity of the previous existence, proceeded to torment Pārśva by throwing at him brick, stone, and the like. But Pārśvanātha remained unshaken and unperturbed. Thus failed Kamaṭha, next conjured up a downpour with thunder so as to drown him. In the meanwhile the two serpents which were led to the heavenly path at the time of their death, had been born as Dharaṇendra Yakṣa and Padmāvatī Yakṣī in the *Pātālaloka.* No sooner did they know about the calamity inflicted on their guru than did they rush to the spot of *upasarga* to help him. Padmāvatī supported him on her crown and Dharaṇendra spread his hoods over his head. And at that moment Pārśvanātha got enlightenment.

In the light of the above Purāṇic story, the sculpture described represents obviously Pārśvanātha with Dharaṇendra and Padmāvatī and the two serpents beneath them in it indicate to the immediately past life of the Yakṣa and Yakṣī.

Some other aspects during the Cālukya and Hoysaḷa periods

In northern Karnataka during the Kalyāṇa-Cālukya period, the back-seat of Jina Pārśvanātha seated in *padmāsana,* shows the finely carved *makara-tōraṇa.*

Under the Hoysaḷas, in south Karnataka, the Jina images in general are characterised by the *parikara*-background intricately carved with minutest details, especially of the *mukkoḍe* under which the Jina is represented in *khaḍgāsana* and also the ornaments of the Indras on the sides attending upon the meditating Jina.

In the Jina sculptures of the Kalyāṇa-Cālukya and Hoysaḷa periods, the difference is only in the degree of excellence connected with an intricate carving of the *mukkoḍe* and the Indras as *cāmaradharas.* Besides, in many cases, the spiral hair ringlets above the head are artistically rendered. The spiral body of the snake and the seven hoods are realistically depicted by detailing the skin-scales and the naturalistic treatment of the rest of the body. But the narrational aspect of the Jina's portrayal with Yakṣa and Yakṣī engaged in the protective action and the Kamaṭha charging with stones etc. are no longer represented. The Yakṣa and Yakṣī are depicted as seated in *padmāsana* or in a standing posture in an attractive *dvibhaṅga*. The Dharaṇendra and Padmāvatī in *dvibhaṅga* from the Pārśvanātha-basadi in Halebiḍu are instances of fine workmanship. However, even when graceful, they lack the dynamism and power of depiction of the preceding examples.

In the Vijayanagara period, the erection of *jinālayas* was largely in the Ghāṭ-coastal region in Biḷgi-Gersoppā-Bhatkal and the neighbouring Mudabidre-Kārkala tracts. These were foundations largely by the Vijayanagara-feudatories. Generally, the depiction of the *Tīrthaṅkaras* is somewhat rigid, lacking as they do the supplementary details and artistic innovations. The dramatic representation of the surroundings, the unshaken and serene meditative personality of Pārśvanātha in the sculptures of the early period degenerated first into ornamental and next into ossified form as the image probably of the Caṇḍogra-Pārśvanātha from the old Gersoppa site illustrates (Plate 67).

NOTES AND REFERENCES

1. This had been the case not only in early Kadamba times but also, and even with greater frequency, in all subsequent periods in Karnataka.
2. The main deity today seen in the Huṁca temple is Pārśvanātha, Padmāvatī sitting next to the Jina on the altar.
3. These need to be published.
4. However, in the Kuṣāṇa period inscriptions at Mathurā, names of such Jinas as Sambhavanātha and Munisuvrata — the third and the 20th *tīrthaṅkara* — do figure. Ariṣṭanemi, the 22nd, also frequently figures there as he can be identified by the presence, on his flanks, of Vāsudeva and Balarāma. There may be other *tīrthaṅkaras* in the lot there; but the absence at that date of the *lāñchana*-cognizance does not help identifying these other Jinas.
5. For his paper *see* here the bibliographical references.

SELECT BIBLIOGRAPHY

1. *Annual Report of the Mysore Archaeological Department* (MAR), 1930. Directorate of Archaeology and Museums, Government of Karnataka, Mysore 1934.
2. M.A. Dhaky, "Śāntara Sculpture," *Journal of the Indian Society of Oriental Art*, New Series, Vol. IV (1971-72), 78-96.
3. Madhusudan Dhanky (M.A. Dhaky), "Gersappā-nāñ Jinamandiro," (Gujarātī), *Svādhyāya*, Vol. XIX, No. 1 (1982).

4. *Epigraphia Carnatica* (EC), Vol. II (Revised edition), Institute of Kannada Studies, University of Mysore, Mysore 1973.
5. B.R. Gopal, *Corpus of Kadamba Inscriptions*, Vol. I, 1985. Kadamba Institute of Cultural Studies, Sirsi (North Kanara Dist., Karnataka).

LIST OF ILLUSTRATIONS

(All illustrations are published here by the courtesy and kindness, American Institute of Indian Studies, Center for Art & Archaeology, Ramnagar, Varanasi.)

राजस्थान में पार्श्वनाथ के तीर्थ स्थान

महोपाध्याय विनयसागर

वर्तमान अवसर्पिणी काल के चौबीस तीर्थंकरों में से मुख्यत: केवल तीन तीर्थंकरों के लिये ही आगम-साहित्य में नाम के साथ विशेषण प्राप्त होते हैं — ऋषभदेव के लिये ''अरहा कोसलिए'' अर्हत् कौशलिक, पार्श्वनाथ के लिये ''अरहा पुरिसादाणीए'' अर्हत् पुरुषादानीय, और महावीर के लिए ''समणे भगवं महावीरे'' श्रवण भगवान् महावीर । यश नाम कर्म की अत्यधिक अतिशयता के कारण समग्र तीर्थंकरों में से केवल पुरुषादानीय पार्श्वनाथ का नाम ही अत्यधिक संस्मरणीय, संस्तवनीय और अर्चनीय रहा है । अधिष्ठायक धरणेन्द्र और पद्मावती देवी की जागृति एवं चमत्कार प्रदर्शन के कारण वीतराग होते हुए भी मनोभिलाषा पूरक के रूप में पार्श्व का नाम ही प्रभुखता को धारण किये हुए है । यही कारण है कि मन्त्र साहित्य और स्तोत्र साहित्य तो विपुलता के साथ पार्श्व के नाम से ही समृद्ध हैं ।

सामान्यत: तीर्थों की गणना में वे ही स्थल आते हैं जहाँ तीर्थंकरों के पांचों कल्याणक—च्यवन, जन्म, दीक्षा, ज्ञान, निर्वाण—हुए हों । सिद्धतीर्थों में उनकी गणना की जाती है जहाँ कोई-न-कोई महापुरुष सिद्ध, बुद्ध, और मुक्त हुए हों अथवा विचरण किया हो । किन्तु अतिशय तीर्थ या चमत्कारी तीर्थ वे कहलाते हैं जहाँ कोई भी महापुरुष सिद्ध तो नहीं हुए हों, परन्तु उन क्षेत्रों में स्थापित उन महापुरुषों/तीर्थंकरो की मूर्तियां अतिशय चमत्कारपूर्ण होती हों ।

भगवान पार्श्वनाथ के कई तीर्थ तो उनके जन्म से पूर्व एवं विद्यमानता में ही स्थापित हो गये थे । परम्परागत श्रुति के अनुसार आचार्य जिनप्रभसूरि ने **विविध तीर्थकल्प** नामक ग्रन्थ (र० सं० १३८९) में लिखा है-

१. दशग्रीव रावण के समय में निर्मित पार्श्वनाथ प्रतिमा ही कालान्तर में श्रीपुर में स्थापित हुई, वही अन्तरिक्ष पार्श्वनाथ के नाम से प्रसिद्ध है ।

२. भगवान नेमिनाथ के समय में कृष्ण और जरासन्ध में भीषण युद्ध हुआ था । इस संग्राम में जरासन्ध ने जरा विद्या के प्रयोग से कृष्ण की सेना को निश्चेष्ट कर दिया था । उस समय पन्नगेन्द्र से पार्श्व प्रभु की प्रतिमा प्राप्त की और उसके न्हवण जल/स्नान जल के छिटकाव से कृष्ण की सेना पूर्णत: स्वस्थ हो गई थी । वही स्थल शंखेश्वर पार्श्वनाथ के नाम से तीर्थ रूप में प्रसिद्ध हुआ और आज भी इसकी प्रसिद्धि चरम सीमा पर है ।

३. स्तम्भन पार्श्वनाथ कल्प के अनुसार भगवान् मुनिसुव्रत स्वामी के समय में निर्मित पार्श्व प्रतिमा ही नागराज से नवम वासुदेव श्रीकृष्ण ने प्राप्त की थी । यही प्रतिमा कालान्तर में नवांगीटीकाकार अभयदेवसूरि ने सेढी नदी के तट पर भूमि से प्रकट कर स्तम्भनपुर (थांभणा) में स्थापित की थी; जो आज भी तीर्थ स्थल के रूप में प्रसिद्ध है ।

इसी **विविध तीर्थकल्प** के अन्तर्गत ''अहिच्छत्रानगरीकल्प'' और ''कलिकुण्ड कुर्कुटेश्वरकल्प'' में लिखा है कि प्रभु पार्श्वनाथ दीक्षा ग्रहण कर छद्मस्तावस्थ में विचरण कर रहे थे, तभी ये दोनों तीर्थ क्षेत्र स्थापित हो गए थे। अर्थात् उनकी विद्यमानता में ही ये दोनों स्थल तीर्थ के रूप में मान्य हो गए थे ।

भारत के प्रत्येक प्रदेश में पुरुषादानीय पार्श्वनाथ के अतिशयपूर्ण एवं विख्यात कई-कई तीर्थ स्थल हैं। जिनप्रभसूरि ने ही ''चतुरशीति महातीर्थनाम संग्रह कल्प'' में पार्श्वनाथ के १५ महातीर्थों का उल्लेख किया है—

१. अजाहरा में नवनिधि पार्श्वनाथ, २. संभाल में भवभयहर, ३. फलवर्धि में विश्वकल्पलता, ४. करहेड़ा में उपसर्गहर, ५. अहिच्छत्रा में त्रिभुवनभानु, ६-७. कलिकुण्ड और नागह्रद में श्री पार्श्वनाथ, ८. कुर्कुटेश्वर में विश्वगज, ९. महेन्द्र पर्वत पर छाया, १०. ओंकार पर्वत पर सहस्रफणा, ११. वाराणसी में भव्य पुष्करावर्तक, १२. महाकाल के अन्तर में पाताल चक्रवर्ती, १३. मथुरा में कल्पद्रुम, १४. चम्पा में अशोक और, १५. मलयगिरि पर श्री पार्श्वनाथ भगवान् हैं। साथ ही पार्श्व के दस तीर्थों पर कल्प भी लिखे हैं ।

वि० सं० ०१६६८ में विनयकुशल ने गोडी पार्श्वनाथ स्तवन में तथा १८८१ में खुशलविजय ने पार्श्वनाथ छन्द में प्रभु पार्श्वनाथ के १०८ तीर्थों का उल्लेख किया है । वहीं धीरविमल के शिष्य नयविमल ने पार्श्वनाथ के १३५ तीर्थ-मन्दिरों का वर्णन किया है ।

इस प्रकार देखा जाए तो चिन्ताचूरक, चिन्तमणिरत्न के समान मनोवांछापूरक पार्श्वप्रभु के नाम से वर्तमान समय में भारतवर्ष में शताधिक तीर्थ हैं, सहस्र के लगभग मन्दिर हैं और मूर्तियों की तो गणना भी सम्भव नहीं है; क्योंकि प्रत्येक मन्दिर में पाषाण एवं धातु की अनेकों प्रतिमाएं प्राप्त होती हैं ।

राजस्थान प्रदेश में तीर्थंकरों विशेषत: पार्श्वनाथ के पाँचों कल्याणकों में से कोई कल्याणक नहीं होने से यहाँ के पुरुषादानीय पार्श्वनाथ के सारे तीर्थं क्षेत्र अतिशय/चमत्कारी तीर्थों की गणना में ही आते हैं । राजस्थान में प्रभु पार्श्वनाथ के नाम से निम्न स्थल तीर्थ के रूप में अत्यधिक विख्यात हैं; जिनका संक्षिप्त परिचय अकारानुक्रम से प्रस्तुत है ।

१. **करहेड़ा पार्श्वनाथ**—उदयपुर-चित्तौड़ रेलवे मार्ग पर करहेड़ा स्टेशन है । स्टेशन से एक कि०मी० पर यह गाँव है । यहाँ उपसर्गहर पार्श्वनाथ की श्यामवर्णी प्रतिमा विराजमान है । नाहार जी के लेखानुसार सं० १०३९ में संडेरकगच्छीय यशोभद्रसूरि ने पार्श्वनाथ बिम्ब की प्रतिष्ठा की थी । यहाँ १३०३, १३०६, १३४१ आदि के प्राचीन मूर्तिलेख भी प्राप्त हैं । सुकृतसागर काव्य के अनुसार मांड्वगढ़ के पेथड़ और झांझण ने यहाँ के प्राचीन मंदिर का जीर्णोद्धार करवा कर सात मंजिला भव्य मंदिर बन्धवाया था, किन्तु आज वह प्राप्त नहीं है । सं० १४३१ में खरतरगच्छ के आचार्यों के द्वारा बड़ा महोत्सव हुआ और सं० १६५६ में इसका जीर्णोद्धार हुआ था और वर्तमान में फक्कड वल्लभदत्तविजय जी के उपदेश से जीर्णोद्धार हुआ है।

जिनप्रभसूरि रचित फलवर्दि पार्श्वनाथ कल्प के अनुसार यह करहेड़ा पार्श्वनाथ तीर्थ प्रसिद्ध तीर्थों में से था । खरतरगच्छ की पिघलक शाखा का यहाँ विशेष प्रभाव रहा है ।

मेवाड़ के तीर्थों में पार्श्वनाथ का यह एकमात्र प्राचीन तीर्थ है ।

२. **कापरड़ा पार्श्वनाथ**—जोधपुर से बिलाड़ा-अजमेर रोड़ पर यह तीर्थ है । प्राचीन उल्लेखों में इसका नाम कर्पटहेडक, कापड़हेड़ा मिलता है । जैतारण निवासी सेठ भानाजी भंडारी ने भूमि से ९९ फीट ऊँचा चार मंजिला यह विशालकाय शिखरबद्ध मन्दिर बनवाया था । इस मन्दिर की उन्नतता और विशालता की तुलना कुमारपाल भूपति निर्मापित तारांगा के मन्दिर से की जा सकती है । यह मन्दिर चतुर्मुख है और मूलनायक स्वयम्भू पार्श्वनाथ हैं । मूलनायक की मूर्ति जिनचन्द्रसूरि ने सं० १६७४ पौष बदि १० को भूमि

से प्राप्त की थी । इसकी प्रतिष्ठा वि० सं० १६७८ वैशाख सूदि पूर्णमा को खरतरगच्छ की आद्यपक्षीय शाखा के जिनदेवसूरि के पट्टधर पंचायण भट्टारक जिनचन्द्रसूरि ने करवाई थी । मूलनायक की चारों मूर्तियां परिकरयुक्त है ।

३. चंवलेश्वर पार्श्वनाथ—जहाजपुर तहसील में पारोली से ६ मि०मी० की दूरी पर वर्तमान में प्रसिद्ध चंवलेश्वर पार्श्वनाथ का मन्दिर है । अधुना श्वेताम्बर-ध्गिम्बर के विवाद में उलझा हुआ है।

पं० कल्याणसागर रचित पार्श्वनाथ चैत्य परिपाटी में, मेघविजयोपाध्याय कृत पार्श्वनाथ नाममाला में और जिनहर्षगणि कृत पार्श्वनाथ १०८ नाम स्तवन में इस तीर्थ का उल्लेख प्राप्त है।

४. चित्तौड़ सोमचिन्तामणि पार्श्वनाथ—राजगच्छीय हीरकलश द्वारा १५वीं शती में रचित मेदपाटदेश तीर्थमाला स्तव पद्य १६ के अनुसार यहाँ श्री सोमचिन्तामणि पार्श्वनाथ का तीर्थ स्वरूप विशाल मन्दिर विद्यमान था, किन्तु आज नामोनिशान भी नहीं है ।

उत्खनन में प्राप्त कमलदल चित्र काव्य मय शिलापट्ट के अनुसार अनुमानतः ११६२ में जिनवल्लभगणि (जिवल्लभसूरि) ने पार्श्वनाथविधि चैत्य की प्रतिष्ठा की थी।

५. जीरावाला पार्श्वनाथ—खराड़ी से आबू-देलवाड़ा के मार्ग पर ३० कि०मी० और अणादरा गाँव से १३-१४ कि०मी० की दूरी पर यह गाँव है । इसका प्राचीन नाम जीरिकापल्ली, जीरापल्ली, जीरावल्ली प्राप्त होता है । उपदेश सप्तति के अनुसार ११०९ एवं **वीरवंशावली** के अनुसार ११९१ में श्रेष्ठि धांधल ने देवीत्री पर्वत की गुफा से प्राप्त प्रतिमा की इस गाँव में नवीन मंदिर बनवाकर स्थापना की थी और प्रतिष्ठा अजितदेवसूरि ने की थी । यह तीर्थ जीरावला पार्श्वनाथ के नाम से प्रसिद्ध हुआ । अलाउद्दीन खिलजी द्वारा १३६८ में यह प्रतिमा खंडित कर दी गई। विलेपन करने पर भी नवअंग (भाग) स्पष्ट दिखाई देते थे । खंडित मूर्ति मुख्य स्थान में शोभा नहीं देती, अतः परवर्ती आचार्यों ने मुख्य स्थान पर नेमिनाथ की मूर्ति स्थापित कर दी और इस मूर्ति को दाईं ओर विराजमान कर दी ।

उपदेश तरंगिणी (प० १८) के अनुसार संधपति पेथड़ शाह और झांझण शाह ने यहाँ एक विशाल मन्दिर बनवाया था और महेश्वर कवि रचित **काव्य मनोहर** (सर्ग ७ श्लो० ३२) के अनुसार सोनगिरा श्रीमालवंशीय श्रेष्टि झांझक्ण के पुत्र संधपति आल्हराज ने भी इस महातीर्थ पर उन्नत तोरण युक्त विशाल मन्दिर बनवाया था, किन्तु आज इनका कोई अता-पता नहीं है।

इस महातीर्थ की प्रसिद्धि इतनी अधिक हुई कि आज भी प्रतिष्ठा के समय भगवान की गद्दी पर विराजमान करने के पूर्व गद्दी पर जीरावला पार्श्वनाथ का मन्त्र लिखा जाता है । देलवाड़ा के सं० १४९१ के लेख के प्रारम्भ में ''नमो जीरावलाय'' लिखा है, जो इसकी प्रसिद्धि का सूचक है ।

जीरावाला नाम इतना अधिक विख्यात हुआ कि जीरावला पार्श्वनाथ के नाम से अनेकों स्थानों पर मन्दिर निर्माण हुए; जिनमें से मुख्य-मुख्य हैं — धाणेराव, नाडलाई, नंदोल, बतोल, सिरोही, गिरनार, घाटकोपर (बम्बई) आदि।

६. नवलखा पार्श्वनाथ—पाली मारवाड़ में नवलखा दरवाजा के पास बावन जिनालय वाला विशाल नवलखा पार्श्वनाथ का प्रसिद्ध मन्दिर है । इस स्थान का प्राचीन नाम पल्लिका, पल्ली था । सं० ११२४, ११७८, १२०१ के प्राप्त लेखानुसार मूलतः यह महावीर स्वामी का मन्दिर था । सं० १६८६ के लेखानुसार नवलखा मन्दिर का जीर्णोद्धार हुआ था और पुर्नप्रतिष्ठा के समय पार्श्वनाथ की सपरिवार मूर्ति स्थापित की गई थी।

७. नाकोड़ा पार्श्वनाथ—जोधपुर से बाड़मेर रेलवे के मध्य में बालोतरा स्टेशन से १० कि० मी० दूरी पर मेवानगर ग्राम में यह तीर्थ है । वस्तुत: ग्राम का नाम वीरमपुर या नगर था किन्तु महेवा और नगर का मिश्रण होकर यह स्थान अभी मेवानगर कहलाता है । नाकोड़ा ग्राम के तालाब से प्रकट इस पार्श्वनाथ प्रतिमा की इस स्थान पर स्थापना/प्रतिष्ठा अनुमानत: वि०सं० १५१२ में खरतरगच्छीय कीर्तिरत्नसूरि ने की थी । संस्थापक कीर्तिरत्नसूरि की मूर्ति भी (१५३६ में प्रतिष्ठित) मूल मण्डप के बाहर बायीं ओर के आले में विराजमान है । नाकोड़ा में प्रकटित होने के कारण ही नाकोड़ा पार्श्वनाथ के नाम से इसकी प्रसिद्धि हुई है । यहाँ के अधिष्ठायक भैरव भी नाकोड़ा भैरव के नाम से सारे भारत में विख्यात हैं । वर्तमान में श्रद्धालु यात्री भी ४००-५०० के लगभग प्रतिदिन आते हैं। राजस्थान के समस्त तीर्थों की तुलना में आय भी इसकी सर्वाधिक है । मन्दिर भी विशाल और रमणीय है । व्यवस्था भी सुन्दर है ।

८. नागफणा पार्श्वनाथ—यह मन्दिर उदयपुर में है । साराभाई म० नवाब की पुस्तक ''पुरिसादाणी श्री पार्श्वनाथजी'' के अनुसार महाराणा प्रताप ने धरणेन्द्र-पद्मावती सहित पार्श्वनाथ की आराधना से ही पिछले युद्धों में विजय प्राप्त कर इस मन्दिर का निर्माण करवाया था, जो नागफणा पार्श्वनाथ के नाम से आज भी प्रभावशाली माना जाता है ।

९. नागह्रद नवखण्डा पार्श्वनाथ—उदयपुर से २२ कि०मी० पर नागदा गाँव है । यहाँ वर्तमान में सं० १४९४ में खरतरगच्छीय जिनसागरसूरि प्रतिष्ठित शान्तिनाथ का मन्दिर है । किन्तु मुनिसुन्दरसूरि रचित नागह्रद तीर्थस्तोत्र, जिनप्रभसूरि के फलविधि पार्श्वनाथ तीर्थकल्प में नागह्रद पार्श्वनाथ के उल्लेख प्राप्त हैं। राजगच्छीय हीरकलश रचित (१५वीं शती) मेदपाट देश **तीर्थमाला-स्तव** पद्य ३ में नवखण्डा पार्श्वनाथ का उल्लेख है।

यहाँ पार्श्वनाथ का जीर्ण मन्दिर भी है । मंदिरस्थ मूर्ति के एक पभासण के नीचे ११९२ का लेख प्राप्त है ।

आलोक पार्श्वनाथ—नागदा में ही एकलिंग जी के मन्दिर के पास ही दिगम्बर परम्परा का आलोक पार्श्वनाथ का मन्दिर था जिसे समुद्रसूरि ने श्वेताम्बर तीर्थ के रूप में परिवर्तित कर दिया था । १७वीं शताब्दी से अनेकों श्वे० शिलालेख प्राप्त है ।

आलोक पार्श्वनाथ मंदिर का उल्लेख बिजोलिया के १२३६ वाले शिलालेख में भी प्राप्त है।

१०. फलवर्द्धि पार्श्वनाथ—मेड़ता रोड़ जंक्सन स्टेशन से एक फर्लांग की दूरी पर फलोधी नामक गाँव है जो फलौधी पार्श्वनाथ या मेड़ता फलौधी के नाम से मशहूर है । राजस्थान के प्राचीन तीर्थस्थानों में इसकी गणना की जाती है । जिनप्रभसूरि रचित फलवर्द्धि पार्श्वनाथकल्प के अनुसार मालवंशीय धांधल और ओसवाल वंशीय शिवकर ने भूमि से प्राप्त सप्तफला पार्श्वनाथ की प्रतिमा नवीन विशाल गगनस्पर्शी मन्दिर बनवाकर स्थापित की और इसकी प्रतिष्ठा वि०सं० ११८१ में राजगच्छ (धर्मघोषगच्छ) के शीलभद्रसूरि के शिष्य धर्मघोषसूरि ने की थी । सं० १२३३ में शहाबुद्दीन गौरी ने मूर्ति का अंग-भंग किया, तथापि प्राचीन एवं देवाधिष्ठित होने के कारण यही मूर्ति मूलनायक के रूप में ही रही ।

पुरातन-प्रबन्ध-संग्रह के अनुसार पारस श्रेष्ठि ने वाद विजेता वादीदेवसूरि के तत्त्वावधान में इस गगनचुम्बी मन्दिर का निर्माण ११९९ में करवाया और इसकी प्रतिष्ठा वादिदेवसूरि के पट्टधर मुनिचन्द्रसूरि ने १२०४ में करवाई ।

इस तीर्थ की महिमा का वर्णन करते हुए जिनप्रभसूरि तो यहाँ तक लिखते है—

"इस महातीर्थभूत पार्श्वनाथ के दर्शन से कलिकुण्ड, कुर्कुटेश्वर, श्रीपर्वत, शंखेश्वर, सेरीसा, मथुरा, वाराणसी; अहिच्छता, स्तंभ, अजाहर, प्रवरनगर, देवपत्तन, करहेड़ा, नागदा, श्रीपुर, सामिणि, चारूप, ढिंपुरी, उज्जैन, शुद्धदन्ती; हरिकंखी, लिम्बोडक आदि स्थानों में विद्यमान पार्श्वनाथ प्रतिमाओं का यात्रा करने का फल होता है ।"

१५वीं शती में हेमराज सुराणा ने इसका जीर्णोद्धार करवाया था । आज भी यह मन्दिर दर्शनीय है और चमत्कारपूर्ण है ।

११. बिजोलिया पार्श्वनाथ—यह भीलवाड़ा जिले की बूंदी की सीमा पर स्थित है । यहां चट्टान पर खुदा हुआ "उत्तम शिखर पुराण" एवं वि० सं० १२२६ का चौहान-कालीन महत्वपूर्ण लेख है । मन्दिर भग्न हो गया है, केवल शिखर का भाग ही अवशिष्ट है । यह मन्दिर दिगम्बर परम्परा का है । चौहान-कालीन १२२६ के लेख में ९२ पद्य एवं कुछ गद्य भाग है । लेख के ५६वें पद्य में लिखा है—श्रेष्ठि लोलाक की पत्नी ललिता को स्वप्न में यहाँ मन्दिर बनवाने का देव-निर्देश मिला था । इस लेख में यह उल्लेख भी मिलता है कि यहाँ कमठ ने उपसर्ग किया था ।

उत्तम शिखर पुराण दूसरी चट्टान पर खुदा हुआ है । इसमें २९४ श्लोक हैं । इसके तीसरे सर्ग में कमठ के उपसर्ग का विस्तृत वर्णन भी मिलता है ।

१२. रतनपुर पार्श्वनाथ—रतनपुर मारवाड़ के पार्श्वनाथ मन्दिर का तीर्थ रूप में उल्लेख मिलता है । वि० सं० १२०९, १३३३, १३४३, १३४६ के लेखों से इसकी प्राचीनता और प्रसिद्धि स्पष्ट है, किन्तु आज यह तीर्थ महत्व-शून्य है ।

१३. रावण पार्श्वनाथ—अलवर से ५ कि०मी० दूर जंगल में रावण पार्श्वनाथ मन्दिर जीर्ण दशा में प्राप्त है । परम्परागत श्रुति के अनुसार यह मूर्ति रावण-मन्दोदरी द्वारा निर्मित थी । सं० १६४५ में श्रेष्ठि हीरानन्द ने रावण पार्श्वनाथ का भव्य मन्दिर बनवाकर खरतरगच्छीय आद्यपक्षीय शाखा के जिनचन्द्रसूरि के आदेश से वाचक रंग कलश से प्रतिष्ठा करवाई थी ।

१४४९ की कल्पसूत्र की प्रशस्ति तथा अनेक तीर्थ-मालाओं आदि में भी रावण तीर्थ का उल्लेख मिलता है ।

१४. लौद्रवा पार्श्वनाथ—जैसलमेर से १५ किलोमीटर पर यह तीर्थ है सहजकीर्ति निर्मित शतदलपद्म गर्भित चित्रकाव्य के अनुसार श्रीधर और राझधर ने चिन्तामणि पार्श्वनाथ का मन्दिर बनवाया। श्रेष्ठि खीमसा ने मन्दिर भग्न होने पर नूतन मन्दिर बनवाया । इसके भी जीर्ण-क्षीर्ण होने पर जैसलमेर निवासी भणसाली गोत्रीय थाहरू शाह ने प्राचीन मन्दिर के नींव पर ही पंचानुत्तर विमान की आकृति पर नव्य एवं भव्य मन्दिर बनवाकर चिन्तामणि पार्श्वनाथ की श्यामवर्णी प्रतिमा विराजमान की इसकी प्रतिष्ठा खरतरगच्छीय जिनराजसूरि ने सं० १६७५ मिगसर सुदि १२ गुरुवार को की थी । मन्दिर के दायीं ओर समवसरण पर अष्टापद और उस पर कल्पवृक्ष की मनोहर रचना भी है । मन्दिर शिखरबद्ध है और शिल्पकला की दृष्टि से अनूठा है।

१५. वरकाणा पार्श्वनाथ—राणीस्टेशन से ३ कि०मी० पर वरकाणा गांव है । "वरकनकपुर", प्राचीन नाम मिलता है । गोडवाड की प्रसिद्ध पंचतीर्थी में इस तीर्थ का प्रमुख स्थान है । कई बार इसका जीर्णोद्धार होने से प्राचीनता नष्ट हो गई है । शिवराजगणि ने **आनन्दसुन्दर** ग्रन्थ (र०सं० १५५९) के प्रारंभ में ही "वरकाणा पार्श्व प्रसन्नो भव" लिखकर इस तीर्थ की महिमा गाई है । महाराणा जगतसिंह ने सं० १६८७

के लेख मे मेले के लिये जफात में छूट का उल्लेख है।

अन्य तीर्थ—इसी प्रकार तिंवरी पार्श्वनाथ, पोसलिया पार्श्वनाथ सोजत के पास मुंडेवा पार्श्वनाथ, नाडलाई में सोमटिया पार्श्वनाथ, सुजानगढ़ में जगवल्लभ पार्श्वनाथ के मन्दिर भी दर्शनीय हैं ।

गोंडी पार्श्वनाथ के नाम से बीकानेर, आहोर, धानेरा, नाड़लाई, सोजत के मन्दिर प्रसिद्ध और दर्शनीय हैं ।

वस्तुत: देखा जाए तो यह राजस्थान प्रदेश अतिशय/चमत्कारी तीर्थ-स्थलों का ही प्रदेश है । इस लघु निबन्ध में पार्श्वनाथ के प्रसिद्ध एवं मुख्य-मुख्य तीर्थ-स्थलों का उल्लेख मात्र किया गया है । ऐतिहासिक विश्लेषण प्राचीनत्व और विशिष्टताओं का लेखा-जोखा नहीं । अनुसन्धान करने पर इस प्रदेश में अन्य अनेक प्राचीन तीर्थ क्षेत्रों का परिचय भी प्राप्त किया जा सकता है ।

THE TĪRTHAS OF PĀRŚVANĀTHA IN GUJARAT

M. A. Dhaky

The early āgamic and related commentaries composed from the late sixth to the ninth century refer to no place as a *tīrtha* sacred to Jina Pārśvanātha in western India including Gujarat. The ancient sites then very famous as *tīrthas* within the present-day province of Gujarat were Ujjayantagiri (Girnār Hills), Śatruñjayagiri (Setrunjo), and Prabhāsa, the first was sacred to Arhat Ariṣṭanemi, the second to Jina Ṛṣabha, and the third to Jina Candraprabha, Pārśvanātha thus not figuring in their context as the principal deity. Likewise, the temples sacred to Jinas that existed in Valabhī (ancient capital of the Maitrakas in Saurāṣṭra) before its destruction in A.D. 784 did not include that of Jina Pārśva.[1] It was only in the medieval period that one hears of some sites sacred to that Jina: these were Stambhanaka (Thāmbhaṇā), Śaṅkhapura (Śaṅkheśvara), Cārūpa, Seriṣaka (Serisā) and a few others, the first two being far more famous in the past, the second also so in the present times, than the remaining sites.[2] For their images were believed to be endowed with miraculous powers including the cure of leucoderma by bathing in the lustral water of the images of the Jinas concerned. The myths relating to the origin of the first two *tīrthas* have been incorporated in the *Kalapradīpa* of Jinaprabha Sūri (*c.* A.D. 1333)[3]; these are best left to the faithful. Historically speaking, the following facts about the *tīrthas* concerned are available in the medieval and late medieval Śvetāmbara literature. The other sites sacred to Pārśvanātha were Ajāharā (Ajārā), Ghoghā, and Maṅgalpura (Maggrol), all located on Saurāṣṭra's western and south-eastern sea-board. And in Aṇahillapāṭaka, the capital of Gujarat, was the famous temple of Pañcāsarā-Pārśvanātha.

Stambhana - Pārśvanātha

A head of an image of Pārśva had been exposed near a tree in the environs of the village Stambhana situated on the bank of River Seḍhī near Cambay or Khambhāt. The exhumed image subsequently was set up in a shrine built for it and was consecrated by Abhayadeva Sūri of Candra-gaccha, the famous commentator on the nine *aṅga*-works of the *āgama* literature of the northern Nirgrantha tradition inherited by the Śvetāmbara sect. The date of consecration has been reported to be A.D. 1053 (or 1063). Abhayadeva Sūri next composed a *stotra* in Apabhraṁśa in praise of the Stambhana-Pārśvanātha, the psalm famous as *Jaya Tihuaṇa-thotta.*[4] Thereafter followed several similar compositions, in Sanskrit as well as Prākṛta, which sing the glory of the image of that *tīrtha*.[5] Among these the earliest was by Vardhamāna Sūri — disciple of Abhayadeva Sūri — followed by other brilliant compositions till the 15th century. From these, the beginning of a *stuti* by Nayacandra of Bṛhad-gaccha, dated S. 1257/A.D. 1201, is cited below:[6]

सेढीतटस्तम्भनकप्रतिष्ठः श्री पार्श्वनाथः सुगुणैर्गरिष्ठः ।
पायादपायादलिनीलकायः सिद्धयङ्गनासङ्घटनाभ्युपायः ॥ १ ॥

The glorificatory myths of the early and late medieval epochs speak in most glowing terms the merits that can be accrued by visiting (and worshipping) the Lord Jina Pārśva in the Stambhana shrine. By about A.D. 1232, minister Vastupāla had founded the "*avatāra-tīrtha*" — shrine incarnate — of Stambhana Pārśvanātha on the Śatruñjayagiri as well as Ujjayantagiri.

The image of the Jina had been transferred, in early years of the 14th century, from Stambhana to Stambhatīrtha (Khambhāt) for ensuring its safety; but it could not have survived the Muslim conquest and subsequent occupation of Gujarat when, by A.D. 1325, all Brahmanical and Jaina temples in Khambhāt — which indeed existed in very large number — had been completely destroyed. A shrine of Stambhana Pārśvanātha today does exist in Khambhāt, but is a building of a very late date, of late British period, the old glory of the *tīrtha* has by now been considerably dimmed.

Śaṅkhapura - Pārśvanātha

The image had turned up in the present village of Śaṅkheśvara at the fag end of the 11th century. One Sajjana built a temple for it in S. 1155/A.D. 1099. Minister Vastupāla had renovated or rebuilt in marble (or made additions to) the temple early in the second quarter of the 13th century;[7] he also founded its *avatāra*-shrine on the holy hills of Śatruñjaya. Many pilgrim congregations had visited the shrine in the past and even today its fame is fairly considerable. A few hymns due to the Lord Pārśva of Śaṅkhapura are known, that by Municandra Sūri of an unknown *gaccha* and probably of *c*. mid-13th century, which is of historical importance, is appended at the end. This *tīrtha* of Pārśvanātha has been noticed also in several other hymnic compositions by authors of the centuries between the 13th and 15th; and Upādhyāya Yaśovijaya, in the 17th century, had sung the glory of the lord in dazzling phrases. The mythical literature commensurate with the glory of the *tīrtha* was also duly created. It is said in the hymn of Municandra that the local ruler Durjanaśalya (13th century) was cured of leucoderma by bathing in the lustral water of the Jina. Even today the lustral water of this Jina here is believed among the Jainas to be restoring the skin pigment. The original temple was, to all seeming, destroyed during the Muslim occupation of Gujarat some time early in the 14th century. On its site was built another temple, now in brick, in early 17th century in Mughal times. This, too, seems to have been desecrated and damaged in the time plausibly of Aurangzeb. The present shrine, situated at a different location in the village, is the result of construction late in the British period.

Aṇahillapāṭaka, Pañcāsara - Pārśvanātha

The image had been brought from an old shrine in his ancestral town Pañcāsara by Vanarāja, the progenitor of the Cāpotkaṭa dynasty, and set up in late ninth century in a temple — Vanarāja-vihāra — an abbey-temple founded by him in his new capital, Aṇahillapāṭaka or Aṇhillapattana, present-day Pāṭaṇ in north Gujarat. The temple and the ancient image of course have not survived since almost the entire old Pāṭaṇ was completely devastated by the Muslim invasion and occupation of Gujarat in *c.* A.D. 1304. Even the ancient site of the temple has been forgotten, though it could not be far from the present new structure. The image of Pārśvanātha of Pañcāsara, though famous becuase it was ancient, perhaps of sixth or seventh century, was not reputed for performing miracles. A few late *stavanas* and a number of notices on this temple, however, are known from the pilgrim psalms in late Maru-Gurjara-bhāṣā and in Gujarātī.

Cārupa - Pārśvanātha

The temple's image was believed to be ancient. A hymn by Ratnaśekhara Sūri of Tapā-gaccha (2nd quarter of the 15th century) sang the glory of the *tīrtha*. The *tīrtha* exists but does not enjoy the importance it did in the medieval period.

Ajāharā - Pārśvanātha

The foundation of the Ajāharā Pārśvanātha near Unā seemingly was of the time as early as the eighth century. It was in all probability destroyed when Mahmūd of Gaznā, after devastating Unnatapura (Unā) was proceeding to Prabhāsa for the destruction of the temple of Somanātha in late weeks of December 1025. The original temple may have been built by the adherents of the Nirgrantha-Yāpanīya sect who had settled for some time in Saurāṣṭra. The shrine was perhaps rebuilt in the 13th century, possibly by the Śvetāmbaras. The original, desecrated, damaged, and discarded lime stone image of Pārśva, highly corroded by centuries of exposure to weathering in the temple's outer surroundings, is now preserved in the Government Museum, Junāgaḍh. The *tīrtha*, though ancient, is now of minor importance. It had inspired a couple of hymns, perhaps in the 17th century, when its glory was somewhat revived.

Ghoghā - Pārśvanātha

The ancient image of Jina Pārśva at Ghoghā had been broken into nine fragments but joined into one piece some time after the retreat of the Muslim army in early 14th century; hence it is called Navakhaṇḍā Pārśvanātha. Its glory was re-established in the 15th century and the famous pontiff Somasundara Sūri (and his confrère Jñānasāgara) of Tapā-gaccha and a couple of his disciples composed fine hymns in adoration of the Jina. Today, of course, the *tīrtha*, though visited by pilgrims, is of secondary importance.

Maṅgalapura - Pārśvanātha

The original image had belonged to a foundation called Kumāra-vihāra, built probably by the Solaṅkī emperor Kumārapāla some time between 1160-1170. The temple had been destroyed during the Muslim rule. The ceiling of its great hall is now in the Jumā Masjid to the west of the township. A single hymn by Lakṣmilābha (*c.* 16th-17th century?) on this Jina is known. The present shrine is of the British period. It hardly attracts pilgrims excepting for the stray Śvetāmbara Jainas visiting this decaying town.

Serisā - Pārśvanātha

The Pārśva image and other old images (possibly along with the temple) were consecrated in a temple in Seriṣaka by Devendra Sūri in emperor Kumārapāla's times; the Sūri is said to have belonged to the hagiographical line of the Navāṅga-vṛttikāra Abhayadeva Sūri (Candra-gaccha) according to the *Kalpapradīpa* (A.D. 1333) of Jinaprabha Sūri[9] and to the lineage of the Nāgendra-gaccha according to the *Nābhinandana-Jinoddhāna-prabandha* of Kakka Suri (A.D. 1337).[10] In the middle of the 13th century, Minister Ālhādana and next Dharmaghoṣa Sūri of Tapā-gaccha (A.D. 1260-1300) alluded to this *tīrtha* in their psalms. The temple has been referred to also in the *tīrthamālās* and allied literature in old Gujarātī of the 16th and 17th century. Before the destruction of the temple in the Muslim period, the old images had been interred for safety, the temple though was destroyed and stood as a very battered ruin till some decades ago. The images, however, had been recovered and re-established in a new building that was built in A.D. 1946. The glory of this medieval *tīrtha* has been, to some extent, revived.

श्रीमुनिचन्द्रसूरिप्रणीतप्रबन्धगतं

श्रीशङ्खेश्वर-पार्श्वनाथ-स्तवनम् ।

समस्तकल्याणनिधानकोशं वामाङ्गकुक्ष्येकमृणालहंसम् ।
अलङ्कृतेक्ष्वाकुविशालवंशं वन्दे सदा शङ्खपुरावतंसम् ॥ १ ॥
आराधित: श्री ऋषभस्य काले विद्याधरेन्द्रेण नमीश्वरेण ।
पूर्व हि वैताढयगिरौ जिनं तं वन्दे सदा शङ्खपुरावतंसम् ॥ २ ॥
य: पूजित: पन्नगनायकेन पातालभूमौ भवनाधिपेन ।
कालं कियन्तं जिननायकं तं वन्दे सदा शङ्खपुरावतंसम् ॥ ३ ॥
यदा जरासन्धजयोद्यतेन कृष्णेन नेमीश्वरशासितेन ।
पातालतो बिम्बमिदं तदानीमानीय संस्थापितमेव तीर्थम् ॥ ४ ॥
जराऽऽर्त्तभूतं स्वबलं विलोक्य यत्स्तात्रपीयूषजलेन सिक्तम् ।
सज्जीकृतं तत्क्षणमेव सर्वं वन्दे सदा शङ्खपुरावतंसम् ॥ ५ ॥
पञ्चाशदादौ किल पञ्चयुक्ते एकादशे वर्षशते व्यतीते ।
निवेशित: सज्जनश्रेष्ठिनाऽयं वन्दे सदा शङ्खपुरावतंसम् ॥ ६ ॥
काले कलौ कामगवी प्रणष्टा चिन्तामणि: कल्पतरूश्च नष्ट: ।
धत्ते ह्यसौ तत्प्रतिहस्तकत्वं वन्दे सदा शङ्खपुरावतंसम् ॥ ७ ॥
प्रभुतरोगेण विनष्टदेह आराध्य यं दुर्जनशल्यदेव: ।
चकार देहं मदनस्य तुल्यं वन्दे सदा शङ्खपुरावतंसम् ॥ ८ ॥
राज्यार्थिनां राज्यसुखप्रदाता सुतार्थिनां सन्ततिदायको य: ।
नेत्रार्थिनां लोचनदोऽसि नित्यं वन्दे सदा शङ्खपुरावतंसम् ॥ ९ ॥
इति स्तुत: श्रीमुनिचन्द्रसूरिणा कृपाकर: शङ्खपुरावतार ।
प्रबन्धकादौ प्रणतासुभाजां प्रचच्छ नित्यं निजपादसेवाम् ॥ १० ॥

NOTES AND REFERENCES

1. The late medieval *prabandhas* mention the departure of the images of Valabīnātha, Ṛṣabha, Vardhamāna, and Candraprabha to safer havens. Since this is only a side issue, I forgo citations from the original work.
2. More will be said while describing these *tīrthas*.
3. *Vividha Tīrthakalpa*, Ed. Jina Vijaya, Śāntiniketan 1934, "Ayodhyānagrīkalpa," p. 24; and Mohanlal Dalichand Deshai, *Jaina Sāhitya-no Saṁskṣipta Itihās*, (Gujarātī), Bombay 1933, p. 341, para 495.
4. For the quotation therefrom and the references to the publication sources, *see* here my paper "Arhat Pārśva with Dharaṇendra in hymnic literature".
5. Seemingly, the *tīrtha* in the 12th and the 13th century was at its height of glory. Some of the hymns of that period for the Stambhana-Jina are tāntric.
6. *Jainasotrasandoha*, pt. 1, Ed. Muni Chaturavijaya, Ahmedabad 1932, p. 106.
7. I had noticed a fragment of a *śikharikā* piece in marble showing the 13th century style of carving at the *garbhagṛha's* site, that was some 35 years ago.
8. The temple has been thoroughly renovated.
9. I forgo citations from the original sources.
10. *Ibid*.

ate 1. *Upasarga* of
Pārśvanātha,
Indian Museum,
Calcutta, *c.* late
9th century A.D.

Plate 3. Pañcatīrthi c. 10th Century A.D.
Sravasthi—Baharaich (U.P.)

Plate 2. Haḷebiḍ (Bastihaḷḷi) Pārśvanātha temple,
← *mūlanāyaka* image of Pārśvanātha, A.D. 1133.
(Founder *daṇḍanāyaka* Boppadēva, son of
Gaṅgarāja, prime minister of Hoysaḷa
Viṣṇuvardhana.)

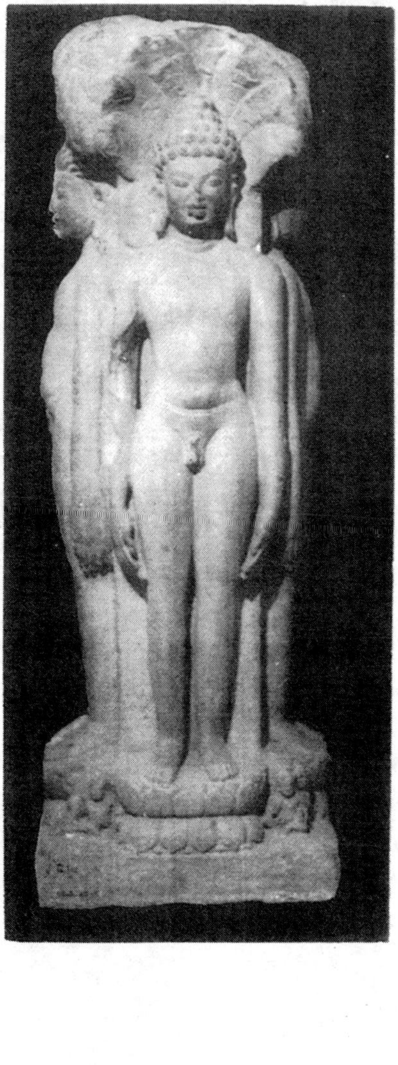

Plate 4. Pārśvanatha c. 9th Century A.D. Agatsarai
Aligarh (U.P.)

Plate 5. Pārśvanatha seated under snake canopy *Saṃ*. 1134-57 (1077 A.D.) Sravasthi—Baharaich (U.P.)

Plate 6. Pārśvanatha white marbel *c*. 12th Century A.D. Mahoba

Plate 7. Udaigiri (Udayagiri), Cave 20, general view, *c.* A.D. 425-426.

Plate 8. Vidiśā, Pārśvanātha-Sarvatobhadrikā image, *c.* 7th century A.D. Vidisha Museum No.357-1225.

Plate 9. Kāritalāi, Pārśvanātha-Sarvatobhadrikā image, *c.* 7th century A.D. Raipur, M.G.M. Museum.

Plate 10. Nāchnā-Kuṭhārā, Pārśvanātha, seated, *c.* 6th century A.D. Ramban, Tulsi Sangrahalaya.

Plate 11: Madhya Pradesh, Pārśvanātha, *c.* 6th century A.D. Calcutta, Indian Museum, A25111.

Plate 12 Gwalior Fort, Pārśvanātha, *c.* 9th century A.D.

Plate 13. Amrol, Pārśvanātha, *c*. 9th century A.D.

Plate 14. Vidiśā, Pārśvanātha, *c*. 9th century A.D. Vidisha State Museum.

Plate 15. Cirainti village, Pārśvanātha, Sarvatobhadrikā, c. 9th century A.D.

Plate 16. Deogarh, Pārśvanātha, c. 9th century A.D.

Plate 17. Deogarh, Jain temple 15, garbhagrha, Pārśvanātha, *c.* 9th century A.D.

Plate 18. Deogarh, Jaina temples 12 & 15, Pārśvanātha, *c.* 9th century A.D.

Plate 19. Kāritalāi, Pārśvanātha, *c.* 10th century A.D. Raipur, M.G.M. Museum (35).

Plate 20. Jabalpur, Pārśvanātha, *c.* 11th century. A.D. Jabalpur, Rani Durgavati Museum.

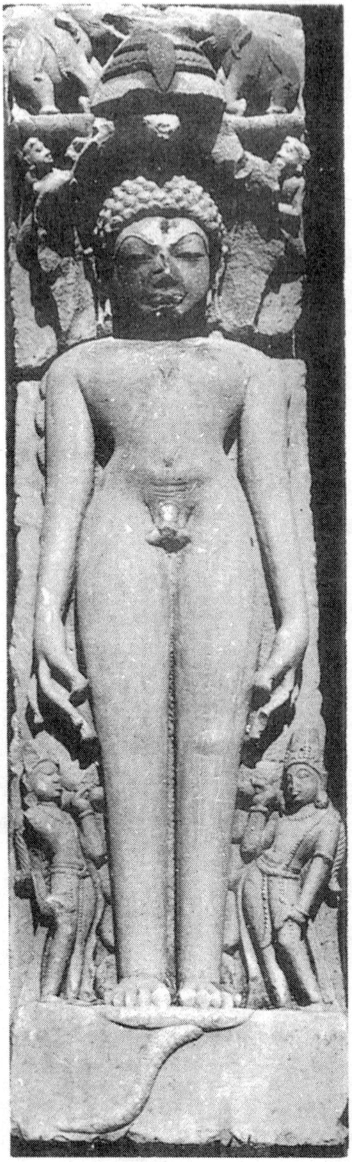

Plate 21. Siṅghanpur, Pancamaṭha temple, Pārśvanātha, mid 10th century A.D.

Plate 22. Singhanpur, Pañcamaṭha temple, Pārśvanātha, mid 10th century A.D.

Plate 23. Madhya Pradesh, Pārśvanātha, Sarvatobhadrikā, *c.* 10th century A.D. Dhubela Museum.

Plate 24. Khajurāho. Pārśvanātha, *c.* 10th century A.D. Khajurāho Archaeological Museum No.1618.

Plate 25. Deogarh, Jaina temple 4, Pārśvanātha, 11th century A.D.

Plate 26. Siron, Pārśvanātha, *c.* 10th century A.D.

Plate 27. Siron, Pārśvanātha, *c.* 11th century A.D.

Plate 28. Hiṅgalājagarh, Pārśvanātha, *c.* 9th-10th century A.D. Bhānpur, State Museum No. 290.

Plate 29. Hiṅgalājagarh, Pārśvanātha, *c.* 10th cent. A.D. Indore, Central Museum.

Plate 30. Bhojpur, Jaina temple, *garbhagṛha*, Pārśvanātha, *c.* 11th cent. A.D.

Plate 31. Udaigiri, Cave 20, Pārśvanātha, *c.* 10th-11th cent. A.D.

Plate 32. Ayodhyā, Pārśvanātha. (Courtesy: Archaeological Survey of India, Calcutta.)

Plate 33. Podasiṅgiḍi, seated Pārśvanātha. (Courtesy and kindness: R.P. Mohapatra.)

Plate 34. Pratāpanagarī, Pārśvanātha. (Courtesy: Archaeological Survey of India, Calcutta.)

Plate 35. Khaṇḍagiri, Cave 7, right wall, seated image of Pārśvanātha.

Plate 36. Khaṇḍagiri, Cave 7, Padmāvatī under the seated Pārśvanātha.

Plate 37. Khaṇḍagiri, Cave 8, Padmāvatī under the seated Pārśvanātha.

Plate 38. Purī, stele with haloed Tīrthaṅkaras flanking Pārśvanātha. (Courtesy: Indian Museum, Calcutta.)

Plate 39. Nandapur, Padmāvatī with Pārśvanātha above.

Plate 40. Deulbhirā, perforated grille with figure of seated Pārśvanātha. (Courtesy: Indian Museum, Calcutta.)

Plate 41. Beharasai, Pārśvanātha, upper part of the image. (Courtesy and kindness: Tarapada Santra.)

Plate 42. Beharasai, Pārśvanātha, lower part of the image. (Courtesy and kindness: Tarapada Santra.)

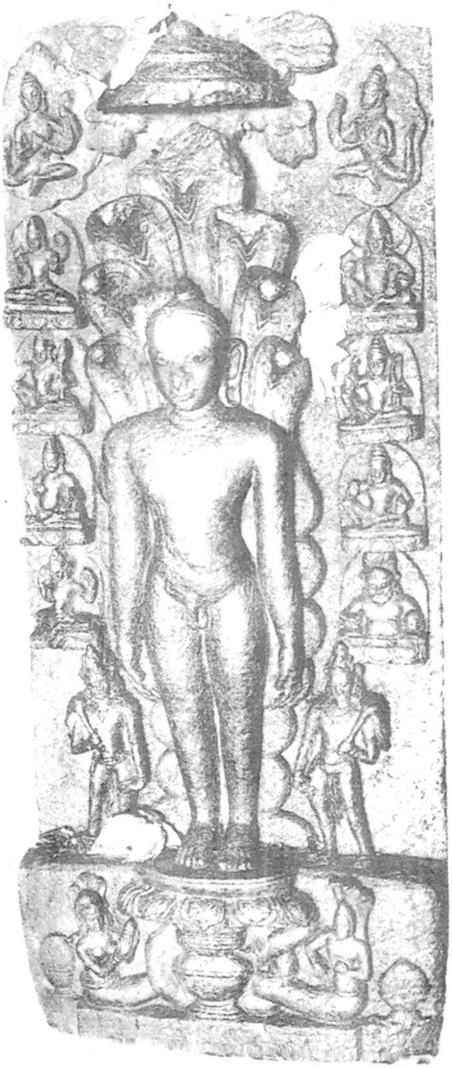

Plate 43. Bahulārā, standing Pārśvanātha. (Courtesy: Archaeological Survey of India.)

Plate 44. Bānkurā, standing Pārśvanātha. (Courtesy: Indian Museum, Calcutta.)

Plate 45. Pakbirrā, seated Pārśvanātha. (Courtesy and kindness: Krishnajivan Bhattacharyya.)

Plate 46. Pakbirrā, Pārśvanātha, lower portion of the image. (Courtesy: Archaeological Survey of India, Calcutta.)

Plate 47. Pakbirrā, Pārśvanātha, lower portion of the image. (Courtesy: Archaeological Survey of India, Calcutta.)

Plate 48. Anai-Jambad, standing Pārśvanātha.

Plate 49. Pakbirrā, votive caumukha. (Courtesy: Archaeological Survey of India, Calcutta.)

Plate 50. Puruliā, votive caumukha. (Courtesy: Haripada Sahitya Mandir, Purulia.)

Plate 51. Barjorā, votive caumukha (Courtesy: Vangiya Sahitya Parishad, Vishnupur.)

Plate 52. Sāt Deuliyā, votive caumukha. (Courtesy: Asutosh Museum, Calcutta.)

Plate 53. Burdwan, Viṣṇu-Lokeśvara. (Courtesy: Asutosh Museum, Calcutta.)

Plate 54. Aihoḷe,-Jaina Cave, vīthikā, Pārśvanātha, *c.* last quarter of the 6th century A.D.

Plate 55. Ellorā, cave 31, Pārśvanātha, south wall, c. ninth century A.D.

Plate 56. Ellorā, cave 31, Pārśvanātha, north wall, *c.* ninth century A.D.

Plate 57. Ellorā, cave 32, Pārśvanātha, south wall, *c.* ninth century A.D.

Plate 58. Ellorā, cave 32, Indrasabhā, Pārśvanātha, south wall, *c.* ninth century A.D.

Plate 59. Ellorā, cave 32, Indrasabhā, Pārśvanātha, *c.* ninth century A.D.

Plate 60. Ellorā, cave 32, Indrasabhā, Pārśvanātha, upper series, east, *c.* ninth century A.D.

Plate 61. Ellorā, cave 33, Pārśvanātha with the figure of Kamaṭha (?), *c.* ninth century A.D.

Plate 62. Ellorā, cave 33, Pārśvanātha, *c.* ninth century A.D.

Plate 63. Ellorā, cave 34, Pārśvanātha, south wall, *c.* ninth century A.D.

Plate 64. Badāmi, Cave IV, vīthikā, Pārśvanātha, *c.* late 6th century A.D.

Plate 65.

Hum̐ca, Pārśvanātha-basadi, gūḍhamaṇḍapa, stele showing the upsarga of Pārśvanātha, *c.* late ninth A.D.

Plate 66. Śravaṇa Belgoḷa, Candragiri, Pārśvanātha-basadi, garbhagṛha, cult image of Pārśvanātha, c. early 11th century A.D.

Plate 67. Gerīsoppa, forest, ruined Jaina temple, Pārśvanātha, *c.* 15th century A.D.